OPENSOURCES

Voices from the Open Source Revolution

OPENSOURCES

Voices from the Open Source Revolution

Edited by Chris DiBona, Sam Ockman & Mark Stone

O'REILLY®

Beijing · Cambridge · Köln · London · Paris · Sebastopol · Taipei · Tokyo

Open Sources: Voices of the Open Source Revolution

Edited by Chris DiBona, Sam Ockman, and Mark Stone

Published by O'Reilly & Associates, Inc., 101 Morris Street, Sebastopol, CA 95472.

Production Editor: Jane Ellin

Printing History:

January 1999:   First Edition.

This book is printed on acid-free paper with 85% recycled content, 15% post-consumer waste. O'Reilly & Associates is committed to using paper with the highest recycled content available consistent with high quality.

ISBN: 1-56592-582-3

Table of Contents

Acknowledgments vii

Introduction 1
Chris DiBona, Sam Ockman, and Mark Stone

A Brief History of Hackerdom 19
Eric S. Raymond

Twenty Years of Berkeley Unix: From AT&T–Owned to
  Freely Redistributable 31
Marshall Kirk McKusick

The Internet Engineering Task Force 47
Scott Bradner

The GNU Operating System and the Free Software Movement 53
Richard Stallman

Future of Cygnus Solutions: An Entrepreneur's Account 71
Michael Tiemann

Software Engineering 91
Paul Vixie

The Linux Edge 101
Linus Torvalds

Giving It Away: How Red Hat Software Stumbled Across a New
  Economic Model and Helped Improve an Industry 113
Robert Young

Diligence, Patience, and Humility 127
Larry Wall

Open Source as a Business Strategy 149
Brian Behlendorf

The Open Source Definition 171
Bruce Perens

Hardware, Software, and Infoware...................................... 189
Tim O'Reilly

Freeing the Source: The Story of Mozilla............................. 197
Jim Hamerly and Tom Paquin with Susan Walton

The Revenge of the Hackers... 207
Eric S. Raymond

Appendix A: The Tanenbaum-Torvalds Debate 221

Appendix B: The Open Source Definition, Version 1.0 253

Contributors.. 265

Acknowledgments

No book like this happens without the help and counsel of a number of people, so I thank my Mom, Dad, Trish, Denise, Neil, and Mickey. I'd also like to thank the folks at the Coffeenet, who have been there for me. And of course my thanks to the contributors who have wasted valuable coding time to work on this book; I appreciate it!

To the people at VA Research Linux Systems, I couldn't have hoped for a better collection of smart, dedicated people; thanks for putting up with me during the writing of this book.

This book would not have happened without the continual support and dedication of Mark Stone. He is the true hero behind this book's creation. He has said that "A book could be written about how this book was written," which I'm sure he means in the nicest way possible. I'm sure one day he will look back and laugh at this time—right, Mark? Mark?

In the initial brainstorming period for the book, a number of people contributed ideas and support that eventually led to Open Sources. These people include Paul Crowley, Paul Russell, Corey Saltiel, Edward Avis, Jeff Licquia, Jeff Knox, Becky Wood, and the guy whose site (*http://slashdot.org*) acted as the catalyst, Rob Malda. Thanks to all; I hope this book is everything you had wished it to be.

Finally, I could not have completed this work without the morale of Christine Hillmer, who selflessly unpacked our apartment while I toiled away at my keyboard. You are all that I ever could have wished for and I am reminded each day how lucky I am.

—*Chris DiBona*

I'd like to thank the following people for the many ways that they have supported me: Joe McGuckin, Peter Hendrickson, Jo Schuster, Ruth Ockman, Allison Huynh, and Nina Woodard. I'd also like to thank my favorite hackers: David S. Miller and H. Peter Anvin.

—Sam Ockman

I'd like to thank Sam and Chris for bringing this crazy idea to me in the first place. I'm sure they had no idea what they were getting into, but I'm equally sure it has been worth it. I'd also like to thank each of the contributors; each is a creative spirit with more ideas than time to execute them, but each understood the importance of this project and the need to make time for it.

For every book there are people behind the scenes who work their magic to make the book a success. On this book especially, some of these quiet heroes deserve acknowledgment: Troy Mott, Katie Gardner, Tara McGoldrick, Jane Ellin, Robert Romano, Rhon Porter, Nancy Wolfe Kotary, Sheryl Avruch, Mike Sierra, and Edie Freeman. Of course I'd also like to thank my friends and family who have supported me through yet another of Dad's crazy book projects. Finally, my thanks to the good people at Lytton Coffee Roasting Company, my "office away from home."

—Mark Stone

Introduction

Chris DiBona, Sam Ockman,
and Mark Stone

Prologue

Linux creator Linus Torvalds reports that the name "Linus" was chosen for him because of his parents' admiration for Nobel laureate Linus Pauling. Pauling was the rarest of men: a scientist who won the Nobel Prize not once, but twice. We find a cautionary tale for the Open Source community in the story of Pauling's foundational work that made possible the discovery of the structure of DNA.

The actual discovery was made Francis Crick and James Watson, and is famously chronicled in Watson's book *The Double Helix*. Watson's book is a remarkably frank account of the way science is actually done. He recounts not just the brilliance and insight, but the politics, the competition, and the luck. The quest for the secret of DNA became a fierce competition between, among others, Watson and Crick's lab in Cambridge, and Pauling's lab at Cal Tech.

Watson describes with obvious unease the way in which Pauling came to know that Watson and Crick had solved the mystery, and created a model of DNA's helical structure. The story here centers on Max Delbruk, a mutual friend who traveled between Cambridge and Cal Tech. While sympathetic to Watson and Crick's desire to keep the discovery secret until all results could be confirmed, Delbruk's allegiance ultimately was to science itself. In this passage, Watson describes how he learned that Pauling had heard the news:

> Linus Pauling first heard about the double helix from Max Delbruk. At the bottom of the letter that broke the news of the complementary chains, I had asked that he not tell Linus. I was still slightly afraid something would go wrong and did not want Pauling to think about hydrogen-bonded base pairs until we had a few more days to digest our position. My request, however, was ignored. Delbruk wanted to tell everyone in his lab and knew that within hours the gossip would travel from his lab in biology to their friends working under Linus. Also, Pauling made him promise to let him know the minute he heard from me. Then there was the even more important

consideration that Delbruk hated any form of secrecy in scientific matters and did not want to keep Pauling in suspense any longer.

Clearly the need for secrecy made Watson uncomfortable. One of the poignant themes that runs throughout the book is Watson's acknowledgment that competition kept parties from disclosing all they knew, and that the progress of science may have been delayed, if ever so slightly, by that secrecy.

Science, after all, is ultimately an Open Source enterprise. The scientific method rests on a process of discovery, and a process of justification. For scientific results to be justified, they must be replicable. Replication is not possible unless the source is shared: the hypothesis, the test conditions, and the results. The process of discovery can follow many paths, and at times scientific discoveries do occur in isolation. But ultimately the process of discovery must be served by sharing information: enabling other scientists to go forward where one cannot; pollinating the ideas of others so that something new may grow that otherwise would not have been born.

What Is Free Software and How Does It Relate to Open Source?

In 1984, Richard Stallman, a researcher at the MIT AI Lab, started the GNU project. The GNU project's goal was, simply put, to make it so that no one would ever have to pay for software. Stallman launched the GNU project because essentially he feels that the knowledge that constitutes a running program—what the computer industry calls the source code—should be free. If it were not, Stallman reasons, a very few, very powerful people would dominate computing.

Where proprietary commercial software vendors saw an industry guarding trade secrets that must be tightly protected, Stallman saw scientific knowledge that must be shared and distributed. The basic tenet of the GNU project and the Free Software Foundation (the umbrella organization for the GNU project) is that source code is fundamental to the furthering of computer science and freely available source code is truly necessary for innovation to continue.

Stallman worried how the world would react to free software. Scientific knowledge is often in the public domain; it is one function of academic publishing to put it there. With software, however, it was clear that just letting the source code go into the public domain would tempt businesses to co-opt the code for their own profitability. Stallman's answer to this threat was the GNU General Public License, known as the GPL (see Appendix B).

The GPL basically says that you may copy and distribute the software licensed under the GPL at will, provided you do not inhibit others from doing the same, either by charging them for the software itself or by restricting them through further licensing.

The GPL also requires works derived from work licensed under the GPL to be licensed under the GPL as well.

When Stallman and others in this book talk about free software, they are really talking about free speech. English handles the distinction here poorly, but it is the distinction between *gratis* and *liberty*, as in "Free as in speech, not as in beer." This radical message (the freedom part, not the beer part) led many software companies to reject free software outright. After all, they are in the business of making money, not adding to our body of knowledge. For Stallman, this rift between the computer industry and computer science was acceptable, maybe even desirable.

What Is Open Source Software?

In the spring of 1997, a group of leaders in the free software community assembled in California. This group included Eric Raymond, Tim O'Reilly, and VA Research president Larry Augustin, among others. Their concern was to find a way to promote the ideas surrounding free software to people who had formerly shunned the concept. They were concerned that the Free Software Foundation's anti-business message was keeping the world at large from really appreciating the power of free software.

At Eric Raymond's insistence, the group agreed that what they lacked in large part was a marketing campaign, a campaign devised to win mind share, and not just market share. Out of this discussion came a new term to describe the software they were promoting: Open Source. A series of guidelines were crafted to describe software that qualified as Open Source.

Bruce Perens had laid much of the groundwork for the Open Source Definition. One of the GNU project's states goals was to create a freely available operating system that could serve as the platform for running GNU software. In a classic case of software bootstrapping, Linux had become that platform, and Linux had been created with the help of GNU tools. Perens had headed the Debian project, which managed a distribution of Linux that included within the distribution only software that adhered to the spirit of GNU. Perens had laid this out explicitly in a document called the "Debian Social Contract." The Open Source definition is a direct descendant of the "Debian Social Contract," and thus Open Source is very much in the spirit of GNU.

The Open Source Definition allows greater liberties with licensing than the GPL does. In particular, the Open Source Definition allows greater promiscuity when mixing proprietary and open-source software.

Consequently, an Open Source license could conceivably allow the use and redistribution of open-source software without compensation or even credit. As an example you can take great swaths of the Netscape browser source code and distribute it with another, possibly proprietary, program without even notifying Netscape. Why would

Netscape wish this? For a number of reasons, but the most compelling is that it gets greater market share for their client code, which works very well with their commercial offerings. In this way, giving away source code is a very good way to build a platform. This is also one of the reasons why the people at Netscape did not use the GPL.

This is not a small issue in the community. Late in 1998, there was an important dispute that threatened to fracture the Linux community. This fracture was caused by the advent of two software systems, GNOME and KDE, each of which aims to build an object-oriented desktop interface. On the one hand, KDE utilized Troll Technology's Qt library, a piece of code that was proprietary, but quite stable and mature. On the other hand, the GNOME people decided to use the GTK+ library, which was a completely free library, though not as mature as Qt.

In the past, Troll Technology would have had to choose between using the GPL and maintaining their proprietary stance. The rift between GNOME and KDE would have continued. With the advent of Open Source, however, Troll was able to change their license to one that met the Open Source definition, while still giving Troll the control over the technology they wanted. The rift between two important parts of the Linux community appears to be closing.

The Dark Side of the Force

Though he may not have realized it at the time, Watson stood at the threshold of a new era in biological science. At the time of the discovery of the double helix, science in biology and chemistry was essentially a craft, a practical art. It was practiced by a few men working in small groups, primarily under the auspices of academic research. The seeds of change had already been planted, however. With the advent of several medical breakthroughs, notably the polio vaccine and the discovery of penicillin, biological science was about to become an industry.

Today organic chemistry, molecular biology, and basic medical research are not practiced as a craft by a small body of practitioners, but pursued as an industry. While research continues in academia, the vast majority of researchers, and the vast majority of research dollars, belong to the pharmaceutical industry. This alliance between science and industry is an uneasy one at best. While pharmaceutical companies can fund research at a level undreamed of in academic institutions, they also fund research with a vested interest. Consider: would a pharmaceutical company rather put major funding into research for a cure for an illness that is therapy-based or medication-based?

Computer science, too, must exist in an uneasy alliance with industry. Once new ideas came primarily from academic computer scientists; now the computer industry drives innovation forward. While the rank and file of Open Source programmers are still the many computer science undergrads and graduate students around the world, more and more Open Source programmers are working in industry rather than academic settings.

Industry has produced some marvelous innovations: Ethernet, the mouse, and the Graphical User Interface (GUI) all came out of Xerox PARC. But there is an ominous side to the computer industry as well. No one outside of Redmond really thinks that it is a good idea for Microsoft to dictate, to the extent they do, what a computer desktop should look like or have on it.

Industry can have a negative impact on innovation. The Graphical Image Manipulation Program (GIMP) languished incomplete for a year at beta release 0.9. Its creators, two students at Berkeley, had left school to take jobs in industry, and left their innovation behind.

Use the Source, Luke

Open Source was not an idea decreed from the top. The Open Source movement is a genuine grass roots revolution. While evangelists like Eric Raymond and Bruce Perens have had great success changing the language around free software, that change would have been impossible if the conditions were not right. We have reached the stage where an entire generation of students who learned computer science under the influence of GNU is now at work in industry, and have quietly been bringing free software in through the back doors of industry for years. They do so not from altruistic motives, but rather to bring better code to their work.

The revolutionaries are in place. They are the network engineers, system administrators, and programmers who have thrived on open-source software throughout their education, and want to use open-source software to thrive professionally as well. Free software has become a vital part of many companies, often unwittingly, but in some cases quite deliberately. Open Source has come of age: there is such a thing as an Open Source business model.

Bob Young's company, Red Hat Software, Inc., thrives on giving away its core product: Red Hat Linux. One good way to deliver free software is to package it as a full-featured distribution with a nice manual. Young is primarily selling convenience, as most do not want to have to bother with downloading all the pieces that make up a full-featured Linux system.

But he is not the only one doing this. So why does Red Hat dominate the U.S. market? Why does SuSE Linux dominate Europe? Open-source software is a commodity market. In any commodity market, customers value a brand they can trust. Red Hat's strength comes from brand management: consistent marketing and community outreach that makes the community recommend them when their friends ask them which distribution to use. The same is true for SuSE, and the two companies own their respective markets mostly because they were first to take brand management seriously.

Supporting the community is essential. Red Hat, SuSE, and other companies in the Linux space understand that to just make money off of Linux without giving anything back would cause two problems. First, people would consider such a company a freeloader and would recommend a competitor instead. Second, a company must be able to differentiate itself from competitors. Companies like CheapBytes and Linux Central merely provide low-cost distribution, selling CDs for as little as a dollar. For Red Hat to be perceived as offering greater value than these budget distributors, Red Hat must give something back. In a wonderful irony of the Open Source model, Red Hat can afford to charge $49.95 for their distribution only because they support the development of new code and return that code to the community at large as Open Source.

This kind of brand management is new to Open Source, but an old-fashioned model of simply providing good service has been a part of the Open Source business model for a long time. Michael Tiemann helped found Cygnus on the idea that though the world's best compiler, GCC, was freely available, companies would still be willing to pay for support of and enhancements to that compiler. Co-founder John Gilmore's description of Cygnus is apt: "Making free software affordable."

In fact this model of giving away the product and selling the support is proliferating rapidly in the Open Source world now. VA Research has been making and supporting high-quality Linux systems since late 1993. Penguin Computing offers similar products and services. LinuxCare does full, soup-to-nuts support for Linux in all of its flavors. Sendmail creator Eric Allmen has now created Sendmail Inc. to provide service and enhancements for the mail server software that holds about 80% of the market share. Sendmail is an interesting case because they have a two-tiered approach to the market. It has the proprietary Sendmail Pro, and the Free Software Sendmail, which is one year behind Sendmail Pro's development cycle.

Along those same lines, Paul Vixie, the president of Vixie Enterprises and a contributor to this book, enjoys a practical monopoly through his program BIND. This unassuming program is used every time you send an email or go to a web site or download a file via ftp. BIND is the program that handles the conversion of addresses like "www.dibona.com" to their actual IP address (in this case, 209.81.8.245). Vixie enjoys a thriving consultancy derived from his program's ubiquity.

Innovation Through the Scientific Method

The most fascinating development in the Open Source movement today is not the success of companies like Red Hat or Sendmail Inc. What's intriguing is to see major corporations within the computer industry, companies like IBM and Oracle, turn their attention to Open Source as a business opportunity. What are they looking for in Open Source?

Innovation.

Science is ultimately an Open Source enterprise. The scientific method rests on a process of discovery, and a process of justification. For scientific results to be justified, they must be replicable. Replication is not possible unless the source is shared: the hypothesis, the test conditions, and the results. The process of discovery can follow many paths, and at times scientific discoveries do occur in isolation. But ultimately the process of discovery must be served by sharing information: enabling other scientists to go forward where one cannot; pollinating the ideas of others so that something new may grow that otherwise would not have been born.

Where scientists talk of replication, Open Source programmers talk of debugging. Where scientists talk of discovering, Open Source programmers talk of creating. Ultimately, the Open Source movement is an extension of the scientific method, because at the heart of the computer industry lies computer science. Consider the words of Grace Hopper, inventor of the compiler, who said, in the early 60s:

> To me programming is more than an important practical art. It is also a gigantic undertaking in the foundations of knowledge.

Computer science, though, differs fundamentally from all other sciences. Computer science has only one means of enabling peers to replicate results: share the source code. To demonstrate the validity of a program to someone, you must provide them with the means to compile and run the program.

Replication makes scientific results robust. One scientist cannot expect to account for all possible test conditions, nor necessarily have the test environment to fully test every aspect of a hypothesis. By sharing hypotheses and results with a community of peers, the scientist enables many eyes to see what one pair of eyes might miss. In the Open Source development model, this same principle is expressed as "Given enough eyes, all bugs are shallow." By sharing source code, Open Source developers make software more robust. Programs get used and tested in a wider variety of contexts than one programmer could generate, and bugs get uncovered that otherwise would not be found. Because source code is provided, bugs can often be removed, not just discovered, by someone who otherwise would be outside the development process.

The open sharing of scientific results facilitates discovery. The scientific method minimizes duplication of effort because peers will know when they are working on similar projects. Progress does not stop simply because one scientists stops working on a project. If the results are worthy, other scientists will follow up. Similarly, in the Open Source development model, sharing source code facilitates creativity. Programmers working on complimentary projects can each leverage the results of the other, or combine resources into a single project. One project may spark the inspiration for another project that would not have been conceived without it. And worthy projects need not be orphaned when a programmer moves on. With the source code available, others can step in and take over the direction of a project. The GIMP sat idle for a year, but ultimately development did continue, and today the GIMP is pointed to with pride when Open Source developers consider what they can do in an area that is new territory for them: end-user applications.

Fortune 500 companies want to leverage off of this powerful model for innovation. IBM will happily charge a tidy sum to set up and administer the integration of Apache into MIS departments. This is a net win for IBM; they can install an exceptionally stable platform, which reduces the cost of supporting the platform, and really deliver service that can truly help their customers out. Just as important, IBM engineers share in the cross-pollination of ideas with other independent developers in the Apache Team.

This is precisely the reasoning behind Netscape's decision to make its browser Open Source. Part of the goal was to stabilize or increase market share. But more importantly, Netscape looked to the community of independent developers to drive innovation and help them build a superior product.

IBM was quick to see that tightly integrating software technologies like Apache into server platforms like the AS400 and the RS6000 line can only help in winning contracts and selling more IBM hardware. IBM is taking this to the next step and is porting their popular DB2 database to the Linux operating system. While many took this as being a response to Oracle releasing its Oracle 8 line on Linux, IBM has taken its role in the community seriously and has dedicated resources to the open software cause. By porting Apache to the AS400 platform, IBM has taken its most popular mainframe and legitimized the open technologies in ways only IBM can do.

It will be interesting to see what will happen in the competitive bids that companies like Coleman (of Thermo-electron), SAIC, BDM, and IBM make to the federal government and to industry. Consider the software cost of installing 1,000 seats with NT or Solaris and compare them with installing 1,000 seats with Linux. When you can drop your bid price by over a quarter of a million dollars, you can compete more effectively for these sorts of bids. Companies like CSC, who have a reputation of commonly forgoing a percent or two of profit margin to get more contracts, are probably just trying to figure out how to leverage technologies like Linux.

While companies like IBM, Oracle, and Netscape have begun to integrate their business model with Open Source, many traditional software companies continue to focus on purely proprietary solutions. They do so at their peril.

In the web server space, Microsoft's complete denial of the Open Source phenomenon is almost amusing. The Apache web server has, at the time of writing, more than

50% of the web serving market according the Netcraft survey (*http://www.netcraft. com/survey*). When you look at advertisements for Microsoft's Internet Information Server (IIS) you see them tout that they own over half the market in web serving— over half the commercial server market, that is. When compared against competitors like Netscape and Lotus, they have a substantial edge in the market share, but that "edge" looks puny in the overall server market where Microsoft's 20% is dwarfed by Apache's 53%.

The irony deepens, however. The fact is that 29% of the Web now runs on Linux-based servers, according the surveys conducted by the QUESO and WTF. QUESO is a tool that can determine the operating system a machine is running by sending TCP/IP packets to it and analyzing how the server responds to them. When run in conjunction with the likes of the Netcraft query engine, which analyzes the identification tags that the server responds with, it can produce a telling picture of the Web by OS and server type.

In fact, proprietary software vendors have already suffered a number of quiet casualties. Linux and Free BSD have really eliminated opportunities to successfully sell a proprietary Unix on PC hardware. One such company, Coherent, has already foundered. The Santa Cruz Operation (SCO) has gone from a leading Unix vendor to an afterthought in the span of a couple of years. SCO, the company, will probably find a way to survive, but will its flagship product, SCO Unix, be another casualty of Open Source?

Sun Microsystems has in many ways provided support for open-source development over the years, whether through donations of hardware and resources to help with the SPARC port of Linux, or through supporting development of John Ousterhout's Tcl scripting language. It's ironic, then, that the company that grew out of the joyous free software roots at Berkeley that Kirk McKusick describes so often struggles to grasp the significance of the Open Source phenomenon.

Let's take a moment to do some comparison and contrast with SCO and Sun.

Sun makes the majority of their money from supporting and servicing their OS and hardware. Sun's product line goes from a desktop workstation that is competitively priced with a PC to large enterprise class server-clusters that compete in the mainframe space. Their profits in the hardware realm do not come from their low-end Ultra series so much as they do from the service, sales, and support of their highly specialized and customized E and A series servers. It's estimated that Sun enjoys fully 50% of their profits from support, training, and consulting services.

SCO, on the other hand, makes money by selling the SCO Unix operating system, programs like compilers and servers, and training and education on the use of the SCO products. So while SCO has a nicely put together organization, it is in danger the same way that a farm with one crop can be vulnerable to a single blight destroying a harvest.

Sun sees the development of Linux as perhaps more concern for the lower end of their product offering. Sun's strategy is to make sure that Linux can run on the Sun hardware so people can choose to run Linux on Sun hardware. This is interesting because Sun can then continue to offer hardware support for their machines. In the future, we would not be surprised to see Sun offer software support for Linux on their lower-end machines.

In many ways, this is a short step for Sun. In fact, if you were to call a Sun administrator right now and ask him or her what's the first thing they do when they receive a new Sun box, they will tell you "Download the GNU tools and compilers and install my favorite shells." Sun will perhaps finally get this message from their customer base and just do this for people as an outreach measure. However, Sun will operate at a disadvantage until they see the service their customer base can provide for them: innovation through cross-pollination of ideas based on source code release.

SCO, on the other hand, has a less flexible model. SCO's pricing model sells the OS first, with additional costs for tools that the Linux user takes for granted, such as compilers and text processing languages. This model simply can't be sustained in the face of competition from a robust free OS. Unlike Sun, which has added value in its broad hardware line, SCO has no hardware to tie profits to. Their OS is essentially all they have, and in SCO's case, that's not good enough. What will SCO do?

Their response so far has not been enlightened. In the beginning of 1998, SCO sent out a letter to its vast mailing list of users slamming open Unixes like Linux and FreeBSD as unstable and unprofessional while offering a reduced price on the SCO base OS. They were widely scorned for this move and had to do some serious back-pedaling. The letter insulted a number of people by blatantly lying about the credentials of Linux. SCO didn't give their customers credit for being smart enough to see through the FUD. SCO eventually published a retraction on their web site.

In late 1998, SCO sent out a press release talking about how SCO Unix now has a Linux compatibility layer, so that your favorite Linux programs can be run under SCO Unix. The response was underwhelming. Why spend money on an OS just to make it compatible with a competitive free offering?

SCO is in a unique position to benefit from the Open Source movement. SCO has some very valuable intellectual property that they can leverage into a real position of power in the Open Source future. They must, however, make a leap of faith. Instead of seeing Open Source as a threat that would erode SCO's intellectual property, they need to see Open Source as an opportunity to bring innovation to that intellectual property.

Of course the maneuverings of a company like SCO or even Sun with respect to Open Source pale compared to the actions of Microsoft. So far Microsoft remains locked in its proprietary model, and seems determined to see that model through at least the release of Windows 2000.

Our guess is that Windows 2000 will ship in the latter part of 2000 or early 2001 to great fanfare. This will be the great merging event of NT and 98 after all. Somewhere around this event, or six months before, there will be an announcement for a new Microsoft Windows operating system. Microsoft has always coveted the "Lucrative Enterprise Market," a place where the machines serve a company's lifeblood of data. So far, however, there's no evidence that Microsoft can deliver a Windows NT system or Windows 2000 system with the greater stability this market requires. So this new system will be decreed as the coming solution.

Let's call the product that represents this phantom change "Windows Enterprise" or WEnt. Microsoft will look at NT and say, essentially, how can we make it more reliable and stable? OS theory, as Linus Torvalds points out in his essay, really hasn't changed much in the last 20 years, and so Microsoft engineering will essentially come back and say that a nice, tightly-written kernel without any pollution in the executive level of execution is the best way to accomplish reliability and speed. Thus to fix the major errors of the Windows NT kernels, namely the inclusion of ill tested or ill-chosen third party drivers and making the GUI part of the kernel, Microsoft will have to either write a monster slow emulation layer, or just break a ton of old applications. Microsoft is certainly capable of pursuing either course. But open-source programs may well have reached the maturity where corporations who are buying software will ask themselves if they trust Microsoft to give them what is already available under the guise of Linux, namely a stable kernel.

The answer will of course show itself with time. No one really knows if Microsoft can actually write solid stable software at this level. The "Halloween Documents" that Eric Raymond refers to suggest that even within Microsoft there are serious doubts.

Perils to Open Source

Most software ventures, like most scientific enterprises, fail. As Bob Young points out, making successful open-source software is not so very different from making successful proprietary software. In both cases real success is rare, and the best innovators are those who learn from mistakes.

The rampant creativity that leads to innovation in both science and software comes at a cost. Maintaining control of an active Open Source project can be difficult. This fear of losing control prevents some individuals and many companies from active participation. Specifically, one concern when embarking or joining an open-source software project is that a large competitor or group of people will come in and create what is called a fork in the code base. Much like a fork in the road, a code base can at times diverge into two separate, incompatible, roads and never the twain shall meet. This is not an idle problem; look, for instance, at the multiple forks that the BSD-based operating systems have taken, leading to NetBSD, OpenBSD, FreeBSD, and many others. What is to keep this from happening to Linux?

One thing that keeps this happening is the open methods used in the development of the Linux kernel. Linus Torvalds, Alan Cox, and the rest run a tight ship and are the central authority for adding and accessing the kernel. The Linux kernel project has been called a benign dictatorship, with Linus as its dictator, and so far this model has produced a nicely written tight kernel without too much extraneous cruft in it.

What's ironic is that while Linux has experienced little actual forking, there exist large patches that convert the Linux kernel into a hard real-time kernel, suitable for tight critical device control, and additionally there exist versions of Linux that can run under dramatically weird architectures. These patches could be considered forks, as they are based on a set kernel and grow from there out, but because they occupy special niche application areas for Linux, they do not have a fracturing effect on the Linux community as a whole.

Think, by way of analogy, of a scientific theory applied on special cases. Most of the world gets along just fine using Newton's laws of motion for mechanical calculations. Only under special circumstances of large masses or high velocities must we make recourse to Einstein's theory of relativity. Einstein's theory could grow and extend without undermining the application of the older Newtonian theoretical base.

But competing software ventures often conflict just as competing scientific theories often conflict. Look at the history of Lucid. Lucid was a company formed to exploit and develop a streamlined version of the popular programmer's editor Emacs and sell it to the development community as a replacement for the original Emacs, written by Richard Stallman. Lucid's alternative was called Lucid Emacs and then Xemacs. When the Lucid team went to pitch the Xemacs solution to various companies, they found that they could not draw enough of a distinction in the results produced by Xemacs versus Emacs. Combined with the lackluster state of the computer market at the time, Lucid was short-lived.

Interestingly, Lucid did GPL its Xemacs code before it went out of business. Even this failed enterprise is a testament to the longevity of open-source software. As long as people find a use for the software, they will maintain it to work with new systems and architectures. Even now, Xemacs enjoys terrific popularity, and you can spark an interesting debate among Emacs hackers by asking them which Emacs they prefer. Xemacs, with very few people working on the program, is still a vital advancing product, changing, keeping up, and adapting to the new times and architectures.

Motivating the Open Source Hacker

The Lucid experience shows that programmers often have loyalty to a project that goes beyond direct compensation for working on the project. Why do people write free software? Why do they give away freely what they could charge hundreds of dollars an hour for? What do they get out of it?

The motivation is not just altruism. The contributors here may not be loaded down with Microsoft stock options, but each has achieved a reputation that should assure him opportunities that pay the rent and feeds the kids. From the outside this can seem like a paradox; you can't eat free software after all. The answer lies, in part, in thinking beyond conventional notions of work and compensation. We are witnessing a new economic model take shape, not just a new culture.

Eric Raymond has become a kind of self-appointed participant anthropologist to the Open Source community, and in his writings he touches on the reasons why the people develop software only to give it away.

Keep in mind that these people have been, for the most part, coding for years, and don't see programming itself as burdensome, or as work. A very complex project like Apache or the Linux kernel brings the satisfaction of the ultimate in intellectual exercise. Much like the rush a runner feels while running a race, a true programmer will feel this same rush after writing a perfect routine or tight piece of code. It is difficult to describe the joy felt after completing or debugging a hideously tricky piece of recursive code that has been a source of trouble for days.

The point is that many programmers code because it is what they love to do, and in fact it is how they define their intellect. Without coding, a programmer feels less of a person, much like an athlete deprived of an opportunity to compete. Discipline can be a problem with programmers as much as with athletes; many programmers really don't enjoy maintaining a piece of code after having mastered it.

Still, other programmers don't take this "macho" view of their craft, and take a more scholarly view. Many programmers consider themselves, rightly, to be scientists. Scientists aren't supposed to hoard profits from their inventions, they are supposed to publish and share their inventions for all to benefit from. A scientist isn't supposed to let profits come at the expense of the pursuit of knowledge.

What all these introspections on programming have in common is an emphasis on reputation. Programming is a gift culture: the value of a programmer's work can only come from sharing it with others. That value is enhanced when the work is more widely shared, and that value is enhanced when the work is more completely shared by showing the source, not just the results from a pre-compiled binary.

Programming is also about empowerment, what Eric Raymond calls "scratching an itch." Most Open Source projects began with frustration: looking for a tool to do a job and finding none, or finding one that was broken or poorly maintained. Eric Raymond began fetchmail this way; Larry Wall began Perl this way; Linus Torvalds began Linux this way. Empowerment, in many ways, is the most important concept underlying Stallman's motivation for starting the GNU project.

The Venture and Investment Future of Linux

A hacker's motivations may be intellectual, but the result need not be a lifestyle of sacrifice. More and more, enterprises and individual Open Source programmers are coming together in a new spirit of pragmatism and opportunity.

In Silicon Valley, where we work and live, there is a history of investment and venture capital that powers the economy of the region. It can be traced back to the years when the transistor was first being exploited for commercial gain and the microprocessor became a force in the industry, replacing cumbersome logic boards with thousands of chips and individual transistors on them.

At any given time there is a hot technology that venture capital concentrates on. While they don't ignore other companies and opportunities, they realize that to achieve their benchmarks of economic performance, they don't just need successful companies, they need hot companies that can do an Initial Public Offering (IPO) within three years of investment or be sold for hundreds of millions to companies like Oracle or Cisco.

In 1998, the great wave of the Internet is ebbing; the rash of Internet IPOs that began with Netscape's spectacular debut has begun to decline. In a fitting act of symbolism, America Online's purchase of Netscape really does signal the end of an era. Internet stocks are now looked at more closely by the investment community, and generally Internet companies are held to the same standards as other companies: they must have some plausible expectation of profitability ahead.

So where will venture go? Our guess is that Linux and open-source software related companies are and will be the hot investment through the end of the millennium. With any luck, you will see a great rash of Linux and Open Source IPOs starting with Red Hat software in late 1999. The money out there to be invested is nothing less than staggering, and companies like Scriptics, Sendmail, and Vix.com are well poised to take advantage of the favorable market conditions and build their dream companies.

The question really is not whether venture capital funding will flow to Open Source, but why the flow has only begun to trickle in that direction. Keep in mind, free software is not new; Richard Stallman started the FSF in 1984 and was building on a tradition dating back long before that. Why did it take so long to catch on?

Taking a look at the computing landscape, you've got a situation where a very large company with very deep pockets controls the lion's share of the commercial market. In Silicon Valley, hopeful applications vendors looking for backing from the angel and venture capital community learn very quickly that if they position themselves against Microsoft, they will not get funded. Every startup either has to play Microsoft's game or not play at all.

This creatively oppressive environment is clearly where the original impetus for the rise of free software began to take root. Any programmer who has had to deal with creating programs for Microsoft's Windows operating systems will tell you that it is a daunting collection of cumbersome interfaces designed to serve the goal of making the program completely dependent on Microsoft libraries. The number of interfaces presented to the programmer from Microsoft serve the purpose of making any Windows native program very difficult to port to other operating systems.

The biggest arena that Microsoft has yet to dominate—the Internet—has no such restriction. As Scott Bradner describes, the Internet is built on a powerful collection of open standards maintained on the merit of individual participation, not the power of a corporate wallet. The Internet is, in many ways, the original Open Source venture. Keeping the Internet firmly based on open standards made it possible for a wide and diverse range of programmers to work on developing Internet applications. The Internet's spectacular growth is a testament to the power of this open standards model.

The structures inherent in the Internet's success are present in the Open Source movement as well. Linux distributors like Red Hat and SuSE compete, yes, but they compete based on open standards and shared code. Both use Red Hat Package Manager (RPM) as their package management tool, for example, rather than trying to lock developers in to individual package management systems. Debian uses a different package management tool, but because both Debian's and Red Hat's tools are open-source programs, compatibility between the two has been achieved.

So the infrastructure that made Internet technologies a tempting arena for venture capitalists is present in Open Source, and should make Open Source technologies equally tempting.

More importantly, though, the Internet has created a new infrastructure off of which Open Source can leverage. We are moving from the era of software enterprises to the era of infoware enterprises that Tim O'Reilly describes. To make this move, the barriers to entry and the costs of distribution had to be lowered dramatically. The Internet has lowered the bar.

Science and the New Renaissance

The Open Source development model of today has its roots in the academic computer science of a decade or more ago. What makes Open Source dramatically more successful today, however, is the rapid dissemination of information made possible by the Internet. When Watson and Crick discovered the double helix, they could reasonably expect the information to travel from Cambridge to Cal Tech in a matter of days, or weeks at most. Today the transmission of such information is effectively instantaneous. Open Source has been born into a digital renaissance made possible by the Internet, just as modern science was made possible during the Renaissance by the invention of the printing press.

The Middle Ages lacked an affordable information infrastructure. Written works had to be copied by hand at great expense, and hence the information had to have an immediate value attached to it. Trade records, banking transactions, diplomatic correspondence; this information was concise enough and carried enough immediate value to be transmitted. The speculative writings of alchemists, priests, and philosophers—the men who would later be called scientists—took a much lower priority, and hence the information was disseminated much more slowly. The printing press changed all this by dramatically lowering the barriers to entry in the information infrastructure. Scholars who had previously worked in isolation could, for the first time, establish a sense of community with other scholars all over Europe. But this exercise in community building required an absolute commitment to the open sharing of information.

What was born out of this community was the notion of academic freedom, and ultimately the process we now call the Scientific Method. None of this would have been possible without the need to form community, and the open sharing of information has, for centuries, been the cement that has held the scientific community together.

Imagine for a moment if Newton had withheld his laws of motion, and instead gone into business as a defense contractor to artillerists following the 30 Years War. "No, I won't tell you how I know about parabolic trajectories, but I'll calibrate your guns for a fee." The very idea, of course, sounds absurd. Not only did science not evolve this way, but it could not have evolved this way. If that had been the mindset of those scientifically inclined, their very secrecy would have kept science from developing and evolving at all.

The Internet is the printing press of the digital age. Once again, the barriers to entry for the information infrastructure have been dramatically lowered. No longer does source code need to be distributed on paper tape as with the original version of Unix, or floppy disks, as in the early days of DOS, or even on CD-ROM. Any ftp or web server can now serve as a distribution point that is cheap and effectively instantaneous.

While this renaissance holds great promise, we must not forget the centuries old scientific heritage on which the Open Source development model is based. Computer science and the computer industry do exist in an uneasy alliance today. There is pressure from industry giants like Microsoft to keep new developments proprietary for the sake of short-term financial gain. But as more and more of the development work in computer science has its origins in industry rather than academia, industry must take care to nourish computer science through the open sharing of ideas— namely, the Open Source development model. The computer industry must do this not out of any altruistic motives to serve a greater cause, but for the most basic pragmatic reasons: enlightened self-interest.

First of all, it would be shortsighted of those in the computer industry to believe that monetary reward is the primary concern of Open Source's best programmers. To involve these people in industry, their priorities must be respected. These people are involved in a reputation game, and history has shown that scientific success outlives financial success. We remember a few of the great industrialists of the last hundred years: Carnegie, Rockefeller. We remember a great many more of the scientists and inventors from the last hundred years: Einstein, Edison . . . Pauling. When the history of this time is written a hundred years from now, people will perhaps remember the name of Bill Gates, but few other computer industrialists. They are much more likely to remember names like Richard Stallman and Linus Torvalds.

Second, and more important, industry needs the innovation science can provide. Open Source can develop and debug new software with the speed and creativity of science. The computer industry needs the next generation of ideas that will come from Open Source development.

Consider the example of Linux once again. Linux is a project that was conceived some five years after Microsoft began development of Windows NT. Microsoft has spent tens of thousands of man-hours and millions of dollars on the development of Windows NT. Yet today Linux is considered a competitive alternative to NT as a PC-based server system, an alternative that major middleware and backend software is being ported to by Oracle, IBM, and other major providers of enterprise software. The Open Source development model has produced a piece of software that would otherwise require the might and resources of someone like Microsoft to create.

To sustain the digital renaissance we need Open Source development. Open Source development drives progress not just in computer science, but in the computer industry as well.

A Brief History of Hackerdom

Eric S. Raymond

Prologue: The Real Programmers

In the beginning, there were Real Programmers.

That's not what they called themselves. They didn't call themselves "hackers," either, or anything in particular; the sobriquet "Real Programmer" wasn't coined until after 1980. But from 1945 onward, the technology of computing attracted many of the world's brightest and most creative minds. From Eckert and Mauchly's ENIAC onward there was a more or less continuous and self-conscious technical culture of enthusiast programmers, people who built and played with software for fun.

The Real Programmers typically came out of engineering or physics backgrounds. They wore white socks and polyester shirts and ties and thick glasses and coded in machine language and assembler and FORTRAN and half a dozen ancient languages now forgotten. These were the hacker culture's precursors, the largely unsung protagonists of its prehistory.

From the end of World War II to the early 1970s, in the great days of batch computing and the "big iron" mainframes, the Real Programmers were the dominant technical culture in computing. A few pieces of revered hacker folklore date from this era, including the well-known story of Mel (included in the Jargon File), various lists of Murphy's Laws, and the mock-German "Blinkenlights" poster that still graces many computer rooms.

Some people who grew up in the "Real Programmer'" culture remained active into the 1990s. Seymour Cray, designer of the Cray line of supercomputers, is said to have once toggled an entire operating system of his own design into a computer of his own design. In octal. Without an error. And it worked. Real Programmer macho supremo.

On a lighter note, Stan Kelly-Bootle, author of *The Devil's DP Dictionary* (McGraw-Hill, 1981) and folklorist extraordinaire, programmed on the Manchester Mark I, the first fully-operational stored-program digital computer, in 1948. Nowadays he writes technical humor columns for computing magazines which often take the form of a vigorous and knowing dialogue with today's hacker culture.

Others, such as David E. Lundstrom, have written anecdotal histories of those early years (*A Few Good Men From UNIVAC*, 1987).

What did the "Real Programmer" culture in was the rise of interactive computing, the universities, and the networks. These gave birth to a continuous engineering tradition that, eventually, would evolve into today's open-source hacker culture.

The Early Hackers

The beginnings of the hacker culture as we know it today can be conveniently dated to 1961, the year MIT acquired the first PDP-1. The Signals and Power committee of MIT's Tech Model Railroad Club adopted the machine as their favorite tech-toy and invented programming tools, slang, and an entire surrounding culture that is still recognizably with us today. These early years have been examined in the first part of Steven Levy's book *Hackers* (Anchor/Doubleday, 1984).

MIT's computer culture seems to have been the first to adopt the term "hacker." The TMRC's hackers became the nucleus of MIT's Artificial Intelligence Laboratory, the world's leading center of AI research into the early 1980s. And their influence was spread far wider after 1969, the first year of the ARPAnet.

The ARPAnet was the first transcontinental, high-speed computer network. It was built by the Defense Department as an experiment in digital communications, but grew to link together hundreds of universities and defense contractors and research laboratories. It enabled researchers everywhere to exchange information with unprecedented speed and flexibility, giving a huge boost to collaborative work and tremendously increasing both the pace and intensity of technological advance.

But the ARPAnet did something else as well. Its electronic highways brought together hackers all over the U.S. in a critical mass; instead of remaining in isolated small groups each developing their own ephemeral local cultures, they discovered (or reinvented) themselves as a networked tribe.

The first intentional artifacts of hackerdom—the first slang lists, the first satires, the first self-conscious discussions of the hacker ethic—all propagated on the ARPAnet in its early years. (The first version of the Jargon File, as a major example, dated from 1973.) Hackerdom grew up at the universities connected to the Net, especially (though not exclusively) in their computer science departments.

Culturally, MIT's AI Lab was first among equals from the late 1960s. But Stanford University's Artificial Intelligence Laboratory (SAIL) and (later) Carnegie-Mellon University (CMU) became nearly as important. All were thriving centers of computer science and AI research. All attracted bright people who contributed great things to hackerdom, on both the technical and folkloric levels.

To understand what came later, though, we need to take another look at the computers themselves, because the Lab's rise and its eventual fall were both driven by waves of change in computing technology.

Since the days of the PDP-1, hackerdom's fortunes had been woven together with Digital Equipment Corporation's PDP series of minicomputers. DEC pioneered commercial interactive computing and time-sharing operating systems. Because their machines were flexible, powerful, and relatively cheap for the era, lots of universities bought them.

Cheap time sharing was the medium the hacker culture grew in, and for most of its lifespan the ARPAnet was primarily a network of DEC machines. The most important of these was the PDP-10, first released in 1967. The 10 remained hackerdom's favorite machine for almost fifteen years; TOPS-10 (DEC's operating system for the machine) and MACRO-10 (its assembler) are still remembered with nostalgic fondness in a great deal of slang and folklore.

MIT, though it used the same PDP-10's as everyone else, took a slightly different path; they rejected DEC's software for the PDP-10 entirely and built their own operating system, the fabled ITS.

ITS stood for "Incompatible Timesharing System," which gives one a pretty good fix on their attitude. They wanted it their way. Fortunately for all, MIT's people had the intelligence to match their arrogance. ITS, quirky and eccentric and occasionally buggy though it always was, hosted a brilliant series of technical innovations and still arguably holds the record for time-sharing system in longest continuous use.

ITS itself was written in assembler, but many ITS projects were written in the AI language LISP. LISP was far more powerful and flexible than any other language of its day; in fact, it is still a better design than most languages of today, twenty-five years later. LISP freed ITS's hackers to think in unusual and creative ways. It was a major factor in their successes, and remains one of hackerdom's favorite languages.

Many of the ITS culture's technical creations are still alive today; the Emacs program editor is perhaps the best-known. And much of ITS's folklore is still "live" to hackers, as one can see in the Jargon File.*

SAIL and CMU weren't asleep, either. Many of the cadre of hackers that grew up around SAIL's PDP-10 later became key figures in the development of the personal computer and today's window/icon/mouse software interfaces. And hackers at CMU

---

* *http;//www.tuxedo.org*

were doing the work that would lead to the first practical large-scale applications of expert systems and industrial robotics.

Another important node of the culture was Xerox PARC, the famed Palo Alto Research Center. For more than a decade, from the early 1970s into the mid-1980s, PARC yielded an astonishing volume of groundbreaking hardware and software innovations. The modern mice, windows, and icons style of software interface was invented there. So was the laser printer, and the local-area network; and PARC's series of D machines anticipated the powerful personal computers of the 1980s by a decade. Sadly, these prophets were without honor in their own company; so much so that it became a standard joke to describe PARC as a place characterized by developing brilliant ideas for everyone else. Their influence on hackerdom was pervasive.

The ARPAnet and the PDP-10 cultures grew in strength and variety throughout the 1970s. The facilities for electronic mailing lists that had been used to foster cooperation among continent-wide special-interest groups were increasingly also used for more social and recreational purposes. DARPA deliberately turned a blind eye to all the technically "unauthorized" activity; it understood that the extra overhead was a small price to pay for attracting an entire generation of bright young people into the computing field.

Perhaps the best-known of the "social" ARPAnet mailing lists was the SF-LOVERS list for science-fiction fans; it is still very much alive today, in fact, on the larger "Internet" that ARPAnet evolved into. But there were many others, pioneering a style of communication that would later be commercialized by for-profit time-sharing services like CompuServe, GEnie, and Prodigy.

The Rise of Unix

Meanwhile, however, off in the wilds of New Jersey, something else had been going on since 1969 that would eventually overshadow the PDP-10 tradition. The year of ARPAnet's birth was also the year that a Bell Labs hacker named Ken Thompson invented Unix.

Thompson had been involved with the development work on a time-sharing OS called Multics, which shared common ancestry with ITS. Multics was a test-bed for some important ideas about how the complexity of an operating system could be hidden inside it, invisible to the user and even to most programmers. The idea was to make using Multics from the outside (and programming for it!) much simpler, so that more real work could get done.

Bell Labs pulled out of the project when Multics displayed signs of bloating into an unusable white elephant (the system was later marketed commercially by Honeywell but never became a success). Ken Thompson missed the Multics environment, and began to play at implementing a mixture of its ideas and some of his own on a scavenged DEC PDP-7.

Another hacker named Dennis Ritchie invented a new language called "C" for use under Thompson's embryonic Unix. Like Unix, C was designed to be pleasant, unconstraining, and flexible. Interest in these tools spread at Bell Labs, and they got a boost in 1971 when Thompson and Ritchie won a bid to produce what we'd now call an office-automation system for internal use there. But Thompson and Ritchie had their eye on a bigger prize.

Traditionally, operating systems had been written in tight assembler to extract the absolute highest efficiency possible out of their host machines. Thompson and Ritchie were among the first to realize that hardware and compiler technology had become good enough that an entire operating system could be written in C, and by 1974 the whole environment had been successfully ported to several machines of different types.

This had never been done before, and the implications were enormous. If Unix could present the same face, the same capabilities, on machines of many different types, it could serve as a common software environment for all of them. No longer would users have to pay for complete new designs of software every time a machine went obsolete. Hackers could carry around software toolkits between different machines, rather than having to re-invent the equivalents of fire and the wheel every time.

Besides portability, Unix and C had some other important strengths. Both were constructed from a "Keep It Simple, Stupid" philosophy. A programmer could easily hold the entire logical structure of C in his head (unlike most other languages before or since) rather than needing to refer constantly to manuals; and Unix was structured as a flexible toolkit of simple programs designed to combine with each other in useful ways.

The combination proved to be adaptable to a very wide range of computing tasks, including many completely unanticipated by the designers. It spread very rapidly within AT&T, in spite of the lack of any formal support program for it. By 1980, it had spread to a large number of university and research computing sites, and thousands of hackers considered it home.

The workhorse machines of the early Unix culture were the PDP-11 and its descendant, the VAX. But because of Unix's portability, it ran essentially unaltered on a wider range of machines than one could find on the entire ARPAnet. And nobody used assembler; C programs were readily portable among all these machines.

Unix even had its own networking, of sorts—Unix-to-Unix Copy Protocol (UUCP): low-speed and unreliable, but cheap. Any two Unix machines could exchange point-to-point electronic mail over ordinary phone lines; this capability was built into the system, not an optional extra. Unix sites began to form a network nation of their own, and a hacker culture to go with it. In 1980, the first Usenet board that would quickly grow bigger than ARPAnet.

A few Unix sites were on the ARPAnet themselves. The PDP-10 and Unix cultures began to meet and mingle at the edges, but they didn't mix very well at first. The PDP-10 hackers tended to consider the Unix crowd a bunch of upstarts, using tools that looked ridiculously primitive when set against the baroque, lovely complexities of LISP and ITS. "Stone knives and bearskins!" they muttered.

And there was yet a third current flowing. The first personal computer had been marketed in 1975. Apple was founded in 1977, and advances came with almost unbelievable rapidity in the years that followed. The potential of microcomputers was clear, and attracted yet another generation of bright young hackers. Their language was BASIC, so primitive that PDP-10 partisans and Unix aficionados both considered it beneath contempt.

The End of Elder Days

So matters stood in 1980: three cultures, overlapping at the edges but organized around very different technologies. The ARPAnet/PDP-10 culture, wedded to LISP and MACRO and TOPS-10 and ITS. The Unix and C crowd with their PDP-11s and VAXen and pokey telephone connections. And an anarchic horde of early microcomputer enthusiasts bent on taking computer power to the people.

Among these, the ITS culture could still claim pride of place. But storm clouds were gathering over the Lab. The PDP-10 technology ITS depended on was aging, and the Lab itself was split into factions by the first attempts to commercialize AI technology. Some of the Lab's (and SAIL's and CMU's) best were lured away to high-paying jobs at startup companies.

The death blow came in 1983, when DEC cancelled its follow-on to the PDP-10 in order to concentrate on the PDP-11 and VAX lines. ITS no longer had a future. Because it wasn't portable, it was more effort than anyone could afford to move ITS to new hardware. The Berkeley variant of Unix running on a VAX became the hacking system par excellence, and anyone with an eye on the future could see that microcomputers were growing in power so rapidly that they were likely to sweep all before them.

It was around this time that Levy wrote *Hackers*. One of his prime informants was Richard M. Stallman (inventor of Emacs), a leading figure at the Lab and its most fanatical holdout against the commercialization of Lab technology.

Stallman (who is usually known by his initials and login name, RMS) went on to form the Free Software Foundation and dedicate himself to producing high-quality free software. Levy eulogized him as "the last true hacker," a description that happily proved incorrect.

Stallman's grandest scheme neatly epitomized the transition hackerdom underwent in the early 80s—in 1982 he began the construction of an entire clone of Unix, written in C and available for free. Thus, the spirit and tradition of ITS was preserved as an important part of the newer, Unix- and VAX-centered hacker culture.

It was also around this time that microchip and local-area network technology began to have a serious impact on hackerdom. Ethernet and the Motorola 68000 microchip made a potentially potent combination, and several different startups had been formed to build the first generation of what we now call workstations.

In 1982, a group of Unix hackers from Berkeley founded Sun Microsystems on the belief that Unix running on relatively inexpensive 68000-based hardware would prove a winning combination for a wide variety of applications. They were right, and their vision set the pattern for an entire industry. While still priced out of reach of most individuals, workstations were cheap for corporations and universities; networks of them (one to a user) rapidly replaced the older VAXes and other timesharing systems.

The Proprietary Unix Era

By 1984, when AT&T divested and Unix became a commercial product for the first time, the most important fault line in hackerdom was between a relatively cohesive "network nation" centered around the Internet and Usenet (and mostly using minicomputer- or workstation-class machines running Unix), and a vast disconnected hinterland of microcomputer enthusiasts.

The workstation-class machines built by Sun and others opened up new worlds for hackers. They were built to do high-performance graphics and pass around shared data over a network. During the 1980s, hackerdom was preoccupied by the software and tool-building challenges of getting the most use out of these features. Berkeley Unix developed built-in support for the ARPAnet protocols, which offered a solution to the networking problem and encouraged further growth of the Internet.

There were several attempts to tame workstation graphics. The one that prevailed was the X Window System. A critical factor in its success was that the X developers were willing to give the sources away for free in accordance with the hacker ethic, and were able to distribute them over the Internet. X's victory over proprietary graphics systems (including one offered by Sun itself) was an important harbinger of changes which, a few years later, would profoundly affect Unix itself.

There was a bit of factional spleen still vented occasionally in the ITS/Unix rivalry (mostly from the ex-ITSers' side). But the last ITS machine shut down for good in

1990; the zealots no longer had a place to stand and mostly assimilated to the Unix culture with various degrees of grumbling.

Within networked hackerdom itself, the big rivalry of the 1980s was between fans of Berkeley Unix and the AT&T versions. Occasionally you can still find copies of a poster from that period, showing a cartoony X-wing fighter out of the *Star Wars* movies streaking away from an exploding Death Star patterned on the AT&T logo. Berkeley hackers liked to see themselves as rebels against soulless corporate empires. AT&T Unix never caught up with BSD/Sun in the marketplace, but it won the standards wars. By 1990, AT&T and BSD versions were becoming harder to tell apart, having adopted many of each others' innovations.

As the 1990s opened, the workstation technology of the previous decade was beginning to look distinctly threatened by newer, low-cost and high-performance personal computers based on the Intel 386 chip and its descendants. For the first time, individual hackers could afford to have home machines comparable in power and storage capacity to the minicomputers of ten years earlier—Unix engines capable of supporting a full development environment and talking to the Internet.

The MS-DOS world remained blissfully ignorant of all this. Though those early microcomputer enthusiasts quickly expanded to a population of DOS and Mac hackers orders of magnitude greater than that of the "network nation" culture, they never become a self-aware culture themselves. The pace of change was so fast that fifty different technical cultures grew and died as rapidly as mayflies, never achieving quite the stability necessary to develop a common tradition of jargon, folklore, and mythic history. The absence of a really pervasive network comparable to UUCP or the Internet prevented them from becoming a network nation themselves. Widespread access to commercial online services like CompuServe and Genie was beginning to take hold, but the fact that non-Unix operating systems don't come bundled with development tools meant that very little source was passed over them. Thus, no tradition of collaborative hacking developed.

The mainstream of hackerdom, (dis)organized around the Internet and by now largely identified with the Unix technical culture, didn't care about the commercial services. They wanted better tools and more Internet, and cheap 32-bit PCs promised to put both in everyone's reach.

But where was the software? Commercial Unixes remained expensive, in the multiple-kilobuck range. In the early 1990s, several companies made a go at selling AT&T or BSD Unix ports for PC-class machines. Success was elusive, prices didn't come down much, and (worst of all) you didn't get modifiable and redistributable sources with your operating system. The traditional software-business model wasn't giving hackers what they wanted.

Neither was the Free Software Foundation. The development of HURD, RMS's long-promised free Unix kernel for hackers, got stalled for years and failed to produce anything like a usable kernel until 1996 (though by 1990 FSF supplied almost all the other difficult parts of a Unix-like operating system).

Worse, by the early 1990s it was becoming clear that ten years of effort to commercialize proprietary Unix was ending in failure. Unix's promise of cross-platform portability got lost in bickering among half a dozen proprietary Unix versions. The proprietary-Unix players proved so ponderous, so blind, and so inept at marketing that Microsoft was able to grab away a large part of their market with the shockingly inferior technology of its Windows OS.

In early 1993, a hostile observer might have had grounds for thinking that the Unix story was almost played out, and with it the fortunes of the hacker tribe. And there was no shortage of hostile observers in the computer trade press, many of whom had been ritually predicting the imminent death of Unix at six-month intervals ever since the late 1970s.

In those days it was conventional wisdom that the era of individual techno-heroism was over, that the software industry and the nascent Internet would increasingly be dominated by colossi like Microsoft. The first generation of Unix hackers seemed to be getting old and tired (Berkeley's Computer Science Research group ran out of steam and lost its funding in 1994). It was a depressing time.

Fortunately, there had been things going on out of sight of the trade press, and out of sight even of most hackers, that would produce startlingly positive developments in later 1993 and 1994. Eventually, these would take the culture in a whole new direction and to undreamed-of successes.

The Early Free Unixes

Into the gap left by the HURD's failure had stepped a Helsinki University student named Linus Torvalds. In 1991 he began developing a free Unix kernel for 386 machines using the Free Software Foundation's toolkit. His initial, rapid success attracted many Internet hackers to help him develop Linux, a full-featured Unix with entirely free and redistributable sources.

Linux was not without competitors. In 1991, contemporaneously with Linus Torvalds's early experiments, William and Lynne Jolitz were experimentally porting the BSD Unix sources to the 386. Most observers comparing BSD technology with Linus's crude early efforts expected that BSD ports would become the most important free Unixes on the PC.

The most important feature of Linux, however, was not technical but sociological. Until the Linux development, everyone believed that any software as complex as an operating system had to be developed in a carefully coordinated way by a relatively small, tightly-knit group of people. This model was and still is typical of both commercial software and the great freeware cathedrals built by the Free Software Foundation in the 1980s; also of the freeBSD/netBSD/OpenBSD projects that spun off from the Jolitzes' original 386BSD port.

Linux evolved in a completely different way. From nearly the beginning, it was rather casually hacked on by huge numbers of volunteers coordinating only through the Internet. Quality was maintained not by rigid standards or autocracy but by the naively simple strategy of releasing every week and getting feedback from hundreds of users within days, creating a sort of rapid Darwinian selection on the mutations introduced by developers. To the amazement of almost everyone, this worked quite well.

By late 1993, Linux could compete on stability and reliability with many commercial Unixes, and hosted vastly more software. It was even beginning to attract ports of commercial applications software. One indirect effect of this development was to kill off most of the smaller commercial Unix vendors—without developers and hackers to sell to, they folded. One of the few survivors, BSDI (Berkeley Systems Design, Incorporated), flourished by offering full sources with its BSD-based Unix and cultivating close ties with the hacker community.

These developments were not much remarked on at the time even within the hacker culture, and not at all outside it. The hacker culture, defying repeated predictions of its demise, was just beginning to remake the commercial-software world in its own image. It would be five more years, however, before this trend became obvious.

The Great Web Explosion

The early growth of Linux synergized with another phenomenon: the public discovery of the Internet. The early 1990s also saw the beginnings of a flourishing Internet-provider industry, selling connectivity to the public for a few dollars a month. Following the invention of the World Wide Web, the Internet's already-rapid growth accelerated to a breakneck pace.

By 1994, the year Berkeley's Unix development group formally shut down, several different free Unix versions (Linux and the descendants of 386BSD) served as the major focal points of hacking activity. Linux was being distributed commercially on CD-ROM and selling like hotcakes. By the end of 1995, major computer companies were beginning to take out glossy advertisements celebrating the Internet-friendliness of their software and hardware!

In the late 1990s the central activities of hackerdom became Linux development and the mainstreaming of the Internet. The World Wide Web has at last made the Internet into a mass medium, and many of the hackers of the 1980s and early 1990s launched Internet Service Providers selling or giving access to the masses.

The mainstreaming of the Internet has even brought the hacker culture the beginnings of mainstream respectability and political clout. In 1994 and 1995, hacker activism scuppered the Clipper proposal, which would have put strong encryption under government control. In 1996 hackers mobilized a broad coalition to defeat the misnamed "Communications Decency Act" (CDA) and prevent censorship of the Internet.

With the CDA victory, we pass out of history into current events. We also pass into a period in which your historian became an actor rather than just an observer. This narrative will continue in "The Revenge of the Hackers."

> All governments are more or less combinations against the people . . . and as rulers have no more virtue than the ruled. . . the power of government can only be kept within its constituted bounds by the display of a power equal to itself, the collected sentiment of the people.
>
> —*Benjamin Franklin Bache, in a Philadelphia Aurora editorial, 1794*

Twenty Years of Berkeley Unix
From AT&T–Owned to Freely Redistributable

Marshall Kirk McKusick

Early History

Ken Thompson and Dennis Ritchie presented the first Unix paper at the Symposium on Operating Systems Principles at Purdue University in November 1973. Professor Bob Fabry, of the University of California at Berkeley, was in attendance and immediately became interested in obtaining a copy of the system to experiment with at Berkeley.

At the time, Berkeley had only large mainframe computer systems doing batch processing, so the first order of business was to get a PDP-11/45 suitable for running with the then-current Version 4 of Unix. The Computer Science Department at Berkeley, together with the Mathematics Department and the Statistics Department, were able to jointly purchase a PDP-11/45. In January 1974, a Version 4 tape was delivered and Unix was installed by graduate student Keith Standiford.

Although Ken Thompson at Purdue was not involved in the installation at Berkeley as he had been for most systems up to that time, his expertise was soon needed to determine the cause of several strange system crashes. Because Berkeley had only a 300-baud acoustic-coupled modem without auto answer capability, Thompson would call Standiford in the machine room and have him insert the phone into the modem; in this way Thompson was able to remotely debug crash dumps from New Jersey.

Many of the crashes were caused by the disk controller's inability to reliably do overlapped seeks, contrary to the documentation. Berkeley's 11/45 was among the first systems that Thompson had encountered that had two disks on the same controller! Thompson's remote debugging was the first example of the cooperation that sprang up between Berkeley and Bell Labs. The willingness of the researchers at the Labs to share their work with Berkeley was instrumental in the rapid improvement of the software available at Berkeley.

Though Unix was soon reliably up and running, the coalition of Computer Science, Mathematics, and Statistics began to run into problems; Math and Statistics wanted to run DEC's RSTS system. After much debate, a compromise was reached in which each department would get an eight-hour shift; Unix would run for eight hours followed by sixteen hours of RSTS. To promote fairness, the time slices were rotated each day. Thus, Unix ran 8 a.m. to 4 p.m. one day, 4 p.m. to midnight the next day, and midnight to 8 a.m. the third day. Despite the bizarre schedule, students taking the Operating Systems course preferred to do their projects on Unix rather than on the batch machine.

Professors Eugene Wong and Michael Stonebraker were both stymied by the confinements of the batch environment, so their INGRES database project was among the first groups to move from the batch machines to the interactive environment provided by Unix. They quickly found the shortage of machine time and the odd hours on the 11/45 intolerable, so in the spring of 1974, they purchased an 11/40 running the newly available Version 5. With their first distribution of INGRES in the fall of 1974, the INGRES project became the first group in the Computer Science department to distribute their software. Several hundred INGRES tapes were shipped over the next six years, helping to establish Berkeley's reputation for designing and building real systems.

Even with the departure of the INGRES project from the 11/45, there was still insufficient time available for the remaining students. To alleviate the shortage, Professors Michael Stonebraker and Bob Fabry set out in June 1974, to get two instructional 11/45's for the Computer Science department's own use. Early in 1975, the money was obtained. At nearly the same time, DEC announced the 11/70, a machine that appeared to be much superior to the 11/45. Money for the two 11/45s was pooled to buy a single 11/70 that arrived in the fall of 1975. Coincident with the arrival of the 11/70, Ken Thompson decided to take a one-year sabbatical as a visiting professor at the University of California at Berkeley, his alma mater. Thompson, together with Jeff Schriebman and Bob Kridle, brought up the latest Unix, Version 6, on the newly installed 11/70.

Also arriving in the fall of 1975 were two unnoticed graduate students, Bill Joy and Chuck Haley; they both took an immediate interest in the new system. Initially they began working on a Pascal system that Thompson had hacked together while hanging around the 11/70 machine room. They expanded and improved the Pascal interpreter to the point that it became the programming system of choice for students because of its excellent error recovery scheme and fast compile and execute time.

With the replacement of Model 33 teletypes by ADM-3 screen terminals, Joy and Haley began to feel stymied by the constraints of the *ed* editor. Working from an editor named *em* that they had obtained from Professor George Coulouris at Queen Mary's College in London, they worked to produce the line-at-a-time editor *ex*.

With Ken Thompson's departure at the end of the summer of 1976, Joy and Haley begin to take an interest in exploring the internals of the Unix kernel. Under Schrieb-man's watchful eye, they first installed the fixes and improvements provided on the "fifty changes" tape from Bell Labs. Having learned to maneuver through the source code, they suggested several small enhancements to streamline certain kernel bottle-necks.

Early Distributions

Meanwhile, interest in the error recovery work in the Pascal compiler brought in requests for copies of the system. Early in 1977, Joy put together the "Berkeley Software Distribution." This first distribution included the Pascal system, and, in an obscure subdirectory of the Pascal source, the editor *ex*. Over the next year, Joy, acting in the capacity of distribution secretary, sent out about thirty free copies of the system.

With the arrival of some ADM-3a terminals offering screen-addressable cursors, Joy was finally able to write *vi*, bringing screen-based editing to Berkeley. He soon found himself in a quandary. As is frequently the case in universities strapped for money, old equipment is never replaced all at once. Rather than support code for optimizing the updating of several different terminals, he decided to consolidate the screen management by using a small interpreter to redraw the screen. This interpreter was driven by a description of the terminal characteristics, an effort that eventually became *termcap*.

By mid-1978, the software distribution clearly needed to be updated. The Pascal system had been made markedly more robust through feedback from its expanding user community, and had been split into two passes so that it could be run on PDP-11/34s. The result of the update was the "Second Berkeley Software Distribution," a name that was quickly shortened to 2BSD. Along with the enhanced Pascal system, *vi* and *termcap* for several terminals was included. Once again Bill Joy single-handedly put together distributions, answered the phone, and incorporated user feedback into the system. Over the next year nearly seventy-five tapes were shipped. Though Joy moved on to other projects the following year, the 2BSD distribution continued to expand. The final version of this distribution, 2.11BSD, is a complete system used on hundreds of PDP-11's still running in various corners of the world.

VAX Unix

Early in 1978, Professor Richard Fateman began looking for a machine with a larger address space on which he could continue his work on Macsyma (originally started on a PDP-10). The newly announced VAX-11/780 fulfilled the requirements and was available within budget. Fateman and thirteen other faculty members put together an NSF proposal that they combined with some departmental funds to purchase a VAX.

Initially the VAX ran DEC's operating system VMS, but the department had gotten used to the Unix environment and wanted to continue using it. So, shortly after the arrival of the VAX, Fateman obtained a copy of the 32/V port of Unix to the VAX by John Reiser and Tom London of Bell Labs.

Although 32/V provided a Version 7 Unix environment on the VAX, it did not take advantage of the virtual memory capability of the VAX hardware. Like its predecessors on the PDP-11, it was entirely a swap-based system. For the Macsyma group at Berkeley, the lack of virtual memory meant that the process address space was limited by the size of the physical memory, initially 1 megabyte on the new VAX.

To alleviate this problem, Fateman approached Professor Domenico Ferrari, a member of the systems faculty at Berkeley, to investigate the possibility of having his group write a virtual memory system for Unix. Ozalp Babaoglu, one of Ferrari's students, set about to find some way of implementing a working set paging system on the VAX; his task was complicated because the VAX lacked reference bits.

As Babaoglu neared the completion of his first cut at an implementation, he approached Bill Joy for some help in understanding the intricacies of the Unix kernel. Intrigued by Babaoglu's approach, Joy joined in helping to integrate the code into 32/V and then with the ensuing debugging.

Unfortunately, Berkeley had only a single VAX for both system development and general production use. Thus, for several weeks over the Christmas break, the tolerant user community alternately found themselves logging into 32/V and "Virtual VAX/Unix." Often their work on the latter system would come to an abrupt halt, followed several minutes later by a 32/V login prompt. By January, 1979, most of the bugs had been worked out, and 32/V had been relegated to history.

Joy saw that the 32-bit VAX would soon make the 16-bit PDP-11 obsolete, and began to port the 2BSD software to the VAX. While Peter Kessler and I ported the Pascal system, Joy ported the editors *ex* and *vi*, the C shell, and the myriad other smaller programs from the 2BSD distribution. By the end of 1979, a complete distribution had been put together. This distribution included the virtual memory kernel, the standard 32/V utilities, and the additions from 2BSD. In December, 1979, Joy shipped the first of nearly a hundred copies of 3BSD, the first VAX distribution from Berkeley.

The final release from Bell Laboratories was 32/V; thereafter all Unix releases from AT&T, initially System III and later System V, were managed by a different group that emphasized stable commercial releases. With the commercialization of Unix, the researchers at Bell Laboratories were no longer able to act as a clearing-house for the ongoing Unix research. As the research community continued to modify the Unix system, it found that it needed an organization that could produce research releases. Because of its early involvement in Unix and its history of releasing Unix-based tools, Berkeley quickly stepped into the role previously provided by the Labs.

DARPA Support

Meanwhile, in the offices of the planners for the Defense Advanced Research Projects Agency (DARPA), discussions were being held that would have a major influence on the work at Berkeley. One of DARPA's early successes had been to set up a nation-wide computer network to link together all their major research centers. At that time, they were finding that many of the computers at these centers were reaching the end of their useful lifetime and had to be replaced. The heaviest cost of replacement was the porting of the research software to the new machines. In addition, many sites were unable to share their software because of the diversity of hardware and operating systems.

Choosing a single hardware vendor was impractical because of the widely varying computing needs of the research groups and the undesirability of depending on a single manufacturer. Thus, the planners at DARPA decided that the best solution was to unify at the operating systems level. After much discussion, Unix was chosen as a standard because of its proven portability.

In the fall of 1979, Bob Fabry responded to DARPA's interest in moving towards Unix by writing a proposal suggesting that Berkeley develop an enhanced version of 3BSD for the use of the DARPA community. Fabry took a copy of his proposal to a meeting of DARPA image processing and VLSI contractors, plus representatives from Bolt, Beranek, and Newman, the developers of the ARPAnet. There was some reservation whether Berkeley could produce a working system; however, the release of 3BSD in December 1979 assuaged most of the doubts.

With the increasingly good reputation of the 3BSD release to validate his claims, Bob Fabry was able to get an 18-month contract with DARPA beginning in April 1980. This contract was to add features needed by the DARPA contractors. Under the auspices of this contract, Bob Fabry sets up an organization which was christened the Computer Systems Research Group, or CSRG for short. He immediately hired Laura Tong to handle the project administration. Fabry turned his attention to finding a project leader to manage the software development. Fabry assumed that since Joy had just passed his Ph.D. qualifying examination, he would rather concentrate on completing his degree than take the software development position. But Joy had other plans. One night in early March he phoned Fabry at home to express interest in taking charge of the further development of Unix. Though surprised by the offer, Fabry took little time to agree.

The project started promptly. Tong set up a distribution system that could handle a higher volume of orders than Joy's previous distributions. Fabry managed to coordinate with Bob Guffy at AT&T and lawyers at the University of California to formally release Unix under terms agreeable to all. Joy incorporated Jim Kulp's job control, and added auto reboot, a 1K block file system, and support for the latest VAX machine, the VAX-11/750. By October 1980, a polished distribution that also included the Pascal compiler, the Franz Lisp system, and an enhanced mail handling system was released as 4BSD. During its nine-month lifetime, nearly 150 copies were shipped. The license arrangement was on a per-institution basis rather than a per machine basis; thus the distribution ran on about 500 machines.

With the increasingly wide distribution and visibility of Berkeley Unix, several critics began to emerge. David Kashtan at Stanford Research Institute wrote a paper describing the results of benchmarks he had run on both VMS and Berkeley Unix. These benchmarks showed severe performance problems with the Unix system for the VAX. Setting his future plans aside for several months, Joy systematically began tuning up the kernel. Within weeks he had a rebuttal paper written showing that Kashtan's benchmarks could be made to run as well on Unix as they could on VMS.

Rather than continue shipping 4BSD, the tuned-up system, with the addition of Robert Elz's auto configuration code, was released as 4.1BSD in June, 1981. Over its two-year lifetime about 400 distributions were shipped. The original intent had been to call it the 5BSD release; however, there were objections from AT&T that there would be customer confusion between their commercial Unix release, System V, and a Berkeley release named 5BSD. So, to resolve the issue, Berkeley agreed to change the naming scheme for future releases to stay at 4BSD and just increment the minor number.

4.2BSD

With the release of 4.1BSD, much of the furor over performance died down. DARPA was sufficiently satisfied with the results of the first contract that a new two-year contract was granted to Berkeley with funding almost five times that of the original. Half of the money went to the Unix project, the rest to other researchers in the Computer Science department. The contract called for major work to be done on the system so the DARPA research community could better do their work.

Based on the needs of the DARPA community, goals were set and work begun to define the modifications to the system. In particular, the new system was expected to include a faster file system that would raise throughput to the speed of available disk technology, support processes with multi-gigabyte address space requirements, provide flexible interprocess communication facilities that allow researchers to do work in distributed systems, and would integrate networking support so that machines running the new system could easily participate in the ARPAnet.

To assist in defining the new system, Duane Adams, Berkeley's contract monitor at DARPA, formed a group known as the "steering committee" to help guide the design work and ensure that the research community's needs were addressed. This committee met twice a year between April 1981 and June 1983. It included Bob Fabry, Bill Joy, and Sam Leffler of the University of California at Berkeley; Alan Nemeth and Rob Gurwitz of Bolt, Beranek, and Newman; Dennis Ritchie of Bell Laboratories; Keith Lantz of Stanford University; Rick Rashid of Carnegie-Mellon University; Bert Halstead of the Massachusetts Institute of Technology; Dan Lynch of The Information Sciences Institute; Duane Adams and Bob Baker of DARPA; and Jerry Popek of the University of California at Los Angeles. Beginning in 1984, these meetings were supplanted by workshops that were expanded to include many more people.

An initial document proposing facilities to be included in the new system was circulated to the steering committee and other people outside Berkeley in July, 1981, sparking many lengthy debates. In the summer of 1981, I became involved with the CSRG and took on the implementation of the new file system. During the summer, Joy concentrated on implementing a prototype version of the interprocess communication facilities. In the fall of 1981, Sam Leffler joined the CSRG as a full-time staff member to work with Bill Joy.

When Rob Gurwitz released an early implementation of the TCP/IP protocols to Berkeley, Joy integrated it into the system and tuned its performance. During this work, it became clear to Joy and Leffler that the new system would need to provide support for more than just the DARPA standard network protocols. Thus, they redesigned the internal structuring of the software, refining the interfaces so that multiple network protocols could be used simultaneously.

With the internal restructuring completed and the TCP/IP protocols integrated with the prototype IPC facilities, several simple applications were created to provide local users access to remote resources. These programs, **rcp**, **rsh**, **rlogin**, and **rwho** were intended to be temporary tools that would eventually be replaced by more reasonable facilities (hence the use of the distinguishing "r" prefix). This system, called 4.1a, was first distributed in April 1982 for local use; it was never intended that it would have wide circulation, though bootleg copies of the system proliferated as sites grew impatient waiting for the 4.2 release.

The 4.1a system was obsolete long before it was complete. However, feedback from its users provided valuable information that was used to create a revised proposal for the new system called the "4.2BSD System Manual." This document was circulated in February 1982 and contained a concise description of the proposed user interfaces to the system facilities that were to be implemented in 4.2BSD.

Concurrent with the 4.1a development, I completed the implementation of the new file system, and by June 1982, had fully integrated it into the 4.1a kernel. The resulting system was called 4.1b and ran on only a few select development machines at

Berkeley. Joy felt that with significant impending changes to the system, it was best to avoid even a local distribution, particularly since it required every machine's file systems to be dumped and restored to convert from 4.1a to 4.1b. Once the file system proved to be stable, Leffler proceeded to add the new file system related system calls, while Joy worked on revising the interprocess communication facilities.

In the late spring of 1982, Joy announced he was joining Sun Microsystems. Over the summer, he split his time between Sun and Berkeley, spending most of his time polishing his revisions to the interprocess communication facilities and reorganizing the Unix kernel sources to isolate machine dependencies. With Joy's departure, Leffler took over responsibility for completing the project. Certain deadlines had already been established and the release had been promised to the DARPA community for the spring of 1983. Given the time constraints, the work remaining to complete the release was evaluated and priorities were set. In particular, the virtual memory enhancements and the most sophisticated parts of the interprocess communication design were relegated to low priority (and later shelved completely). Also, with the implementation more than a year old and the Unix community's expectations heightened, it was decided an intermediate release should be put together to hold people until the final system could be completed. This system, called 4.1c, was distributed in April 1983; many vendors used this release to prepare for ports of 4.2 to their hardware. Pauline Schwartz was hired to take over the distribution duties starting with the 4.1c release.

In June 1983, Bob Fabry turned over administrative control of the CSRG to Professors Domenico Ferrari and Susan Graham to begin a sabbatical free from the frantic pace of the previous four years. Leffler continued the completion of the system, implementing the new signal facilities, adding to the networking support, redoing the standalone I/O system to simplify the installation process, integrating the disc quota facilities from Robert Elz, updating all the documentation, and tracking the bugs from the 4.1c release. In August 1983, the system was released as 4.2BSD.

When Leffler left Berkeley for Lucasfilm following the completion of 4.2, he was replaced by Mike Karels. Karels' previous experience with the 2.9BSD PDP-11 software distribution provided an ideal background for his new job. After completing my Ph.D. in December 1984, I joined Mike Karels full-time at the CSRG.

The popularity of 4.2BSD was impressive; within eighteen months more than 1,000 site licenses had been issued. Thus, more copies of 4.2BSD had been shipped than of all the previous Berkeley software distributions combined. Most of the Unix vendors shipped a 4.2BSD system rather than the commercial System V from AT&T. The reason was that System V had neither networking nor the Berkley Fast filesystem. The BSD release of Unix only held its dominant commercial position for a few years before returning to its roots. As networking and other 4.2BSD improvements were integrated into the system V release, the vendors usually switched back to it. However, later BSD developments continued to be incorporated into System V.

4.3BSD

As with the 4.1BSD release, criticism was quick in coming. Most of the complaints were that the system ran too slowly. The problem, not surprisingly, was that the new facilities had not been tuned and that many of the kernel data structures were not well-suited to their new uses. Karels' and my first year on the project was spent tuning and polishing the system.

After two years of work spent tuning the system and refining the networking code, we made an announcement at the June 1985 Usenix conference that we anticipated releasing 4.3BSD later that summer. However, our release plans were brought to an abrupt halt by the folks at BBN. They correctly pointed out that we had never updated 4.2BSD with the final version of their networking code. Rather, we were still using the much-hacked initial prototype that they had given us many years earlier. They complained to DARPA that Berkeley was to implement the interface while BBN was supposed to implement the protocol, so Berkeley should replace the TCP/IP code in 4.3BSD with the BBN implementation.

Mike Karels got the BBN code and did an evaluation of the work that had been done since the prototype that was handed off to Berkeley. He decided that the best plan was to incorporate the good ideas from the BBN code into the Berkeley code base, but not to replace the Berkeley code base. The reason to retain the Berkeley code base was that it had gotten considerable testing and improvements from the widespread distribution in 4.2BSD. However, as a compromise, he offered to include both implementations on the 4.3BSD distribution and let users select which one to use in their kernel.

After reviewing Mike Karels' decision, DARPA decided that releasing two code bases would lead to unnecessary interoperability problems, and that just one implementation should be released. To decide which code base to use, they gave both to Mike Muuse of the Ballistics Research Laboratory, who was viewed by both Berkeley and BBN as an independent third party. After a month of evaluation, the report came back that the Berkeley code was more efficient but that the BBN code handled congestion better. The tie breaker was that the Berkeley code flawlessly ran all the tests while the BBN code panicked under some stress conditions. The final decision by DARPA was that 4.3BSD would stick with the Berkeley code base.

The polished 4.3BSD system was finally released in June 1986. As expected, it quelled many of the performance complaints, much as the 4.1BSD release quelled many of the complaints about 4BSD. Although most of the vendors had started the switch back to System V, large parts of 4.3BSD were carried over into their systems, particularly the networking subsystem.

In October 1986, Keith Bostic joined the CSRG. One condition of his employment was that he be allowed to finish up a project that he had been working on at his previous job, which was to port 4.3BSD to the PDP-11. While both Karels and I believed that it would be impossible to get a system that compiled to 250 Kbytes on the VAX to fit in the 64-Kbyte address space of the PDP-11, we agreed that Bostic could finish up his attempts to do so. Much to our amazement, the port was done successfully, using an intricate set of overlays and auxiliary processor states found on the PDP-11. The result was the 2.11BSD release, done by Casey Leedom and Bostic, which is still in use on some of the last remaining PDP-11's still in production in 1998.

Meanwhile, it was becoming increasingly obvious that the VAX architecture was reaching the end of its life and that it was time to begin considering other machines for running BSD. A promising new architecture of the time was made by Computer Consoles, Incorporated, and was called the Power 6/32. Unfortunately, the architecture died when the company decided to change its strategic direction. However, they did provide the CSRG with several machines that enabled us to finish the work, started by Bill Joy, of splitting the BSD kernel into machine-dependent and machine-independent parts. The result of this work was released as 4.3BSD-Tahoe in June 1988. The name Tahoe came from the development name used by Computer Consoles, Incorporated, for the machine that they eventually released as the Power 6/32. Although the useful lifetime of the Power 6/32 machine support was short, the work done to split the kernel into machine-independent and machine-dependent parts proved to be extremely valuable as BSD was ported to numerous other architectures.

Networking, Release 1

Up through the release of 4.3BSD-Tahoe, all recipients of BSD had to first get an AT&T source license. That was because the BSD systems were never released by Berkeley in a binary-only format; the distributions always contained the complete source to every part of the system. The history of the Unix system and the BSD system in particular had shown the power of making the source available to the users. Instead of passively using the system, they actively worked to fix bugs, improve performance and functionality, and even add completely new features.

With the increasing cost of the AT&T source licenses, vendors that wanted to build standalone TCP/IP-based networking products for the PC market using the BSD code found the per-binary costs prohibitive. So, they requested that Berkeley break out the networking code and utilities and provide them under licensing terms that did not require an AT&T source license. The TCP/IP networking code clearly did not exist in

32/V and thus had been developed entirely by Berkeley and its contributors. The BSD originated networking code and supporting utilities were released in June 1989 as Networking Release 1, the first freely-redistributable code from Berkeley.

The licensing terms were liberal. A licensee could release the code modified or unmodified in source or binary form with no accounting or royalties to Berkeley. The only requirements were that the copyright notices in the source file be left intact and that products that incorporated the code indicate in their documentation that the product contained code from the University of California and its contributors. Although Berkeley charged a $1,000 fee to get a tape, anyone was free to get a copy from anyone who already had received it. Indeed, several large sites put it up for anonymous ftp shortly after it was released. Given that it was so easily available, the CSRG was pleased that several hundred organizations purchased copies, since their fees helped fund further development.

4.3BSD-Reno

Meanwhile, development continued on the base system. The virtual memory system whose interface was first described in the 4.2BSD architecture document finally came to fruition. As was often the case with the CSRG, we always tried to find existing code to integrate rather than write something from scratch. So, rather than design a new virtual memory system, we looked around for existing alternatives. Our first choice was the virtual memory system that appeared in Sun Microsystem's SunOS. Although there was some discussion about Sun contributing the code to Berkeley, nothing came of those talks. So we went with our second choice, which was to incorporate the virtual memory system from the MACH operating system done at Carnegie-Mellon University. Mike Hibler at the University of Utah merged the core technology from MACH with the user interface described by the 4.2BSD architecture manual (which was also the interface used by SunOS).

The other major addition to the system at the time was a Sun-compatible version of the Network Filesystem (NFS). Again the CSRG was able to avoid writing the actual NFS code, instead getting an implementation done by Rick Macklem at the University of Geulph in Canada.

Although we did not yet have the complete feature set of 4.4BSD ready to ship, the CSRG decided to do an interim release to get additional feedback and experiences on the two major new additions to the system. This licensed interim release was called 4.3BSD-Reno and occurred in early 1990. The release was named after a big gambling city in Nevada as an oblique reminder to its recipients that running the interim release was a bit of a gamble.

Networking, Release 2

During one of our weekly group meetings at the CSRG, Keith Bostic brought up the subject of the popularity of the freely-redistributable networking release and inquired about the possibility of doing an expanded release that included more of the BSD code. Mike Karels and I pointed out to Bostic that releasing large parts of the system was a huge task, but we agreed that if he could sort out how to deal with reimplementing the hundreds of utilities and the massive C library then we would tackle the kernel. Privately, Karels and I felt that would be the end of the discussion.

Undeterred, Bostic pioneered the technique of doing a mass net-based development effort. He solicited folks to rewrite the Unix utilities from scratch based solely on their published descriptions. Their only compensation would be to have their name listed among the Berkeley contributors next to the name of the utility that they rewrote. The contributions started slowly and were mostly for the trivial utilities. But as the list of completed utilities grew and Bostic continued to hold forth for contributions at public events such as Usenix, the rate of contributions continued to grow. Soon the list crossed one hundred utilities and within 18 months nearly all the important utilities and libraries had been rewritten.

Proudly, Bostic marched into Mike Karels' and my office, list in hand, wanting to know how we were doing on the kernel. Resigned to our task, Karels, Bostic, and I spent the next several months going over the entire distribution, file by file, removing code that had originated in the 32/V release. When the dust settled, we discovered that there were only six remaining kernel files that were still contaminated and which could not be trivially rewritten. While we considered rewriting those six files so that we could release a complete system, we decided instead to release just what we had. We did, however, seek permission for our expanded release from folks higher up in the University administration. After much internal debate and verification of our method for determining proprietary code, we were given the go-ahead to do the release.

Our initial thought was to come up with a whole new name for our second freely-redistributable release. However, we viewed getting a whole new license written and approved by the University lawyers as an unnecessary waste of resources and time delay. So, we decided to call the new release Networking Release 2 since we could just do a revision of the approved Networking Release 1 license agreement. Thus, our second greatly expanded freely-redistributable release began shipping in June 1991. The redistribution terms and cost were the same as the terms and cost of the first networking release. As before, several hundred individuals and organizations paid the $1,000 fee to get the distribution from Berkeley.

Closing the gap from the Networking Release 2 distribution to a fully functioning system did not take long. Within six months of the release, Bill Jolitz had written replacements for the six missing files. He promptly released a fully compiled and bootable system for the 386-based PC architecture which he called 386/BSD. Jolitz's 386/BSD distribution was done almost entirely on the Net. He simply put it up for anonymous FTP and let anyone who wanted it download it for free. Within weeks he had a huge following.

Unfortunately, the demands of keeping a full-time job meant that Jolitz could not devote the time needed to keep up with the flood of incoming bug fixes and enhancements to 386/BSD. So, within a few months of the release of 386/BSD, a group of avid 386/BSD users formed the NetBSD group to pool their collective resources to help maintain and later enhance the system. Their releases became known as the NetBSD distribution. The NetBSD group chose to emphasize the support of as many platforms as possible and continued the research style development done by the CSRG. Until 1998, their distribution was done solely over the Net; no distribution media was available. Their group continues to target primarily the hardcore technical users. More information about the NetBSD project can be found at *http://www.netbsd.org*.

The FreeBSD group was formed a few months after the NetBSD group with a charter to support just the PC architecture and to go after a larger and less technically advanced group of users, much as Linux had done. They built elaborate installation scripts and began shipping their system on a low cost CD-ROM. The combination of ease of installation and heavy promotion on the Net and at major trade shows such as Comdex led to a fast, large growth curve. Certainly FreeBSD currently has the largest installed base of all the Release 2-derived systems.

FreeBSD has also ridden the wave of Linux popularity by adding a Linux emulation mode that allows Linux binaries to run on the FreeBSD platform. This feature allows FreeBSD users to use the ever-growing set of applications available for Linux while getting the robustness, reliability, and performance of the FreeBSD system. The group recently opened a FreeBSD Mall (*http://www.freebsdmall.com*), which brings together many parts of the FreeBSD community, including consulting services, derived products, books, and a newsletter.

In the mid-1990s, OpenBSD spun off from the NetBSD group. Their technical focus was aimed at improving the security of the system. Their marketing focus was to make the system easier to use and more widely available. Thus, they began producing and selling CD-ROMs with many of the ease-of-installation ideas from the FreeBSD distribution. More information about the OpenBSD project can be found at *http://www.openbsd.org*.

The Lawsuit

In addition to the groups organized to freely redistribute systems built around the Networking Release 2 tape, a company, Berkeley Software Design, Incorporated (BSDI), was formed to develop and distribute a commercially supported version of the code. (More information about BSDI can be found at *http://www.bsdi.com*.) Like the other groups, they started by adding the six missing files that Bill Jolitz had written for his 386/BSD release. BSDI began selling their system including both source and binaries in January 1992 for $995. They began running advertisements touting their 99% discount over the price charged for System V source plus binary systems. Interested readers were told to call 1-800-ITS-Unix.

Shortly after BSDI began their sales campaign, they received a letter from Unix System Laboratories (USL) (a mostly-owned subsidiary of AT&T spun off to develop and sell Unix). The letter demanded that they stop promoting their product as Unix and in particular that they stop using the deceptive phone number. Although the phone number was promptly dropped and the advertisements changed to explain that the product was not Unix, USL was still unhappy and filed suit to enjoin BSDI from selling their product. The suit alleged that the BSDI product contained proprietary USL code and trade secrets. USL sought to get an injunction to halt BSDI's sales until the lawsuit was resolved, claiming that they would suffer irreparable harm from the loss of their trade secrets if the BSDI distributions continued.

At the preliminary hearing for the injunction, BSDI contended that they were simply using the sources being freely distributed by the University of California plus six additional files. They were willing to discuss the content of any of the six added files, but did not believe that they should be held responsible for the files being distributed by the University of California. The judge agreed with BSDI's argument and told USL that they would have to restate their complaint based solely on the six files or he would dismiss it. Recognizing that they would have a hard time making a case from just the six files, USL decided to refile the suit against both BSDI and the University of California. As before, USL requested an injunction on the shipping of Networking Release 2 from the University and on the BSDI products.

With the impending injunction hearing just a few short weeks away, preparation began in earnest. All the members of the CSRG were deposed as were nearly everyone employed at BSDI. Briefs, counter-briefs, and counter-counter-briefs flew back and forth between the lawyers. Keith Bostic and I personally had to write several hundred pages of material that found its way into various briefs.

In December 1992, Dickinson R. Debevoise, a United States District Judge in New Jersey, heard the arguments for the injunction. Although judges usually rule on injunction requests immediately, he decided to take it under advisement. On a Friday about six weeks later, he issued a forty-page opinion in which he denied the injunction and threw out all but two of the complaints. The remaining two complaints were narrowed to recent copyrights and the possibility of the loss of trade secrets. He also suggested that the matter should be heard in a state court system before being heard in the federal court system.

The University of California took the hint and rushed into California state court the following Monday morning with a counter-suit against USL. By filing first in California, the University had established the locale of any further state court action. Constitutional law requires all state filing to be done in a single state to prevent a litigant with deep pockets from bleeding an opponent dry by filing fifty cases against them in every state. The result was that if USL wanted to take any action against the University in state courts, they would be forced to do so in California rather than in their home state of New Jersey.

The University's suit claimed that USL had failed in their obligation to provide due credit to the University for the use of BSD code in System V as required by the license that they had signed with the University. If the claim were found to be valid, the University asked that USL be forced to reprint all their documentation with the appropriate due credit added, to notify all their licensees of their oversight, and to run full-page advertisements in major publications such as *The Wall Street Journal* and *Fortune* magazine notifying the business world of their inadvertent oversight.

Soon after the filing in state court, USL was bought from AT&T by Novell. The CEO of Novell, Ray Noorda, stated publicly that he would rather compete in the marketplace than in court. By the summer of 1993, settlement talks had started. Unfortunately, the two sides had dug in so deep that the talks proceed slowly. With some further prodding by Ray Noorda on the USL side, many of the sticking points were removed and a settlement was finally reached in January 1994. The result was that three files were removed from the 18,000 that made up Networking Release 2, and a number of minor changes were made to other files. In addition, the University agreed to add USL copyrights to about 70 files, although those files continued to be freely redistributed.

4.4BSD

The newly blessed release was called 4.4BSD-Lite and was released in June 1994 under terms identical to those used for the Networking releases. Specifically, the terms allow free redistribution in source and binary form subject only to the constraint that the University copyrights remain intact and that the University receive credit when others use the code. Simultaneously, the complete system was released as 4.4BSD-Encumbered, which still required recipients to have a USL source license.

The lawsuit settlement also stipulated that USL would not sue any organization using 4.4BSD-Lite as the base for their system. So, all the BSD groups that were doing releases at that time, BSDI, NetBSD, and FreeBSD, had to restart their code base with the 4.4BSD-Lite sources into which they then merged their enhancements and improvements. While this reintegration caused a short-term delay in the development of the various BSD systems, it was a blessing in disguise since it forced all the divergent groups to resynchronize with the three years of development that had occurred at the CSRG since the release of Networking Release 2.

4.4BSD-Lite, Release 2

The money received from the 4.4BSD-Encumbered and 4.4BSD-Lite releases was used to fund a part-time effort to integrate bug fixes and enhancements. These changes continued for two years until the rate of bug reports and feature enhancements had died down to a trickle. The final set of changes was released as 4.4BSD-Lite, Release 2 in June 1995. Most of these changes eventually made it into the other systems source bases.

Following the release of 4.4BSD-Lite Release 2, the CSRG was disbanded. After nearly twenty years of piloting the BSD ship, we felt that it was time to let others with fresh ideas and boundless enthusiasm take over. While it might seem best to have a single centralized authority overseeing the system development, the idea of having several groups with different charters ensures that many different approaches will be tried. Because the system is released in source form, the best ideas can easily be picked up by other groups. If one group becomes particularly effective, they may eventually become the dominant system.

Today, the open source software movement is gaining increased attention and respect. Although the Linux system is perhaps the most well-known, about half of the utilities that it comes packaged with are drawn from the BSD distribution. The Linux distributions are also heavily dependent on the complier, debuggers, and other development tools written by the Free Software Foundation. Collectively, the CSRG, the Free Software Foundation, and the Linux kernel developers have created the platform from which the Open Source software movement has been launched. I am proud to have had the opportunity to help pioneer the Open Source software movement. I look forward to the day when it becomes the preferred way to develop and buy software for users and companies everywhere.

The Internet Engineering Task Force

Scott Bradner

For something that does not exist, the Internet Engineering Task Force (IETF) has had quite an impact. Apart from TCP/IP itself, all of the basic technology of the Internet was developed or has been refined in the IETF. IETF working groups created the routing, management, and transport standards without which the Internet would not exist. IETF working groups have defined the security standards that will help secure the Internet, the quality of service standards that will make the Internet a more predictable environment, and the standard for the next generation of the Internet protocol itself.

These standards have been phenomenally successful. The Internet is growing faster than any single technology in history, far faster than the railroad, electric light, telephone, or television, and it is only getting started. All of this has been accomplished with voluntary standards. No government requires the use of IETF standards. Competing standards, some mandated by governments around the world, have come and gone and the IETF standards flourish. But not all IETF standards succeed. It is only the standards that meet specific real-world requirements and do well that become true standards in fact as well as in name.

The IETF and its standards have succeeded for the same sorts of reasons that the Open Source community is taking off. IETF standards are developed in an open, all-inclusive process in which any interested individual can participate. All IETF documents are freely available over the Internet and can be reproduced at will. In fact the IETF's open document process is a case study in the potential of the Open Source movement.

This essay will give a short history of the IETF, a review of the IETF organization and processes and, at the end, some additional thoughts on the importance of open standards, open documents, and Open Source.

The History of the IETF

The IETF started in January of 1986 as a quarterly meeting of U.S. government funded researchers. Representatives from non-government vendors were invited, starting with the fourth IETF meeting in October of that year. Since that time all IETF meetings are open to anyone who would like to attend. The initial meetings were very small, with less than 35 people in attendance at each of the first five meetings and with the peak attendance in the first 13 meetings only 120 attendees, at the 12th meeting in January of 1989. The IETF has grown quite a bit since then, with more than 500 attendees at the 23rd meeting in March 1992, more than 750 attendees at the 29th meeting in March 1994, more than 1,000 attendees at the 31st meeting in December 1994, and almost 2,000 attendees at the 37th meeting in December 1996. The rate of growth in attendance has slowed to the point that there were 2,100 attendees at the 43rd meeting in December 1998. Along the way, in 1991, the IETF reduced the number of meetings from four to three per year.

The IETF makes use of a small Secretariat, currently operating out of Reston, VA, and an RFC Editor, currently operated by the University of Southern California's Information Sciences Institute.

The IETF itself has never been incorporated as a legal entity. It has merely been an activity without legal substance. Up until the end of 1997, the IETF's expenses were covered by a combination of U.S. government grants and meeting fees. Since the beginning of 1998 the expenses have been covered by meeting fees and the Internet Society.

The Internet Society was formed in 1992, partially to provide a legal umbrella over the IETF standards process and to provide some funding for IETF-related activities. The Internet Society, an international membership-based non-profit organization, also evangelizes for the Internet in parts of the world that the Internet has not yet reached. At this time the IETF can be best described as a standards development function operating under the auspices of the Internet Society.

The concept of working groups was introduced at the 5th IETF meeting in February 1987 and there are now over 110 working groups operating within the IETF.

IETF Structure and Features

The IETF can be described as a membership organization without a defined membership. There are no specific criteria for membership other than to note that people and not organizations or companies are members of the IETF. Any individual who participates in an IETF mailing list or attends an IETF meeting can be said to be an IETF member.

At this writing there are 115 officially chartered working groups in the IETF. These working groups are organized into eight areas: Applications, General, Internet, Operations and Management, Routing, Security, Transport, and User Services. Each of the areas is managed by one or two volunteer Area Directors. The Area Directors sitting as a group, along with the chair of the IETF, form the Internet Engineering Steering Group (IESG). The IESG is the standards approval board for the IETF. In addition there is a 12-member Internet Architecture Board (IAB), which provides advice to the IESG on working group formation and the architectural implications of IETF working group efforts.

The members of the IAB and the Area Directors are selected for their two year terms by a nominations committee randomly selected each year from among volunteers who have attended at least two out of the previous three IETF meetings.

IETF Working Groups

One of the principal differences between the IETF and many other standards organizations is that the IETF is very much a bottom-up organization. It is quite rare for the IESG or the IAB to create a working group on their own to work on some problem that is felt to be an important one. Almost all working groups are formed when a small group of interested individuals get together on their own and then propose a working group to an Area Director. This does mean that the IETF cannot create task plans for future work, but at the same time it helps ensure that there is enough enthusiasm and expertise to make the working group a success.

The Area Director works with the people proposing the working group to develop a charter. Working group charters are used to list the specific deliverables of the working group, any liaison activities that might be needed with other groups, and, often most important, the limits on what the working group will explore. The proposed charter is then circulated to the IESG and IAB mailing lists for their comments. If significant issues do not arise within a week the charter is posted to the public IETF list and to a list of liaisons from other standards organizations to see if there is work going on in other forums which the IETF should be aware of. After another week for any additional comments, the IESG can then approve the charter and thereby create the working group.

IETF Documents

All IETF documents are public documents freely available over the Internet. The IETF does get a limited copyright from the authors when the documents are published to ensure the document remains freely available (the author can not decide to withdraw the document at some future time), republishable in its entirety by anyone, and, for most documents, that the IETF can make derivative works within the IETF standards process. The author retains all other rights.

The basic publication series for the IETF is the RFC series. RFC once stood for "Request for Comments," but since documents published as RFCs have generally gone through an extensive review process before publication, RFC is now best understood to mean "RFC." RFCs fall into two basic categories: standards track and non-standards track. Standards track RFCs can have Proposed Standard, Draft Standard, or Internet Standard status. Non-standards track RFCs can be classified as Informational, Experimental, or Historic.

In addition to RFCs, the IETF makes use of Internet-Drafts. These are temporary documents whose purpose is close to the original "request for comment" concept of RFCs and which are automatically removed after six months. Internet-Drafts are not to be cited or otherwise referenced other than as works in progress.

The IETF Process

The IETF motto is "rough consensus and running code." Working group unanimity is not required for a proposal to be adopted, but a proposal that cannot demonstrate that most of the working group members think that it is the right thing to do will not be approved. There is no fixed percentage support that a proposal must achieve, but most proposals that have more than 90% support can be approved and those with less than 80% can often be rejected. IETF working groups do not actually vote, but can resort to a show of hands to see if the consensus is clear.

Non standards track documents can originate in IETF working group activity or from individuals who would like to make their thoughts or technical proposals available to the Internet community. Almost all proposals for RFC publication are reviewed by the IESG, after which the IESG will provide advice to the RFC Editor on the advisability of publishing the document. The RFC Editor then decides whether to publish the document and, if the IESG offers one, weather to include a note from the IESG in the document. IESG notes in this case are used to indicate discomfort with the proposal if the IESG feels that some sort of warning label would be helpful.

In the normal case of a standards track document an IETF working group will produce an Internet-Draft to be published as the RFC. The final step in the working group evaluation of the proposal is a "last call," normally two weeks long, where the working group chair asks the working group mailing list if there are any outstanding issues with the proposal. If the result of the working group last call indicates that the consensus of the group is that the proposal should be accepted, the proposal is then forwarded to the IESG for their evaluation. The first step in the IESG evaluation is an IETF-wide last call sent to the main IETF announcement mailing list. This is so that people who have not been following the working group work can comment on the proposal. The normal IETF last call is two weeks for proposals that come from IETF working groups and four weeks for proposals not originating from IETF working groups.

The IESG uses the results of the IETF last-call as input to its deliberations about the proposal. The IESG can approve the document and request its publication, or it can send the proposal back to the author(s) for revision based on the IESG's evaluation of the proposal. This same process is used for each stage of the standards track.

Proposals normally enter the standards track as Proposed Standards, but occasionally if there is uncertainty about the technology or if additional testing is felt to be useful a document is initially published as an Experimental RFC. Proposed Standards are meant to be good ideas with no known technical flaws. After a minimum of six months as a Proposed Standard, a proposal can be considered for Draft Standard status. Draft Standards must have demonstrated that the documentation is clear and that any intellectual property rights issues with the proposal are understood and resolvable. This is done by requiring that there be at least two genetically independent, interoperable implementations of the proposal with separate exercises of licensing procedures if there are any. Note that it also requires that all of the separate features of the protocol be multiply-implemented. Any feature not meeting these requirements must be removed before the proposal can advance. Thus IETF standards can get simpler as they progress. This is the "running code" part of the IETF motto.

The final step in the IETF standards process is Internet Standard. After being at Draft Standard status for at least four months and demonstrating significant marketplace success, a proposal can be considered for Internet Standard status.

Two major differences stand out if one compares the IETF standards track with the process in other standards organizations. First, the final result of most standards bodies is approximately equivalent to the IETF Proposed Standard status. A good idea but with no requirement for actual running code. The second is that rough consensus instead of unanimity can produce proposals with fewer features added to quiet a noisy individual.

In brief, the IETF operates in a bottom-up task creation mode and believes in "fly before you buy."

Open Standards, Open Documents, and Open Source

It is quite clear that one of the major reasons that the IETF standards have been as successful as they have been is the IETF's open documentation and standards development policies. The IETF is one of the very few major standards organizations that make all of their documents openly available, as well as all of its mailing lists and meetings. In many of the traditional standards organizations, and even in some of the newer Internet-related groups, access to documents and meetings is restricted to members or only available by paying a fee. Sometimes this is because the organizations raise some of the funds to support themselves through the sale of their standards. In other cases it is because the organization has fee-based memberships, and one of the reasons for becoming a member is to be able participate in the standards development process and to get access to the standards as they are being developed.

Restricting participation in the standards development process often results in standards that do not do as good a job of meeting the needs of the user or vendor communities as they might or are more complex than the operator community can reasonably support. Restricting access to work-in-progress documents makes it harder for implementors to understand what the genesis and rational is for specific features in the standard, and this can lead to flawed implementations. Restricting access to the final standards inhibits the ability for students or developers from small startups to understand, and thus make use of, the standards.

The IETF supported the concept of open sources long before the Open Source movement was formed. Up until recently, it was the normal case that "reference implementations" of IETF technologies were done as part of the multiple implementations requirement for advancement on the standards track. This has never been a formal part of the IETF process, but it was generally a very useful by-product. Unfortunately this has slowed down somewhat in this age of more complex standards and higher economic implications for standards. The practice has never stopped, but it would be very good if the Open Source movement were to reinvigorate this unofficial part of the IETF standards process.

It may not be immediately apparent, but the availability of open standards processes and documentation is vital to the Open Source movement. Without a clear agreement on what is being worked on, normally articulated in standards documents, it is quite easy for distributed development projects, such as the Open Sources movement, to become fragmented and to flounder. There is an intrinsic partnership between open standards processes, open documentation, and open sources. This partnership produced the Internet and will produce additional wonders in the future.

The GNU Operating System and the Free Software Movement

Richard Stallman

The First Software-Sharing Community

When I started working at the MIT Artificial Intelligence Lab in 1971, I became part of a software-sharing community that had existed for many years. Sharing of software was not limited to our particular community; it is as old as computers, just as sharing of recipes is as old as cooking. But we did it more than most.

The AI Lab used a time-sharing operating system called ITS (the Incompatible Time-sharing System) that the Lab's staff hackers* had designed and written in assembler language for the Digital PDP-10, one of the large computers of the era. As a member of this community, an AI Lab staff system hacker, my job was to improve this system.

We did not call our software "free software," because that term did not yet exist, but that is what it was. Whenever people from another university or a company wanted to port and use a program, we gladly let them. If you saw someone using an unfamiliar and interesting program, you could always ask to see the source code, so that you could read it, change it, or cannibalize parts of it to make a new program.

The Collapse of the Community

The situation changed drastically in the early 1980s when Digital discontinued the PDP-10 series. Its architecture, elegant and powerful in the 60s, could not extend naturally to the larger address spaces that were becoming feasible in the 80s. This meant that nearly all of the programs composing ITS were obsolete.

The AI Lab hacker community had already collapsed, not long before. In 1981, the spin-off company Symbolics had hired away nearly all of the hackers from the AI

---

* The use of "hacker" to mean "security breaker" is a confusion on the part of the mass media. We hackers refuse to recognize that meaning, and continue using the word to mean, "Someone who loves to program and enjoys being clever about it."

Lab, and the depopulated community was unable to maintain itself. (The book *Hackers*, by Steve Levy, describes these events, and gives a clear picture of this community in its prime.) When the AI Lab bought a new PDP-10 in 1982, its administrators decided to use Digital's non-free timesharing system instead of ITS.

The modern computers of the era, such as the VAX or the 68020, had their own operating systems, but none of them were free software: you had to sign a nondisclosure agreement even to get an executable copy.

This meant that the first step in using a computer was to promise not to help your neighbor. A cooperating community was forbidden. The rule made by the owners of proprietary software was, "If you share with your neighbor, you are a pirate. If you want any changes, beg us to make them."

The idea that the proprietary software social system—the system that says you are not allowed to share or change software—is antisocial, that it is unethical, that it is simply wrong, may come as a surprise to some readers. But what else could we say about a system based on dividing the public and keeping users helpless? Readers who find the idea surprising may have taken the proprietary social system as given, or judged it on the terms suggested by proprietary software businesses. Software publishers have worked long and hard to convince people that there is only one way to look at the issue.

When software publishers talk about "enforcing" their "rights" or "stopping piracy," what they actually *say* is secondary. The real message of these statements is in the unstated assumptions they take for granted; the public is supposed to accept them uncritically. So let's examine them.

One assumption is that software companies have an unquestionable natural right to own software and thus have power over all its users. (If this were a natural right, then no matter how much harm it does to the public, we could not object.) Interestingly, the U.S. Constitution and legal tradition reject this view; copyright is not a natural right, but an artificial government-imposed monopoly that limits the users' natural right to copy.

Another unstated assumption is that the only important thing about software is what jobs it allows you to do—that we computer users should not care what kind of society we are allowed to have.

A third assumption is that we would have no usable software (or would never have a program to do this or that particular job) if we did not offer a company power over the users of the program. This assumption may have seemed plausible, before the free software movement demonstrated that we can make plenty of useful software without putting chains on it.

If we decline to accept these assumptions, and judge these issues based on ordinary common-sense morality while placing the users first, we arrive at very different conclusions. Computer users should be free to modify programs to fit their needs, and free to share software, because helping other people is the basis of society.

There is no room here for an extensive statement of the reasoning behind this conclusion, so I refer you to the web page, *http://www.gnu.org/philosophy/why-free.html*.

A Stark Moral Choice

With my community gone, not continuing as before was impossible. Instead, I faced a moral choice.

The easy choice was to join the proprietary software world, signing nondisclosure agreements and promising not to help my fellow hacker. Most likely I would also be developing software that was released under nondisclosure agreements, thus adding to the pressure on other people to betray their fellows too.

I could have made money this way, and perhaps amused myself writing code. But I knew that at the end of my career, I would look back on years of building walls to divide people, and feel I had spent my life making the world a worse place.

I had already experienced being on the receiving end of a nondisclosure agreement, when someone refused to give me and the MIT AI Lab the source code for the control program for our printer. (The lack of certain features in this program made use of the printer extremely frustrating.) So I could not tell myself that nondisclosure agreements were innocent. I was very angry when he refused to share with us; I could not turn around and do the same thing to everyone else.

Another choice, straightforward but unpleasant, was to leave the computer field. That way my skills would not be misused, but they would still be wasted. I would not be culpable for dividing and restricting computer users, but it would happen nonetheless.

So I looked for a way that a programmer could do something for the good. I asked myself, was there a program or programs that I could write, so as to make a community possible once again?

The answer was clear: what was needed first was an operating system. That is the crucial software for starting to use a computer. With an operating system, you can do many things; without one, you cannot run the computer at all. With a free operating system, we could again have a community of cooperating hackers—and invite anyone to join. And anyone would be able to use a computer without starting out by conspiring to deprive his or her friends.

As an operating system developer, I had the right skills for this job. So even though I could not take success for granted, I realized that I was elected to do the job. I chose to make the system compatible with Unix so that it would be portable, and so that Unix users could easily switch to it. The name GNU was chosen following a hacker tradition, as a recursive acronym for "GNU's Not Unix."

An operating system does not mean just a kernel, barely enough to run other programs. In the 1970s, every operating system worthy of the name included command processors, assemblers, compilers, interpreters, debuggers, text editors, mailers, and much more. ITS had them, Multics had them, VMS had them, and Unix had them. The GNU operating system would include them too. Later I heard these words, attributed to Hillel:*

> If I am not for myself, who will be for me?
>
> If I am only for myself, what am I?
>
> If not now, when?

The decision to start the GNU project was based on the same spirit.

Free as in Freedom

The term "free software" is sometimes misunderstood—it has nothing to do with price. It is about freedom. Here, therefore, is the definition of free software. A program is free software, for you, a particular user, if:

- You have the freedom to run the program, for any purpose.

- You have the freedom to modify the program to suit your needs. (To make this freedom effective in practice, you must have access to the source code, since making changes in a program without having the source code is exceedingly difficult.)

- You have the freedom to redistribute copies, either gratis or for a fee.

- You have the freedom to distribute modified versions of the program, so that the community can benefit from your improvements.

Since "free" refers to freedom, not to price, there is no contradiction between selling copies and free software. In fact, the freedom to sell copies is crucial: collections of free software sold on CD-ROMs are important for the community, and selling them is an important way to raise funds for free software development. Therefore, a program that people are not free to include on these collections is not free software.

---

* As an atheist, I don't follow any religious leaders, but I sometimes find I admire something one of them has said.

Because of the ambiguity of "free," people have long looked for alternatives, but no one has found a suitable alternative. The English language has more words and nuances than any other, but it lacks a simple, unambiguous word that means "free," as in freedom—"unfettered" being the word that comes closest in meaning. Such alternatives as "liberated," "freedom," and "open" have either the wrong meaning or some other disadvantage.

GNU Software and the GNU System

Developing a whole system is a very large project. To bring it into reach, I decided to adapt and use existing pieces of free software wherever that was possible. For example, I decided at the very beginning to use TeX as the principal text formatter; a few years later, I decided to use the X Window System rather than writing another window system for GNU.

Because of this decision, the GNU system is not the same as the collection of all GNU software. The GNU system includes programs that are not GNU software, programs that were developed by other people and projects for their own purposes, but which we can use because they are free software.

Commencing the Project

In January 1984 I quit my job at MIT and began writing GNU software. Leaving MIT was necessary so that MIT would not be able to interfere with distributing GNU as free software. If I had remained on the staff, MIT could have claimed to own the work, and could have imposed their own distribution terms, or even turned the work into a proprietary software package. I had no intention of doing a large amount of work only to see it become useless for its intended purpose: creating a new software-sharing community.

However, Professor Winston, then the head of the MIT AI Lab, kindly invited me to keep using the Lab's facilities.

The First Steps

Shortly before beginning the GNU project, I heard about the Free University Compiler Kit, also known as VUCK. (The Dutch word for "free" is written with a V.) This was a compiler designed to handle multiple languages, including C and Pascal, and to support multiple target machines. I wrote to its author asking if GNU could use it.

He responded derisively, stating that the university was free but the compiler was not. I therefore decided that my first program for the GNU project would be a multi-language, multi-platform compiler.

Hoping to avoid the need to write the whole compiler myself, I obtained the source code for the Pastel compiler, which was a multi-platform compiler developed at Lawrence Livermore Lab. It supported, and was written in, an extended version of Pascal, designed to be a system-programming language. I added a C frontend, and began porting it to the Motorola 68000 computer. But I had to give that up when I discovered that the compiler needed many megabytes of stack space, and the available 68000 Unix system would only allow 64K.

I then determined that the Pastel compiler was designed to parse the entire input file into a syntax tree, convert the whole syntax tree into a chain of "instructions," and then generate the whole output file, without ever freeing any storage. At this point, I concluded I would have to write a new compiler from scratch. That new compiler is now known as GCC; none of the Pastel compiler is used in it, but I managed to adapt and use the C frontend that I had written. But that was some years later; first, I worked on GNU Emacs.

GNU Emacs

I began work on GNU Emacs in September 1984, and in early 1985 it was beginning to be usable. This enabled me to begin using Unix systems to do editing; having no interest in learning to use *vi* or *ed*, I had done my editing on other kinds of machines until then.

At this point, people began wanting to use GNU Emacs, which raised the question of how to distribute it. Of course, I put it on the anonymous ftp server on the MIT computer that I used. (This computer, prep.ai.mit.edu, thus became the principal GNU ftp distribution site; when it was decommissioned a few years later, we transferred the name to our new ftp server.) But at that time, many of the interested people were not on the Internet and could not get a copy by ftp. So the question was, what would I say to them?

I could have said, "Find a friend who is on the Net and who will make a copy for you." Or I could have done what I did with the original PDP-10 Emacs: tell them, "Mail me a tape and a SASE, and I will mail it back with Emacs on it." But I had no job, and I was looking for ways to make money from free software. So I announced that I would mail a tape to whoever wanted one, for a fee of $150. In this way, I started a free software distribution business, the precursor of the companies that today distribute entire Linux-based GNU systems.

Is a Program Free for Every User?

If a program is free software when it leaves the hands of its author, this does not necessarily mean it will be free software for everyone who has a copy of it. For example, public domain software (software that is not copyrighted) is free software; but anyone can make a proprietary modified version of it. Likewise, many free programs are copyrighted but distributed under simple permissive licenses that allow proprietary modified versions.

The paradigmatic example of this problem is the X Window System. Developed at MIT, and released as free software with a permissive license, it was soon adopted by various computer companies. They added X to their proprietary Unix systems, in binary form only, and covered by the same nondisclosure agreement. These copies of X were no more free software than Unix was.

The developers of the X Window System did not consider this a problem—they expected and intended this to happen. Their goal was not freedom, just "success," defined as "having many users." They did not care whether these users had freedom, only that they should be numerous.

This lead to a paradoxical situation where two different ways of counting the amount of freedom gave different answers to the question, "Is this program free?" If you judged based on the freedom provided by the distribution terms of the MIT release, you would say that X was free software. But if you measured the freedom of the average user of X, you would have to say it was proprietary software. Most X users were running the proprietary versions that came with Unix systems, not the free version.

Copyleft and the GNU GPL

The goal of GNU was to give users freedom, not just to be popular. So we needed to use distribution terms that would prevent GNU software from being turned into proprietary software. The method we use is called "copyleft."*

Copyleft uses copyright law, but flips it over to serve the opposite of its usual purpose: instead of a means of privatizing software, it becomes a means of keeping software free.

The central idea of copyleft is that we give everyone permission to run the program, copy the program, modify the program, and distribute modified versions—but not permission to add restrictions of their own. Thus, the crucial freedoms that define "free software" are guaranteed to everyone who has a copy; they become inalienable rights.

For an effective copyleft, modified versions must also be free. This ensures that work based on ours becomes available to our community if it is published. When

---

* In 1984 or 1985, Don Hopkins (a very imaginative fellow) mailed me a letter. On the envelope he had written several amusing sayings, including this one: "Copyleft—all rights reversed." I used the word "copyleft" to name the distribution concept I was developing at the time.

programmers who have jobs as programmers volunteer to improve GNU software, it is copyleft that prevents their employers from saying, "You can't share those changes, because we are going to use them to make our proprietary version of the program."

The requirement that changes must be free is essential if we want to ensure freedom for every user of the program. The companies that privatized the X Window System usually made some changes to port it to their systems and hardware. These changes were small compared with the great extent of X, but they were not trivial. If making changes was an excuse to deny the users freedom, it would be easy for anyone to take advantage of the excuse.

A related issue concerns combining a free program with non-free code. Such a combination would inevitably be non-free; whichever freedoms are lacking for the non-free part would be lacking for the whole as well. To permit such combinations would open a hole big enough to sink a ship. Therefore, a crucial requirement for copyleft is to plug this hole: anything added to or combined with a copylefted program must be such that the larger combined version is also free and copylefted.

The specific implementation of copyleft that we use for most GNU software is the GNU General Public License, or GNU GPL for short. We have other kinds of copyleft that are used in specific circumstances. GNU manuals are copylefted also, but use a much simpler kind of copyleft, because the complexity of the GNU GPL is not necessary for manuals.

The Free Software Foundation

As interest in using Emacs was growing, other people became involved in the GNU project, and we decided that it was time to seek funding once again. So in 1985 we created the Free Software Foundation, a tax-exempt charity for free software development. The FSF also took over the Emacs tape distribution business; later it extended this by adding other free software (both GNU and non-GNU) to the tape, and by selling free manuals as well.

The FSF accepts donations, but most of its income has always come from sales—of copies of free software, and of other related services. Today it sells CD-ROMs of source code, CD-ROMs with binaries, nicely printed manuals (all with freedom to redistribute and modify), and Deluxe Distributions (where we build the whole collection of software for your choice of platform).

Free Software Foundation employees have written and maintained a number of GNU software packages. Two notable ones are the C library and the shell. The GNU C library is what every program running on a GNU/Linux system uses to communicate with Linux. It was developed by a member of the Free Software Foundation staff,

Roland McGrath. The shell used on most GNU/Linux systems is BASH, the Bourne Again Shell,* which was developed by FSF employee Brian Fox.

We funded development of these programs because the GNU project was not just about tools or a development environment. Our goal was a complete operating system, and these programs were needed for that goal.

Free Software Support

The free software philosophy rejects a specific widespread business practice, but it is not against business. When businesses respect the users' freedom, we wish them success.

Selling copies of Emacs demonstrates one kind of free software business. When the FSF took over that business, I needed another way to make a living. I found it in selling services relating to the free software I had developed. This included teaching, for subjects such as how to program GNU Emacs and how to customize GCC, and software development, mostly porting GCC to new platforms.

Today each of these kinds of free software business is practiced by a number of corporations. Some distribute free software collections on CD-ROM; others sell support at levels ranging from answering user questions to fixing bugs to adding major new features. We are even beginning to see free software companies based on launching new free software products.

Watch out, though—a number of companies that associate themselves with the term "Open Source" actually base their business on non-free software that works with free software. These are not free software companies, they are proprietary software companies whose products tempt users away from freedom. They call these "value added," which reflects the values they would like us to adopt: convenience above freedom. If we value freedom more, we should call them "freedom subtracted" products.

Technical Goals

The principal goal of GNU was to be free software. Even if GNU had no technical advantage over Unix, it would have a social advantage, allowing users to cooperate, and an ethical advantage, respecting the user's freedom.

But it was natural to apply the known standards of good practice to the work—for example, dynamically allocating data structures to avoid arbitrary fixed size limits, and handling all the possible 8-bit codes wherever that made sense.

---

* "Bourne Again Shell" is a joke on the name "Bourne Shell," which was the usual shell on Unix.

In addition, we rejected the Unix focus on small memory size, by deciding not to support 16-bit machines (it was clear that 32-bit machines would be the norm by the time the GNU system was finished), and to make no effort to reduce memory usage unless it exceeded a megabyte. In programs for which handling very large files was not crucial, we encouraged programmers to read an entire input file into core, then scan its contents without having to worry about I/O.

These decisions enabled many GNU programs to surpass their Unix counterparts in reliability and speed.

Donated Computers

As the GNU project's reputation grew, people began offering to donate machines running Unix to the project. These were very useful, because the easiest way to develop components of GNU was to do it on a Unix system, and replace the components of that system one by one. But they raised an ethical issue: whether it was right for us to have a copy of Unix at all.

Unix was (and is) proprietary software, and the GNU project's philosophy said that we should not use proprietary software. But, applying the same reasoning that leads to the conclusion that violence in self-defense is justified, I concluded that it was legitimate to use a proprietary package when that was crucial for developing free replacement that would help others stop using the proprietary package.

But, even if this was a justifiable evil, it was still an evil. Today we no longer have any copies of Unix, because we have replaced them with free operating systems. If we could not replace a machine's operating system with a free one, we replaced the machine instead.

The GNU Task List

As the GNU project proceeded, and increasing numbers of system components were found or developed, eventually it became useful to make a list of the remaining gaps. We used it to recruit developers to write the missing pieces. This list became known as the GNU task list. In addition to missing Unix components, we listed various other useful software and documentation projects that, we thought, a truly complete system ought to have.

Today, hardly any Unix components are left in the GNU task list—those jobs have been done, aside from a few inessential ones. But the list is full of projects that some might call "applications." Any program that appeals to more than a narrow class of users would be a useful thing to add to an operating system.

Even games are included in the task list—and have been since the beginning. Unix included games, so naturally GNU should too. But compatibility was not an issue for games, so we did not follow the list of games that Unix had. Instead, we listed a spectrum of different kinds of games that users might like.

The GNU Library GPL

The GNU C library uses a special kind of copyleft called the GNU Library General Public License (LPGL), which gives permission to link proprietary software with the library. Why make this exception?

It is not a matter of principle; there is no principle that says proprietary software products are entitled to include our code. (Why contribute to a project predicated on refusing to share with us?) Using the LGPL for the C library, or for any library, is a matter of strategy.

The C library does a generic job; every proprietary system or compiler comes with a C library. Therefore, to make our C library available only to free software would not have given free software any advantage—it would only have discouraged use of our library.

One system is an exception to this: on the GNU system (and this includes GNU/Linux), the GNU C library is the only C library. So the distribution terms of the GNU C library determine whether it is possible to compile a proprietary program for the GNU system. There is no ethical reason to allow proprietary applications on the GNU system, but strategically it seems that disallowing them would do more to discourage use of the GNU system than to encourage development of free applications.

That is why using the Library GPL is a good strategy for the C library. For other libraries, the strategic decision needs to be considered on a case-by-case basis. When a library does a special job that can help write certain kinds of programs, then releasing it under the GPL, limiting it to free programs only, is a way of helping other free software developers, giving them an advantage against proprietary software.

Consider GNU Readline, a library that was developed to provide command-line editing for BASH. Readline is released under the ordinary GNU GPL, not the Library GPL. This probably does reduce the amount Readline is used, but that is no loss for us. Meanwhile, at least one useful application has been made free software specifically so it could use Readline, and that is a real gain for the community.

Proprietary software developers have the advantages money provides; free software developers need to make advantages for each other. I hope some day we will have a large collection of GPL-covered libraries that have no parallel available to proprietary software, providing useful modules to serve as building blocks in new free software, and adding up to a major advantage for further free software development.

Scratching an Itch?

Eric Raymond says that "Every good work of software starts by scratching a developer's personal itch." Maybe that happens sometimes, but many essential pieces of GNU software were developed in order to have a complete free operating system. They come from a vision and a plan, not from impulse.

For example, we developed the GNU C library because a Unix-like system needs a C library, the Bourne-Again Shell (BASH) because a Unix-like system needs a shell, and the GNU *tar* because a Unix-like system needs a *tar* program. The same is true for my programs, the GNU C compiler, GNU Emacs, GDB, and GNU Make.

Some GNU programs were developed to cope with specific threats to our freedom. Thus, we developed *gzip* to replace the Compress program, which had been lost to the community because of the LZW patents. We found people to develop LessTif, and more recently started GNOME and Harmony, to address the problems caused by certain proprietary libraries (see below). We are developing the GNU Privacy Guard to replace popular non-free encryption software, because users should not have to choose between privacy and freedom.

Of course, the people writing these programs became interested in the work, and many features were added to them by various people for the sake of their own needs or interests. But that is not why the programs exist.

Unexpected Developments

At the beginning of the GNU project, I imagined that we would develop the whole GNU system, then release it as a whole. That is not how it happened.

Since each component of the GNU system was implemented on a Unix system, each component could run on Unix systems, long before a complete GNU system existed. Some of these programs became popular, and users began extending them and porting them—to the various incompatible versions of Unix, and sometimes to other systems as well.

The process made these programs much more powerful, and attracted both funds and contributors to the GNU project. But it probably also delayed completion of a minimal working system by several years, as GNU developers' time was put into maintaining these ports and adding features to the existing components, rather than moving on to write one missing component after another.

The GNU HURD

By 1990, the GNU system was almost complete; the only major missing component was the kernel. We had decided to implement our kernel as a collection of server processes running on top of Mach. Mach is a microkernel developed at Carnegie Mellon University and then at the University of Utah; the GNU HURD is a collection of servers (or "herd of gnus") that run on top of Mach, and do the various jobs of the Unix kernel. The start of development was delayed as we waited for Mach to be released as free software, as had been promised.

One reason for choosing this design was to avoid what seemed to be the hardest part of the job: debugging a kernel program without a source-level debugger to do it with. This part of the job had been done already, in Mach, and we expected to debug the HURD servers as user programs, with the GNU debugger (GDB). But it took a long time to make that possible, and the multi-threaded servers that send messages to each other have turned out to be very hard to debug. Making the HURD work solidly has stretched on for many years.

Alix

The GNU kernel was not originally supposed to be called the HURD. Its original name was Alix—named after the woman who was my sweetheart at the time. She, a Unix system administrator, had pointed out how her name would fit a common naming pattern for Unix system versions; as a joke, she told her friends, "Someone should name a kernel after me." I said nothing, but decided to surprise her with a kernel named Alix.

It did not stay that way. Michael Bushnell (now Thomas), the main developer of the kernel, preferred the name HURD, and redefined Alix to refer to a certain part of the kernel—the part that would trap system calls and handle them by sending messages to HURD servers.

Ultimately, Alix and I broke up, and she changed her name; independently, the HURD design was changed so that the C library would send messages directly to servers, and this made the Alix component disappear from the design.

But before these things happened, a friend of hers came across the name Alix in the HURD source code, and mentioned the name to her. So the name did its job.

Linux and GNU/Linux

The GNU HURD is not ready for production use. Fortunately, another kernel is available. In 1991, Linus Torvalds developed a Unix-compatible kernel and called it Linux. Around 1992, combining Linux with the not-quite-complete GNU system resulted in a complete free operating system. (Combining them was a substantial job in itself, of course.) It is due to Linux that we can actually run a version of the GNU system today.

We call this system version GNU/Linux, to express its composition as a combination of the GNU system with Linux as the kernel.

Challenges in Our Future

We have proved our ability to develop a broad spectrum of free software. This does not mean we are invincible and unstoppable. Several challenges make the future of free software uncertain; meeting them will require steadfast effort and endurance, sometimes lasting for years. It will require the kind of determination that people display when they value their freedom and will not let anyone take it away.

The following four sections discuss these challenges.

Secret Hardware

Hardware manufactures increasingly tend to keep hardware specifications secret. This makes it difficult to write free drivers so that Linux and XFree86 can support new hardware. We have complete free systems today, but we will not have them tomorrow if we cannot support tomorrow's computers.

There are two ways to cope with this problem. Programmers can do reverse engineering to figure out how to support the hardware. The rest of us can choose the hardware that is supported by free software; as our numbers increase, secrecy of specifications will become a self-defeating policy.

Reverse engineering is a big job; will we have programmers with sufficient determination to undertake it? Yes—if we have built up a strong feeling that free software is a matter of principle, and non-free drivers are intolerable. And will large numbers of us spend extra money, or even a little extra time, so we can use free drivers? Yes, if the determination to have freedom is widespread.

Non-Free Libraries

A non-free library that runs on free operating systems acts as a trap for free software developers. The library's attractive features are the bait; if you use the library, you fall into the trap, because your program cannot usefully be part of a free operating system. (Strictly speaking, we could include your program, but it won't *run* with the library missing.) Even worse, if a program that uses the proprietary library becomes popular, it can lure other unsuspecting programmers into the trap.

The first instance of this problem was the Motif toolkit, back in the 80s. Although there were as yet no free operating systems, it was clear what problem Motif would cause for them later on. The GNU Project responded in two ways: by asking individual free software projects to support the free X toolkit widgets as well as Motif, and by asking for someone to write a free replacement for Motif. The job took many years; LessTif, developed by the Hungry Programmers, became powerful enough to support most Motif applications only in 1997.

Around the same time, another non-free GUI toolkit library began to gain in popularity. This was Qt, from Troll Technologies. Ultimately Qt was used in a substantial collection of free software, the desktop KDE.

Free GNU/Linux systems were unable to use KDE, because we could not use the library. However, some commercial distributors of GNU/Linux systems who were not strict about sticking with free software added KDE to their systems—producing a system with more capabilities, but less freedom. The KDE group was actively encouraging more programmers to use Qt, and millions of new "Linux users" had never been exposed to the idea that there was a problem in this. The situation appeared grim.

The free software community responded to the problem in two ways: GNOME and Harmony.

GNOME, the GNU Network Object Model Environment, is GNU's desktop project. Started in 1997 by Miguel de Icaza, and developed with the support of Red Hat Software, GNOME set out to provide similar desktop facilities, but using free software exclusively. It has technical advantages as well, such as supporting a variety of languages, not just C++. But its main purpose was freedom: not to require the use of any non-free software.

Harmony is a compatible replacement library, designed to make it possible to run KDE software without using Qt.

In November 1998, the developers of Qt announced a change of license which, when carried out, should make Qt free software. There is no way to be sure, but I think that this was partly due to the community's firm response to the problem that Qt posed when it was non-free. (The new license is inconvenient and inequitable, so it remains desirable to avoid using Qt.)

How will we respond to the next tempting non-free library? Will the whole community understand the need to stay out of the trap? Or will many of us give up freedom for convenience, and produce a major problem? Our future depends on our philosophy.

Software Patents

The worst threat we face comes from software patents, which can put algorithms and features off-limits to free software for up to twenty years. The LZW compression algorithm patents were applied for in 1983, and we still cannot release free software to produce proper compressed GIFs. In 1998, a free program to produce MP3 compressed audio was removed from distribution under threat of a patent suit.

There are ways to cope with patents: we can search for evidence that a patent is invalid, and we can look for alternative ways to do a job. But each of these methods works only sometimes; when both fail, a patent may force all free software to lack some feature that users want. What will we do what this happens?

Those of us who value free software for freedom's sake will stay with free software anyway. We will manage to get work done without the patented features. But those who value free software because they expect it to be technically superior are likely to call it a failure when a patent holds it back. Thus, while it is useful to talk about the practical effectiveness of the "cathedral" model of development, and the reliability and power of some free software, we must not stop there. We must talk about freedom and principle.

Free Documentation

The biggest deficiency in our free operating systems is not in the software—it is the lack of good free manuals that we can include in our systems. Documentation is an essential part of any software package; when an important free software package does not come with a good free manual, that is a major gap. We have many such gaps today.

Free documentation, like free software, is a matter of freedom, not price. The criterion for a free manual is pretty much the same as for free software: it is a matter of giving all users certain freedoms. Redistribution (including commercial sale) must be permitted, online and on paper, so that the manual can accompany every copy of the program.

Permission for modification is crucial too. As a general rule, I don't believe that it is essential for people to have permission to modify all sorts of articles and books. For example, I don't think you or I are obliged to give permission to modify articles like this one, which describe our actions and our views.

But there is a particular reason why the freedom to modify is crucial for documentation for free software. When people exercise their right to modify the software, and add or change its features, if they are conscientious they will change the manual too—so they can provide accurate and usable documentation with the modified program. A manual which does not allow programmers to be conscientious and finish the job does not fill our community's needs.

Some kinds of limits on how modifications are done pose no problem. For example, requirements to preserve the original author's copyright notice, the distribution terms, or the list of authors, are OK. It is also no problem to require modified versions to include notice that they were modified, even to have entire sections that may not be deleted or changed, as long as these sections deal with non-technical topics.

These kinds of restrictions are not a problem because they don't stop the conscientious programmer from adapting the manual to fit the modified program. In other words, they don't block the free software community from making full use of the manual.

However, it must be possible to modify all the *technical* content of the manual, and then distribute the result in all the usual media, through all the usual channels; otherwise, the restrictions do obstruct the community, the manual is not free, and we need another manual.

Will free software developers have the awareness and determination to produce a full spectrum of free manuals? Once again, our future depends on philosophy.

We Must Talk About Freedom

Estimates today are that there are ten million users of GNU/Linux systems such as Debian GNU/Linux and Red Hat Linux. Free software has developed such practical advantages that users are flocking to it for purely practical reasons.

The good consequences of this are evident: more interest in developing free software, more customers for free software businesses, and more ability to encourage companies to develop commercial free software instead of proprietary software products.

But interest in the software is growing faster than awareness of the philosophy it is based on, and this leads to trouble. Our ability to meet the challenges and threats described above depends on the will to stand firm for freedom. To make sure our community has this will, we need to spread the idea to the new users as they come into the community.

But we are failing to do so: the efforts to attract new users into our community are far outstripping the efforts to teach them the civics of our community. We need to do both, and we need to keep the two efforts in balance.

"Open Source"

Teaching new users about freedom became more difficult in 1998, when a part of the community decided to stop using the term "free software" and say "open-source software" instead.

Some who favored this term aimed to avoid the confusion of "free" with "gratis"—a valid goal. Others, however, aimed to set aside the spirit of principle that had motivated the free software movement and the GNU project, and to appeal instead to executives and business users, many of whom hold an ideology that places profit above freedom, above community, above principle. Thus, the rhetoric of "Open

Source" focuses on the potential to make high quality, powerful software, but shuns the ideas of freedom, community, and principle.

The "Linux" magazines are a clear example of this—they are filled with advertisements for proprietary software that works with GNU/Linux. When the next Motif or Qt appears, will these magazines warn programmers to stay away from it, or will they run ads for it?

The support of business can contribute to the community in many ways; all else being equal, it is useful. But winning their support by speaking even less about freedom and principle can be disastrous; it makes the previous imbalance between outreach and civics education even worse.

"Free software" and "Open Source" describe the same category of software, more or less, but say different things about the software, and about values. The GNU Project continues to use the term "free software," to express the idea that freedom, not just technology, is important.

Try!

Yoda's philosophy (There is no "try") sounds neat, but it doesn't work for me. I have done most of my work while anxious about whether I could do the job, and unsure that it would be enough to achieve the goal if I did. But I tried anyway, because there was no one but me between the enemy and my city. Surprising myself, I have sometimes succeeded.

Sometimes I failed; some of my cities have fallen. Then I found another threatened city, and got ready for another battle. Over time, I've learned to look for threats and put myself between them and my city, calling on other hackers to come and join me.

Nowadays, I'm often not the only one. It is a relief and a joy when I see a regiment of hackers digging in to hold the line, and I realize this city may survive—for now. But the dangers are greater each year, and now Microsoft has explicitly targeted our community. We can't take the future of freedom for granted. Don't take it for granted! If you want to keep your freedom, you must be prepared to defend it.

Future of Cygnus Solutions
An Entrepreneur's Account

Michael Tiemann

Founded in 1989, Cygnus Solutions was the first, and according to a survey by *Forbes* magazine in August 1998, is by far the largest Open Source business today. Cygnus has established its primary product, the GNUPro Developers Kit, as both the leading compiler product and the leading debugger product in the embedded software tools market. Cygnus customers include the world's top microprocessor companies as well as leading consumer-electronics, Internet, telecommunications, office automation, networking, aerospace, and automotive companies. With headquarters in Sunnyvale, CA, and offices in Atlanta (GA), Boston (MA), Cambridge (UK), Tokyo (JP), Toronto (CN), and remote employees working from various locations ranging from Australia to Oregon, Cygnus is the largest privately held company in the embedded software industry, larger than two publicly-held companies and about to overtake the third largest. With a CAGR greater than 65% since 1992, Cygnus has been on the *San Jose Business Journal's* Top 100 Fastest Growing Private Companies three years in a row, and now ranks on the Software 500 list (based on revenue of all software businesses in the world).

In this essay, I will describe the Open Source model that provided the blueprint for our success, and how we are revising and enhancing it for our future endeavors.

It wasn't until November 13th, 1989 that we finally received the letter from the California Department of Corporations informing us that our application had been approved, and that we could deposit our $6,000 startup capital and begin transacting business as "Cygnus Support." That day was the culmination of a vision that began more than two years earlier, and the beginning of a journey which continues today, almost 10 years later.

The vision began innocently enough. My dad once told me, "If you're going to read a book, make sure you read it cover to cover." Like most fatherly advice, I applied it only when it suited me, and in 1987, when I had become bored with my job and interested in GNU software, I decided to read Richard Stallman's self-published book

GNU Emacs Manual cover to cover. (This book was self-published because at that time, no self-respecting publisher would print a book that encouraged people to freely make legal copies of the text. In fact today, it's still a difficult concept for some publishers to grasp.)

Emacs is a fascinating program. More than a text editor, it has been customized to let you read and respond to email, read and post to newsgroups, start a shell, run compilations and debug the resulting programs, and it even gives you interactive access to the LISP interpreter that drives it. Creative users (or similarly bored hackers) have extended emacs with whimsical features, such as "doctor" mode (a Rogerian psychoanalytic program inspired by John McCarthy's ELIZA program), "dissociated-press," which scrambles text in a way that makes for difficult and sometimes hilarious reading, and even a program that will animate the solution of the Towers of Hanoi on a text screen. It was this depth and richness that drove me to want to learn more, to read the *GNU Emacs Manual* and the GNU Emacs source code.

The last chapter of the book, "The GNU Manifesto," was a personal answer from the author to the overarching question that nagged throughout my entire reading: why is such a cool program available as freely redistributable software (a.k.a. Open Source)? Stallman answers in the general question:

> Why I Must Write GNU
>
> I consider that the golden rule requires that if I like a program I must share it with other people who like it. Software sellers want to divide the users and conquer them, make each user agree not to share with others. I refuse to break solidarity with other users in this way.

There is much more to Stallman's manifesto—too much to quote here. (A reference is *http://www.fsf.org/gnu/manifesto.html*.) Suffice it to say that on the surface, it read like a socialist polemic, but I saw something different. I saw a business plan in disguise. The basic idea was simple: Open Source would unify the efforts of programmers around the world, and companies that provided commercial services (customizations, enhancements, bug fixes, support) based on that software could capitalize on the economies of scale and broad appeal of this new kind of software.

Emacs was not the only mind-blowing program to come from the Free Software Foundation. There was the GNU Debugger (GDB), which Stallman had to write because the debuggers from Digital Equipment Corporation (now part of Compaq) and Sun Microsystems were simply not up to the task of debugging something as complex as Emacs. Not only could it handle big tasks, but it handled them elegantly, with commands and extensions that were geared towards programmers. And because GDB was open-source software, programmers began adding more extensions that made GDB even more powerful. This was a kind of scalability that did not exist in proprietary software.

The real bombshell came in June of 1987, when Stallman released the GNU C Compiler (GCC) Version 1.0. I downloaded it immediately, and I used all the tricks I'd read about in the Emacs and GDB manuals to quickly learn its 110,000 lines of code. Stallman's compiler supported two platforms in its first release: the venerable VAX and the new Sun3 workstation. It handily generated better code on these platforms than the respective vendors' compilers could muster. In two weeks, I had ported GCC to a new microprocessor (the 32032 from National Semiconductor), and the resulting port was 20% faster than the proprietary compiler supplied by National. With another two weeks of hacking, I had raised the delta to 40%. (It was often said that the reason the National chip faded from existence was because it was supposed to be a 1 MIPS chip, to compete with Motorola's 68020, but when it was released, it only clocked .75 MIPS on application benchmarks. Note that 140% * 0.75 MIPS = 1.05 MIPS. How much did poor compiler technology cost National?) Compilers, Debuggers, and Editors are the Big 3 tools that programmers use on a day-to-day basis. GCC, GDB, and Emacs were so profoundly better than the proprietary alternatives, I could not help but think about how much money (not to mention economic benefit) there would be in replacing proprietary technology with technology that was not only better, but also getting better faster.

Again, a quote from the GNU Manifesto:

> There is nothing wrong with wanting pay for work, or seeking to maximize one's income, as long as one does not use means that are destructive. But the means customary in the field of software today are based on destruction.

> Extracting money from users of a program by restricting their use of it is destructive because the restrictions reduce the amount and the ways that the program can be used. This reduces the amount of wealth that humanity derives from the program. When there is a deliberate choice to restrict, the harmful consequences are deliberate destruction.

> The reason a good citizen does not use such destructive means to become wealthier is that, if everyone did so, we would all become poorer from the mutual destructiveness.

Heavy stuff, but the GNU Manifesto is ultimately a rational document. It dissects the nature of software, the nature of programming, the great tradition of academic learning, and concludes that regardless of the monetary consequences, there are ethical and moral imperatives to freely share information that was freely shared with you. I reached a different conclusion, one which Stallman and I have often argued, which was that the freedom to use, distribute, and modify software will prevail against any model that attempts to limit that freedom. It will prevail not for ethical reasons, but for competitive, market-driven reasons.

At first I tried to make my argument the way that Stallman made his: on the merits. I would explain how freedom to share would lead to greater innovation at lower cost, greater economies of scale through more open standards, etc., and people would universally respond "It's a great idea, but it will never work, because nobody is going to pay money for free software." After two years of polishing my rhetoric, refining my arguments, and delivering my messages to people who paid for me to fly all over the world, I never got farther than "It's a great idea, but . . .," when I had my second insight: if everybody thinks it's a great idea, it probably is, and if nobody thinks it will work, I'll have no competition!

$$-F = -MA$$

—*Isaac Newton*

You'll never see a physics textbook introduce Newton's law in this way, but mathematically speaking, it is just as valid as "F = ma". The point of this observation is that if you are careful about what assumptions you turn upside down, you can maintain the validity of your equations, though your result may look surprising. I believed that the model of providing commercial support for open-source software was something that looked impossible because people were so excited about the minus signs that they forgot to count and cancel them.

AN INVASION OF ARMIES CAN BE RESISTED, BUT NOT AN IDEA WHOSE TIME HAS COME.

—*Victor Hugo*

There was one final (and deeply hypothetical) question I had to answer before I was ready to drop out of the Ph.D. program at Stanford and start a company. Suppose that instead of being nearly broke, I had enough money to buy out any proprietary technology for the purposes of creating a business around that technology. I thought about Sun's technology. I thought about Digital's technology. I thought about other technology that I knew about. How long did I think I could make that business successful before somebody else who built their business around GNU would wipe me out? Would I even be able to recover my initial investment? When I realized how unattractive the position to compete with open-source software was, I knew it was an idea whose time had come.

THE DIFFERENCE BETWEEN THEORY AND PRACTICE TENDS TO BE VERY SMALL IN THEORY, BUT IN PRACTICE IT IS VERY LARGE INDEED.

—*Anonymous*

In this section, I will detail the theory behind the Open Source business model, and ways in which we attempted to make this theory practical.

We begin with a few famous observations:

> FREE MARKETS ARE SELF-ORGANIZING, PERMITTING THE MOST EFFICIENT USE OF
> RESOURCES FOR THE GREATEST CREATION OF VALUE.
>
> —*Adam Smith*

> INFORMATION, NO MATTER HOW EXPENSIVE TO CREATE, CAN BE REPLICATED
> AND SHARED AT LITTLE OR NO COST.
>
> —*Thomas Jefferson*

The concept of free market economics is so vast that I often like to joke that each year when it comes time to award the Nobel prize in economics, it goes to the economist who most eloquently paraphrases Adam Smith. But behind that joke lies a kernel of truth: there is untapped and unlimited economic potential waiting to be harnessed by using a more true free market system for software.

In the days of Adam Smith, free market economics went as far as one could travel or trade in person, but larger trades, especially trades between nations, were heavily controlled. When a sufficient number of business people became disenchanted with the prevailing royalty-based system, they revolted and created a new government that was designed to take less interest in their affairs than almost any government that had come before it. Indeed, it was freedom that provided the underlying architecture and vision of the Constitution of the American government, and freedom again that seems to be at the root of every important cause or action in today's global economic and political arena. What makes freedom so compelling? And what has made freedom so responsible for economic prosperity? We will address these questions shortly.

> THE MORE YOU UNDERSTAND WHAT IS WRONG WITH A FIGURE,
> THE MORE VALUABLE THAT FIGURE BECOMES.
>
> —*Lord Kelvin*

Clearly, when it came to tools for programmers in 1989, proprietary software was in a dismal state. First, the tools were primitive in the features they offered. Second, the features, when available, often had built-in limitations that tended to break when projects started to get complicated. Third, support from proprietary vendors was terrible; unless you were in the process of buying lots of hardware or renewing a large software site license, and could use the power of the purse to your advantage, you were out of luck when you ran into one of these built-in limitations. And finally, every vendor implemented their own proprietary extensions, so that when you did use the meager features of one platform, you became, imperceptibly at first, then more obviously later, inextricably tied to that platform. All in all, it was quite clear that whatever the merits of free market economics, they were not at work in the software marketplace. The extent to which the proprietary software model was a broken model made the study of that model extremely valuable indeed.

Today, as then, free market economics lives within the walls of proprietary software companies (where competing engineers and product groups vie for funding and favor). Outside their proprietary walls, the use and distribution of that software is heavily controlled by license agreements, patents, and trade secrets. One can only wonder what power, what efficiency is lost by practicing freedom at the micro level, and not at the macro level. By starting a company prepared to support users at the level of source code, we were going to find out.

INVENTION IS 1% INSPIRATION AND 99% PERSPIRATION.

—*Thomas Edison*

The simplistic view of a software company is that once you've created some software that people want to buy, the act of printing copies of that software and distributing it is not unlike printing money: the cost of goods is negligible, and the margin nearly perfect. I believe that one reason software reached such a poor state of affairs in the 1980s was that people focused on perfecting the abstract model of printing money, without concern for what happened once people actually started using the currency. The concept of software support was seen as a degenerate by-product of some flaw in the software product process, and that by minimizing software support investment, one could maximize profits.

This not only frustrated users, but it was bad for the software as well. Features that were easy to implement were often dismissed as "non-strategic." Without access to source code, features that customers would otherwise be able to implement themselves remained points of speculation and contention. And ultimately vendors (and their marketing departments), not customers, defined the arena of competition with a myriad of useless but easy-to-express features. Free market economics had been turned upside down.

NOBODY HAS A MONOPOLY ON THE TRUTH.

—*Anonymous*

COMMON LAW IS LEGAL CODE THAT IS FREE TO ALL PEOPLE EQUALLY.

—*Michael Tiemann*

It is all very well and good to have wonderful theories about how to make the world a better place. It is another thing entirely to get those theories funded to the point that they are self-sustaining. Although service-based companies were rare in the world of software products, there were many cases to study in other areas.

Consider the practice of law in America (or Great Britain). Common law is freely available to all who wish to use it. One need not license a decision such as *Roe v. Wade* in order to use it for arguments. Indeed, the decisions, once made, and at whatever cost, are free to all. Yet for all this freedom, lawyers are among the most expensive professionals to be found. How can a practice of law, which has no primary proprietary code, command such value?

It is not just the act of prosecuting law that people value so highly. It is also the cumulative value of that prosecution. If you hire a good lawyer, and in the course of the prosecution, a decision is made in your favor, that precedent becomes a new part of the law. Justice is not blind; it is full of history.

This is somewhat analogous to the concept of creating and maintaining standards with open-source software. It is very expensive to create a standard and get it right. But it is far more expensive to work without standards or to try to maintain a standard if the standard is bogus. There is great value in having good people working on software whose precedents will set the standards of tomorrow. We believed at the beginning that people would understand this value proposition, and would value the opportunity to pay us to create high-quality, open-source programs that would become the *de facto* standard of the software world.

Cygnus in the Early Years

Having mapped out the theory, it was time to put the theory into practice. Creating a service-based business is easy enough, if you know anything about business. Unfortunately, between the three founders of Cygnus, not one had any experience in running a business.

ALWAYS MAKE NEW MISTAKES.

—*Esther Dyson*

We used books from the Nolo Press to incorporate our business, establish our by-laws, and complete various other formalities. For every penny we saved in the first year, we paid out dollars by the thousands later on down the road. (It's not clear that we could have done any better hiring professional advice since the first such advice we received cost us hundreds per hour, and still cost us tens of thousands later to fix. For the most part, that still says more about our inability at the time to properly judge the scope of legal/corporate problems and to request the proper advice than it does about the particular incompetence of the many lawyers we tried talking to.)

Having created a completely new business model, we also created our own concepts of finance, accounting, marketing, sales, customer information, and support. Each of these creations served us adequately in the first year of business, where everything was chaotic, and everybody was focused on doing whatever job was necessary to get the business off the ground, but each needed to be completely retooled as the business grew.

CYGNUS—WE MAKE FREE SOFTWARE AFFORDABLE

—John Gilmore

To combat the chaos, we worked hard to make the basic business premise as simple as possible: we were going to provide proven technical support for proven technical software, and we were going to use economies of scale to make it profitable. In our estimation, we were going to provide two to four times the quality of support and development capabilities that in-house people could deliver, and we were going to provide these services for a half to a quarter of the cost. We downplayed all the other stuff about open-source software because it was far too nebulous to sell. We just focused on giving people better tools for less money, and contract by contract, we learned how to do that.

We wrote our first contract in February of 1990, and by the end of April, we had already written over $150,000 worth of contracts. In May, we sent letters to 50 prospects we had identified as possibly interested in our support, and in June, to another 100. Suddenly, the business was real. By the end of the first year, we had written $725,000 worth of support and development contracts, and everywhere we looked, there was more opportunity.

For all this success, we were brewing some serious problems. If we were selling our services for half to a quarter what an internal resource would cost, then were writing contracts that would cost in total between $1.5M to $3M to deliver, yet we only had five people in the whole company: one sales person, one part-time graduate student, and three founders doing everything from Ethernet wiring to letterhead proofing. How big would the business have to be before economies of scale really kicked in? At its current rate of growth, how many more all-nighters would we have to pull to get to that point? Nobody knew, because we didn't have any financial or operational models.

GNUPro

We decided that we needed to achieve economies of scale before burnout became a real problem. And, thinking like engineers, we decided that the fastest way to achieve these economies of scale was to ruthlessly focus on the smallest set of open-source technology that we could reasonably sell as a useful solution. The smaller the focus, we reasoned, the easier it would be to achieve some concept of scale.

FIRST, ESTABLISH A FIRM BASE.

—Sun Tzu

Throwing away plans to support shell tools, file utilities, source code control software, and even plans to write a free kernel for the Intel 386, we settled on selling the GNU compiler and debugger as a shrink-wrapped product. There were a dozen or so companies that sold third-party 32-bit compilers, and there were another dozen internal compiler groups at companies like Sun, HP, IBM, etc. Adding up the numbers, we felt that if we could take over the 32-bit compiler market, we'd be big enough to do all the other cool things we had envisioned from the outset (a full-on Open Source play, analogous to the EDS outsourcing model for IBM systems).

The GNU compiler already supported dozens of host environments and over a dozen target architectures (I had written six of the ports myself), making it one of the most widely ported compilers of its time. The GNU debugger ran on about five native platforms, and several people had adapted it to support embedded systems as well. We naively assumed that making a shrink-wrapped product was a mere matter of collecting bits onto a single distribution, writing a README, adding an install script, getting some product collateral, testing it, and shipping it. The reality was far more challenging.

First, GCC was in the process of transitioning from Version 1.42 to Version 2.0. While GCC Version 1 was good enough to beat most compilers on CISC machines like the m68k and the VAX, lots of new optimizations were needed to make it competitive on RISC platforms. When I did the first GCC port to the SPARC in 1988, GCC was 20% *slower* than Sun's compiler. I wrote an instruction scheduler in 1989 that narrowed the gap to 10%, and I worked on a branch scheduler that same year that, with the instruction scheduler, got GCC to within 5% of Sun's compiler. With the world transitioning from CISC to RISC, we went from having hands-down the best compiler in almost every regard to a more complex set of tradeoffs the customer would have to evaluate. It was no longer a simple, straightforward sell.

Second, GNU C++ was falling behind. I wrote GNU C++ in the fall of 1987, making it the first native-code C++ compiler in the world. C++ was a much more complex language than C, and it was still evolving when we started Cygnus. In 1990, several new, even more complex features became "standard," and with all the distractions of Cygnus, I had no time to keep GNU C++ current.

Third, GDB was all over the map. While GCC and G++ had remained reasonably coherent, with regular releases being made from a central location, GDB suffered fragmentation. Open-source opponents will argue that a benefit of proprietary software is that there's only one "true" version, whereas open-source software can fragment into a million out-of-sync releases, not one of them a legitimate "standard." Because there was no strong maintainer of GDB, it fragmented, with hundreds of people around the world making their own versions to meet their own needs.

Fourth, we did not in fact have a complete toolchain: we had an assembler, linker, and other binary utilities (a.k.a. binutils) that worked on some, but not most, of the platforms supported by GCC and GDB. By the time you took the platforms that GCC supported, intersected that with GDB's supported platforms, intersected with GAS, GLD, and so forth, there were exactly zero platforms that worked from a common source base.

Fifth, we had no C library, which was not a problem for native platforms like the Sun or HP, but a Big Deal for embedded systems developers who needed its functionality for their standalone applications.

Sixth, while our competitors had nothing that could match our just-in-time engineering feats, each of them had already-complete products that they sold very effectively in their respective niches. By building and selling a shrink-wrapped product, we were changing our attack plan from an elaborate flanking maneuver to a frontal assault against companies that had 10 to 100 times our revenues.

And finally, there was the matter of our own confidence. The nice thing about being the integrators of many quickly evolving tools is that the need for your services is so obvious. Skeptics challenged the very notion of a shrink-wrapped Open Source product by claiming that as soon as we produced anything of passing quality, there would be no need for our support business, and we'd be out of business in six months. It was a challenge to our business I would hear for the next four years.

THE WORLD IS FULL OF INSURMOUNTABLE OPPORTUNITIES.

—*Yogi Berra*

There was nothing to do but to go for it, and with an initial estimate of 6 months to do the work, we all agreed to "double up" and make it happen. I was tasked with growing the top line by day, and helping complete the work for GCC 2.0 and G++ by night. David Henkel-Wallace (a.k.a. Gumby), the second Cygnus founder, took on the so-called binutils and the library in addition to his duties as CFO and Director of Support. And John Gilmore, the third Cygnus founder, took on GDB. We hired some new people to help us (1) put the whole works into CVS (an open-source source code control system), (2) write configuration and installation scripts that could handle the hundreds of possible platforms our shrink-wrapped product might work on, (3) automate our testing procedures, and (4) help us with the heavy lifting on the new development contracts that we were closing at an accelerating rate.

Six months later, the job had inexplicably grown, and some people had grown bored with our strict (some would say restrictive) product focus. While the GNU product was the bulk of our sales and engineering efforts, we sold contracts for other technology, such as Kerberos (network security software), Emacs, and even our bug tracking and test framework software (which was still under development at that time).

John had sent a message to the Net saying essentially "I'm going to be the new GDB maintainer. If you want the features you've implemented in GDB to be maintained in the next version, send me your complete GDB sources and I'll figure out how to integrate them." In six weeks, he collected 137 versions of GDB (mostly hacks to Version 3.5), all of which had one or more features that needed to be integrated. John began designing the architecture for GDB 4.0 to support all of these features. Who was I to argue that it couldn't be done?

Gumby had decided that all the binary file utilities should use a common library that described all known object file and debugging formats. The reason behind this decision was clear when one looked at the functionality of the various tools that sit behind the compiler:

Tool	Reads	Writes
Compiler	ASCII	ASCII
Assembler	ASCII	Binary
Archiver	Binary	Binary
Linker	Binary	Binary
Size	Binary	Binary
Strip	Binary	Binary
Binary	Binary	Binary
Nm	Binary	Binary
Debugger	Binary	none

Each tool had its own implementation for reading and/or writing binary file formats, and each of these implementations had varying levels of support for each binary format: a.out, b.out, coff, ecoff, xcoff, elf, ieee695, and others. Moreover, when each tool was configured it supported only a single kind of binary file format. A fix to the m68k-a.out assembler might also need to be made in all the other a.out-specific tools, or it might need to propagate as a object file-independent change. Depending on how a utility was written, it might be an a.out-specific change for one tool, and a generic change for another!

By building a single library that supported all functionality from a single source base, it would be possible to achieve economies of scale sooner because everything could be factored and maintained in a consistent fashion. Besides, it would be neat to demonstrate the ability to link a.out object code to a coff library and generate an ieee695 executable! Gumby began designing the library and discussing the design with Stallman. Stallman said that the job was too difficult—it would require a complete rewrite of all the tools, and it would be too difficult to maintain. Gumby told him it wasn't such a "Big F*cking Deal" and hence named this new creation the BFD library. (We explained to our customers that BFD stood for the binary file descriptor library.)

But while John and Gumby hacked, I still had to sell contracts to keep cash coming in. Every quarter I would have new top-line goals that required more resources to fulfill more contracts, and all the best engineers were tied up on this release into which I had no visibility. Tensions rose between sales and engineering while the Open Source model seemed be working in reverse: the more development we did on GNU software, the less we got back from the Net, until we were doing over 50% of all GNU toolchain development.

Neither was this a temporary state of affairs. It would take a year and a half (!) before the first "Progressive Release" was finally completed. On that momentous day, I was assured that for the first time, a complete C and C++ development toolkit could be built from a single source base, and that we could support two platforms: the Sun3 and the Sun4. I was dumbfounded. I had written 6 GCC ports, 3 GDB ports, and a native-code C++ compiler and debugger in less time than it took a team of hackers to get two toolchains to work from a single source base!?

There were two mitigating facts: (1) the tools worked better than they ever worked before, with many new and useful features, and (2) because of all the infrastructure work we'd put into the job (not just rewriting the tools, but implementing a configuration script and an automated testing framework), we could expect to support many more host/target combinations in the future, including a virtually unlimited range of embedded system platforms.

We put this framework to the test, and it passed with flying colors:

Date	Release Name	Native	Embedded	Total Platforms
Mar 1992	p1	2	0	2
June1992	p2	5	0	5
Sep 1992	p3	5	10	15
Dec 1992	p4	5	20	25
Mar 1993	q1	5	30	35
Jun 1993	q2	5	45	50
Sep 1993	q3	7	53	60
Dec 1993	q4	8	67	75
Mar 1994	r1	10	75	85
Jun 1994	r2	10	80	90
Sep 1994	r3	10	85	95
Dec1004	r4	10	90	100

While the engineers were doing great things to create the GNUPro product, our sales team was working out how to sell it. In 1991, we hired a young business student, recently laid off from Applied Materials, who wanted to learn how to sell software. Though her native language was not English, she picked things up very quickly. By no means a hacker (though she spent some weekends at Cygnus teaching herself to program in C), she nevertheless became a really strong advocate of the Open Source approach. After six months of very successful selling, she invited me to see her make a customer presentation. I was floored. I had always sold Open Source the way a hacker would sell it: focusing mainly on the technical merits. She explained the intrinsic complexity of the job we were doing and the business value of the software we delivered, and this helped us finally explain to customers why they should buy from us instead of trying to do the work with their own people. I was selling the fact that our engineers were somehow better than theirs (not a message most managers want to hear), whereas she could explain how their engineers would benefit from having us do the baseline porting, support, and maintenance work. In the end, the mix of our technical prowess and business benefits led to equally powerful sales accomplishments:

Bookings ($K)	Profitability (%)	Cumulative CAGR
1990: 725	epsilon	N/A
1991: 1500	1	106%
1992: 2800	2	96%
1993: 4800	3	87%
1994: 5700	4	67%

WATSON! COME HERE!

—*Alexander Graham Bell*

Out of this effort has come significant new technologies that have been returned to the Net and become standards in their own right: GNU configure (a generic configuration script that can configure software based on three independent variables: a build platform, a host platform, and a target platform), autoconf (a higher-level script for creating configure scripts), automake (a makefile generator for autoconf-driven environments), DejaGNU (a regression testing framework), GNATS (a problem report management system), and others.

Today, the GNUPro toolkit supports over 175 host/target combinations, a number that is now limited by the actual diversity of the market, not a limitation in our release or configuration technology.

In fact, GNUPro has become so dominant that several of our competitors have announced their intention to sell commercial support for GNU software to compete with us! Fortunately, the Open Source model comes to the rescue again. Unless and until a competitor can match the 100+ engineers we have on staff today, most of whom are primary authors or maintainers of the software we support, they cannot displace us from our position as the "true GNU" source (we supply over 80% of all changes made to GCC, GDB, and related utilities). The best they can hope to do is add incremental features that their customers might pay them to add. But because the software is Open Source, whatever value they add comes back to Cygnus as open-source software, for us to integrate if it's good, or ignore if it's not. Unlike proprietary software in which competitors fight in a two-sided win/lose contest, with Open Source it's more like fighting on a Moebius strip, and everything flows to the side of the primary maintainer. So, while our competitors may get some tactical advantage in the "me-too" GNU space, Cygnus benefits in the long run. Founded in 1989, our first-mover advantage is ten years ahead of the competition.

Challenges

As can be seen from the chart above, while our growth rate remained impressive, it slowed as we grew. While we tried to sell the merits and value of Open Source software, skeptics and potential customers challenged our model with respect to:

Sanity
> Why would a customer pay for a competitor's advantage?

Scalability
> How can a service-based business scale?

Sustainability
> Will Cygnus be around when customers need it?

Profitability
> How can open-source software be profitable?

Manageability
> How can open-source software be managed to deliver quality consistently?

Investibility
> How can a company with no software IP ever attract investors?

Can you imagine trying to sell a $10,000 support contract to a manager of five embedded systems programmers, and getting hung up on whether or not Cygnus can go public based on its business model? For all that Open Source was a great way to open doors into the best and most innovative software development groups, it proved to be a major roadblock when selling to the mainstream market. We were about to learn first-hand what Geoffrey Moore meant in his book *Crossing the Chasm*.

This challenge became absolutely clear when I visited a group of developers who were building wireless communications systems at a Fortune 100 company. As part of their quality process, they not only evaluated their own quality, but the quality of their vendors according to a number of metrics. Of all the different vendors with whom they did business, most ranked "Very Good to Excellent" in most or all of the metrics. Their supplier of embedded tools, however, placed dead last with "Poor or

Unacceptable" in all categories for each of the three years this quality monitoring process had been in place. Yet they would not buy our tools because despite our testimonials (from their customers, no less!), superior technical features, and lower price, management did not want to go with an unknown solution. I left wondering why they even bothered to collect data if they'd never use it to act, but that was the wrong question. I should have instead realized that this was typical mainstream behavior, and that the way to fix the problem was not to fault the customer, but to improve our marketing and messaging.

Our problems were not solely external, however. Many customers did not believe that we could hire enough people to scale our support business much beyond whatever we told them was our current state. They were both quite wrong and quite right. When it came to hiring engineers, they were quite wrong. Cygnus was founded by engineers, and our culture, Open Source business model, and the opportunity to join the preeminent Open Source engineering team in the world has always made Cygnus attractive to the developers we've wanted to hire. Turnover, compared to the national average (and especially compared to the average in Silicon Valley) is something like a quarter to a tenth what other companies experience.

But when it came to hiring managers, it was another story altogether. Sharing many of the same concerns and prejudices that our mainstream customers expressed, most managers we contacted had no interest in working for Cygnus. Those that did were not attracted to it. Those who were attracted to it were often attracted to it for the wrong reasons. By the time we had two managers in our engineering department, we had over 50 engineers. Communication, process, management controls, and employee satisfaction all declined as managers struggled, often unsuccessfully, to come to grips with what it meant to be and manage an Open Source company.

Ironically enough, we also disqualified managers who could not accept creating a closed-source component to our business. Open Source was a business strategy, not a philosophy, and we did not want to hire managers who were not flexible enough to manage either open or closed source products to meet overall company objectives.

We have come to accept the fact that you cannot expect to hire managers who understand all the implications of open-source software right away. You have to expect them to make mistakes (which means you have to budget for the costs of those mistakes), and they have to be able to learn from those mistakes. Most managers who bring experience with them try to change things to fit that experience—a recipe for failure at Cygnus. It was very hard to find managers who could both manage from, and quickly learn from, experience. And we needed them by the dozens.

The Open Source model, for all its challenges, proved to be remarkably resilient. Though we did occasionally lose customers through poorly set expectations or poor execution, our annual renewal rate has remained roughly 90% by dollar value since

1993, and the number one reason we lose customers is "retirement": the conclusion of the customer's project. Two factors helped us survive where other companies would have failed: (1) every person, regardless of title or seniority, recognized the importance of meeting customer commitments (nobody was "above" doing customer support), and (2) when all else failed, the customer was empowered to help themselves (because all customers had source code). Thus, despite amazing amounts of turmoil inside Cygnus in those days, very few customers were ever left holding the bag because the software failed to deliver, a stunning contrast to stories we heard about our proprietary competition as well as people who used unsupported open-source software.

Getting Funded Beyond Open Source—eCos

The reality of the embedded systems world is that there are a relatively small number of companies that make the silicon and there are a relatively small number of Outside Equipment Manufacturers (OEMs) who buy the majority of the silicon for use in their embedded systems products. The rest of the market consists of a large number of small-volume players who build interesting stuff, but they do not drive the volumes necessary to mandate new chip designs or software solutions.

Between the semiconductor vendors and the OEMs there are hundreds of little software companies, all of whom are selling their wares. For example, there are over 120 commercially supported Real Time Operating Systems (RTOSes) in the market today. Not one of these RTOSes has more than a 6% market share, according to IDC. It's like the Unix world ten years ago, only twenty times more fragmented! This fragmentation leads to all the classic degenerative cases of free market economics: redundancy, incompatibility, price gouging, etc. What the semiconductor vendors and the OEMs wanted were standards that would accelerate TTM (time to money), and the commercial RTOS vendors were either taking too much time, costing too much money, or both.

In the embedded systems market we were the rising star: we were growing twice as fast as the leader in our market, and we were keeping our top four competitors to single-digit growth. Yet we were not treated like, nor did we act like, true market leaders. In 1995, after many conversations with our key customers about what did and did not work in their embedded systems world, we began to understand that our GNUPro compilers and debuggers could only go so far in addressing their problems. What customers needed was a silicon abstraction layer—a layer of software that sat underneath the standard C library or a real-time POSIX API. There was a new opportunity to expand our product offering in a non-trivial way.

We sharpened our pencils and took note of the obvious: 120+ commercial RTOSes and 1000+ in-house RTOSes meant that at the technical level nobody had yet built a sufficiently configurable RTOS to achieve "one size fits all," and from a business perspective we noted that run-time royalties were killing margins, so the RTOS had to be royalty-free. In other words, to consolidate the market around our solution, we needed to create a completely new, world-class technology, and we needed to give it away. Management kicked the idea around for a year before finally acting on it.

Once we did decide to go forward with this strategy, our management team continued to wrestle with the question "How is it going to make money?" Even as we continued to consolidate the market around GNUPro, it was not obvious to the team how we could repeat that model for an embedded operating system.

We did the smart thing that any business does when faced with a completely inconsistent problem: we made assumptions. Assuming we would figure out how to make money, we asked ourselves what were the N other things we needed to do in order to solve our customers' problems and become #1 in the market? (1) We needed to develop this whizzy new configuration technology, (2) we needed to build the rest of the system so that people would have something to configure, and (3) we needed to do all of this before the market opportunity evaporated. Software development costs money, and product-oriented software development on a timetable costs lots of money.

When we started Cygnus, we had all assumed that the VCs would never understand what we did, and if they did, it would not be until five or more years down the road, when there was nothing useful they could do for us. Happily, we were wrong on both counts.

Our first outside board member, Philippe Courtot, wasted no time in introducing me to leading VCs in early 1992. I was very open with each of them about our model, technology, and goals for the future, and I was equally open about the fact that we had designed Cygnus to be self-funding and hence did not need their money. Indeed, the fact that we could increase profitability a percentage point per year while growing the company at 80% per year was a pretty good indication (as far as I was concerned) that we were maturing the business nicely. Roger McNamee, a leading software industry analyst for the VC community, said it best when he said "I am both amazed and surprised by your business model. I am amazed at how well it is working, but the more I think about it, the more surprised I am that I didn't think of it first!"

While it was gratifying to think that we had aced the problem and didn't need outside funding, the reality was that by 1996, we had created so much opportunity beyond our self-funding GNUPro business that we needed a new plan and new partners.

We found two investors, Greylock Management and August Capital, who understood what we did and how we did it, understood what we could do with the right guidance and discipline, and had access to enough capital to execute our plan. They invested $6.25M, the largest private placement for a software company in the first half of 1997, and the execution began in earnest.

I DO NOT LIKE THEM, SAM-I-AM. I DO NOT LIKE GREEN EGGS AND HAM.

—Dr. Seuss

While the technical team ramped up, the business people continued to thrash on how the money was going to work, because at first we did not see the connection between the architecture of eCos and the business model we could use to commercialize it. On the technical front, we knew that the configurability of the system was key to delivering a "one size fits all" architecture. On the business front, we knew that a "one size fits all" was key to creating a unifying and beneficial standard for embedded systems development. But we still could not figure out who was going to pay for this benefit. The two sides worked on their problem independently for a year and a half. R&D costs mounted. Unable to reconcile the Open Source paradox, many managers didn't make it.

When the technical people were finally able to demonstrate what they first envisioned, it became clear to the business people what we were actually creating: the world's first Open Source architecture. To me, it was as exciting as the first time I looked at GCC.

Open Source is all well and good for the hacker, and the way that Open Source can create standards is great for the end user, but there's a gap between what hackers can do with open-source software and what regular users can do. We wanted eCos to be a product that could be embraced by the mainstream embedded developer, not just the hacker community. Our idea was to empower users with high-level tools that could configure, customize, and perform basic validation of eCos in an automated fashion, replacing the manual steps that in-house RTOS developers perform today. By making the high-level tools control eCos at the source-code level, and by architecting the source code so that it could be managed via these tools, we made it possible for end users to work virtually at the source-code level, without ever needing to read or write a line of C or C++ code. The proof of our success is that eCos can be scaled from 700 bytes (bare minimum silicon abstraction layer) to over 50 Kbytes (full-featured RTOS with Internet stack and filesystem)!

Once we realized that Open Source was not just a feature, but the technical enabler of eCos, and once we proved to ourselves that with this feature, we had a 10x performance advantage over our competition (10x space savings over object-level configurability and 10x–100x programmer efficiency over source-available, but not source-architected RTOSes), we packaged solutions to *deliver* that performance advantage to the market, and the preliminary response from the market has been extremely positive.

When one considers the past impossibilities of our GNU-based business, one can only imagine the possibilities that eCos will create for Cygnus Solutions and the world.

Reflections and Vision of the Future

Open-source software taps the intrinsic efficiency of the technical free market, but it does so in an organic and unpredictable way. Open Source businesses take on the role of Adam Smith's "invisible hand," guiding it to both help the overall market *and* to achieve their own microeconomic goals. The most successful Open Source businesses will be the ones who can successfully guide technologies that engender the greatest cooperation from the Net community and solve the greatest technical and business challenges of the user community.

Created from open-source software, the Internet has been a fantastic enabler for the development of new open-source software. As people continue to connect on the Internet and through Open Source, we will witness changes in the development and use of software in much the same way that the Renaissance changed how we developed and used academic knowledge. With the freedoms provided by open-source software, I expect nothing less!

> HE SET HIS MIND TO WORK ON UNKNOWN ARTS,
> THEREBY CHANGING THE LAWS OF NATURE.
>
> —*James Joyce*

Software Engineering

Paul Vixie

Software engineering is a wider field than "writing programs." Yet, in many Open Source projects, programs are simply written and given away. It's clear from historical examples that software need not be engineered in order to be widely used and enjoyed. In this essay we'll look at some general elements of software engineering, then at the Open Source community's usual equivalents to these elements, and then finally at the implications of the differences between the two approaches.

The Software Engineering Process

The elements of a software engineering process are generally enumerated as:

* Marketing Requirements
* System-Level Design
* Detailed Design
* Implementation
* Integration
* Field Testing
* Support

No element of this process ought to commence before the earlier ones are substantially complete, and whenever a change is made to some element, all dependent elements ought to be reviewed or redone in light of that change. It's possible that a given module will be both specified and implemented before its dependent modules are fully specified—this is called *advanced development or research*.

It is absolutely essential that every element of the software engineering process include several kinds of *review*: peer review, mentor/management review, and cross-disciplinary review.

Software engineering elements (whether documents or source code) must have version numbers and auditable histories. "Checking in" a change to an element should require some form of review, and the depth of the review should correspond directly to the scope of the change.

Marketing Requirements

The first step of a software engineering process is to create a document which describes the target customers and their reason for needing this product, and then goes on to list the features of the product which address these customer needs. The Marketing Requirements Document (MRD) is the battleground where the answer to the question "What should we build, and who will use it?" is decided.

In many failed projects, the MRD was handed down like an inscribed stone tablet from marketing to engineering, who would then gripe endlessly about the laws of physics and about how they couldn't actually build that product since they had no ready supply of Kryptonite or whatever. The MRD is a joint effort, with engineering not only reviewing but also writing a lot of the text.

System-Level Design

This is a high-level description of the product, in terms of "modules" (or sometimes "programs") and of the interaction between these modules. The goals of this document are first, to gain more confidence that the product could work and could be built, and second, to form a basis for estimating the total amount of work it will take to build it.

The system-level design document should also outline the system-level testing plan, in terms of customer needs and whether they would be met by the system design being proposed.

Detailed Design

The detailed design is where every module called out in the system-level design document is described in detail. The interface (command line formats, calling API, externally visible data structures) of each module has to be completely determined at this point, as well as dependencies between modules. Two things that will evolve out of the detailed design is a PERT or GANT chart showing what work has to be done and in what order, and more accurate estimates of the time it will take to complete each module.

Every module needs a *unit test plan*, which tells the implementor what test cases or what kind of test cases they need to generate in their unit testing in order to verify functionality. Note that there are additional, nonfunctional unit tests which will be discussed later.

Implementation

Every module described in the detailed design document has to be *implemented*. This includes the small act of *coding or programming* that is the heart and soul of the software engineering process. It's unfortunate that this small act is sometimes the only part of software engineering that is taught (or learned), since it is also the only part of software engineering which can be effectively self-taught.

A module can be considered implemented when it has been created, tested, and successfully used by some other module (or by the system-level testing process). Creating a module is the old edit-compile-repeat cycle. Module testing includes the unit level functional and regression tests called out by the detailed design, and also performance/stress testing, and code coverage analysis.

Integration

When all modules are nominally complete, system-level integration can be done. This is where all of the modules move into a single source pool and are compiled and linked and packaged as a system. Integration can be done incrementally, in parallel with the implementation of the various modules, but it cannot authoritatively approach "doneness" until all modules are substantially complete.

Integration includes the development of a system-level test. If the built package has to be able to install itself (which could mean just unpacking a tarball or copying files from a CD-ROM) then there should be an automated way of doing this, either on dedicated crash and burn systems or in containerized/simulated environments.

Sometimes, in the middleware arena, the package is just a built source pool, in which case no installation tools will exist and system testing will be done on the as-built pool.

Once the system has been installed (if it is installable), the automated system-level testing process should be able to invoke every public command and call every public entry point, with every possible reasonable combination of arguments. If the system is capable of creating some kind of database, then the automated system-level testing should create one and then use external (separately written) tools to verify the database's integrity. It's possible that the unit tests will serve some of these needs, and all unit tests should be run in sequence during the integration, build, and packaging process.

Field Testing

Field testing usually begins internally. That means employees of the organization that produced the software package will run it on their own computers. This should ultimately include all "production level" systems—desktops, laptops, and servers. The statement you want to be able to make at the time you ask customers to run a new software system (or a new version of an existing software system) is "we run it our-selves." The software developers should be available for direct technical support dur-ing internal field testing.

Ultimately it will be necessary to run the software externally, meaning on customers' (or prospective customers') computers. It's best to pick "friendly" customers for this exercise since it's likely that they will find a lot of defects—even some trivial and obvious ones—simply because their usage patterns and habits are likely to be differ-ent from those of your internal users. The software developers should be close to the front of the escalation path during external field testing.

Defects encountered during field testing need to be triaged by senior developers and technical marketers, to determine which ones can be fixed in the documentation, which ones need to be fixed before the current version is released, and which ones can be fixed in the next release (or never).

Support

Software defects encountered either during field testing or after the software has been distributed should be recorded in a tracking system. These defects should ultimately be assigned to a software engineer who will propose a change to either the definition and documentation of the system, or the definition of a module, or to the implemen-tation of a module. These changes should include additions to the unit and/or sys-tem-level tests, in the form of a regression test to show the defect and therefore show that it has been fixed (and to keep it from recurring later).

Just as the MRD was a joint venture between engineering and marketing, so it is that support is a joint venture between engineering and customer service. The battle-grounds in this venture are the bug list, the categorization of particular bugs, the maximum number of critical defects in a shippable software release, and so on.

Testing Details

Code Coverage Analysis

Code coverage testing begins with the instrumentation of the program code, some-times by a preprocessor, sometimes by an object code modifier, sometimes using a special mode of the compiler or linker, to keep track of all possible code paths in a block of source code and to record, during its execution, which ones were taken.

Consider the following somewhat typical C snippet:

```
1.    if (read(s, buf, sizeof buf) == -1)
2.    error++;
3.    else
4.    error = 0;
```

If the error variable has not been initialized, then the code is buggy, and if line 2 is ever executed then the results of the rest of the program will be undefined. The likelihood of an error in read (and a return value of –1 from it) occurring during normal testing is somewhat low. The way to avoid costly support events from this kind of bug is to make sure that your unit tests exercise every possible code path and that the results are correct in every case.

But wait, it gets better. Code paths are combinatorial. In our example above, the error variable may have been initialized earlier—let's say by a similar code snippet whose predicate ("system call failure") was false (meaning no error occurred). The following example, which is patently bad code that would not pass any kind of code review anyway, shows how easy it is for simple things to become complicated:

```
1.    if (connect(s, &sa, &sa_len) == -1)
2.    error++;
3.    else
4.    error = 0;
5.    if (read(s, buf, sizeof buf) == -1)
6.    error++;
7.    else
8.    error = 0;
```

There are now four code paths to test:

1. lines 1-2-5-6.

2. lines 1-2-5-8.

3. lines 1-4-5-6.

4. lines 1-4-5-8.

It's usually impossible to test every possible code path—there can be hundreds of paths through even a small function of a few dozen lines. And on the other hand, merely ensuring that your unit tests are capable (on successive runs, perhaps) of exercising every line of code is not sufficient. This kind of coverage analysis is not in the tool bag of every software engineer in the field—and that's why QA is its own specialty.

Regression Tests

Fixing a bug is just not enough. "Obvious by inspection" is often a cop-out used to cover the more insidious "writing the smoking gun test would be difficult." OK, so there are many bugs which *are* obvious by inspection, like division by the constant zero. But to figure out what to fix, one must look at the surrounding code to find out what the author (who was hopefully somebody else) intended. This kind of analysis should be documented as part of the fix, or as part of the comments in the source code, or both.

In the more common case, the bug isn't obvious by inspection and the fix will be in a different part of the source code than the place where the program dumped core or otherwise behaved badly. In these cases, a new test should be written which exercises the bad code path (or the bad program state or whatever) and then the fix should be tested against this new unit test. After review and check-in, the new unit test should *also* be checked in, so that if the same bug is reintroduced later as a side effect of some other change, QA will have some hope of catching it before the customers do.

Open Source Software Engineering

An Open Source project can include every single one of the above elements, and to be fair, some have. The commercial versions of BSD, BIND, and Sendmail are all examples of the standard software engineering process—but they didn't start out that way. A full-blown software engineering process is very resource-hungry, and instantiating one usually requires investment, which usually requires some kind of revenue plan.

The far more common case of an open-source project is one where the people involved are having fun and want their work to be as widely used as possible so they give it away without fee and sometimes without restrictions on redistribution. These folks might not have access to so-called "commercial grade" software tools (like code coverage analyzers, bounds-checking interpreters, and memory integrity verifiers). And the primary things they seem to find fun are coding, packaging, and evangelizing—not QA, not MRDs, and usually not hard and fast ship dates.

Let's revisit each of the elements of the software engineering process and see what typically takes its place in an unfunded Open Source project—a labor of love.

Marketing Requirements

Open Source folks tend to build the tools they need or wish they had. Sometimes this happens in conjunction with one's day job, and often it's someone whose primary job is something like system administration rather than software engineering. If, after several iterations, a software system reaches critical mass and takes on a life of its own, it will be distributed via Internet tarballs and other users will start to either ask for features or just sit down and implement them and send them in.

The battleground for an open-source MRD is usually a mailing list or newsgroup, with the users and developers bantering back and forth directly. Consensus is whatever the developers remember or agree with. Failure to consense often enough results in "code splits," where other developers start releasing their own versions. The MRD equivalent for Open Source can be very nurturing but it has sharp edges—conflict resolution is sometimes not possible (or not attempted).

System-Level Design

There usually just is no system-level design for an unfunded Open Source effort. Either the system design is implicit, springing forth whole and complete straight from Zeus's forehead, or it evolves over time (like the software itself). Usually by Version 2 or 3 of an open-source system, there actually *is* a system design even if it doesn't get written down anywhere.

It is here, rather than in any other departure from the normal rules of the software engineering road, that Open Source earns its reputation for being a little bit flakey. You can compensate for a lack of a formal MRD or even formal QA by just having really good programmers (or really friendly users), but if there's no system design (even if it's only in someone's head), the project's quality will be self-limited.

Detailed Design

Another casualty of being unfunded and wanting to have fun is a detailed design. Some people do find DDDs fun to work on, but these people generally get all the fun they can stand by writing DDDs during their day jobs. Detailed design ends up being a side effect of the implementation. "I know I need a parser, so I'll write one." Documenting the API in the form of external symbols in header files or manpages is optional and may not occur if the API isn't intended to be published or used outside of the project.

This is a shame, since a lot of good and otherwise reusable code gets hidden this way. Even modules that are not reusable or tightly bound to the project where they are created, and whose APIs are not part of the feature deliverables, really ought to have manpages explaining what they do and how to call them. It's hugely helpful to the other people who want to enhance the code, since they have to start by reading and understanding it.

Implementation

This is the fun part. Implementation is what programmers love most; it's what keeps them up late hacking when they could be sleeping. The opportunity to write code is the primary motivation for almost all open-source software development effort ever expended. If one focuses on this one aspect of software engineering to the exclusion of the others, there's a huge freedom of expression.

Open-source projects are how most programmers experiment with new styles, either styles of indentation or variable naming or "try to save memory" or "try to save CPU cycles" or what have you. And there are some artifacts of great beauty waiting in tarballs everywhere, where some programmer tried out a style for the first time and it *worked*.

An unfunded Open Source effort can have as much rigor and consistency as it wants—users will run the code if it's functional; most people don't care if the developer switched styles three times during the implementation process. The developers generally care, or they learn to care after a while. In this situation, Larry Wall's past comments about programming being an artistic expression very much hit home.

The main difference in an unfunded Open Source implementation is that review is informal. There's usually no mentor or peer looking at the code before it goes out. There are usually no unit tests, regression or otherwise.

Integration

Integration of an open-source project usually involves writing some manpages, making sure that it builds on every kind of system the developer has access to, cleaning up the Makefile to remove the random hair that creeps in during the implementation phase, writing a README, making a tarball, putting it up for anonymous FTP somewhere, and posting a note to some mailing list or newsgroup where interested users can find it.

Note that the comp.sources.unix newsgroup was rekindled in 1998 by Rob Braun, and it's a fine place to send announcements of new or updated open-source software packages. It also functions as a repository/archive.

That's right, no system-level testing. But then there's usually no system-level test plan and no unit tests. In fact, Open Source efforts are pretty light on testing overall. (Exceptions exist, such as Perl and PostgreSQL.) This lack of pre-release testing is not a weakness, though, as explained below.

Field Testing

Unfunded open-source software enjoys the best system-level testing in the industry, unless we include NASA's testing on space-bound robots in our comparison. The reason is simply that users tend to be much friendlier when they aren't being charged any money, and power users (often developers themselves) are much more helpful when they can read, and fix, the source code to something they're running.

The essence of field testing is its lack of rigor. What software engineering is looking for from its field testers is patterns of use which are inherently unpredictable at the time the system is being designed and built—in other words, real world experiences of real users. Unfunded open-source projects are simply unbeatable in this area.

An additional advantage enjoyed by open-source projects is the "peer review" of dozens or hundreds of other programmers looking for bugs by reading the source code rather than just by executing packaged executables. Some of the readers will be looking for security flaws and some of those found will not be reported (other than among other crackers), but this danger does not take away from the overall advantage of having uncounted strangers reading the source code. These strangers can really keep an Open Source developer on his or her toes in a way that no manager or mentor ever could.

Support

"Oops, sorry!" is what's usually said when a user finds a bug, or "Oops, sorry, and thanks!" if they also send a patch. "Hey, it works for me" is how Open Source developers do bug triage. If this sounds chaotic, it is. The lack of support can keep some users from being willing (or able) to run unfunded Open Source programs, but it also creates opportunities for consultants or software distributors to sell support contracts and/or enhanced and/or commercial versions.

When the Unix vendor community first encountered a strong desire from their users to ship prepackaged open-source software with their base systems, their first reaction was pretty much "Well, OK, but we're not going to support it." The success of companies like Cygnus has prompted reexamination of that position, but the culture clash runs pretty deep. Traditional software houses, including Unix vendors, just cannot plan or budget for the cost of sales of a support business if there are unreviewed changes being contributed by uncounted strangers.

Sometimes the answer is to internalize the software, running it through the normal QA process including unit and system testing, code coverage analysis, and so on. This can involve a reverse-engineered MRD and DDD to give QA some kind of context (i.e., what functionality to test for). Other times the answer is to rewrite the terms of the support agreement to "best efforts" rather than "guaranteed results." Ultimately the software support market will be filled by who can get leverage from all those uncounted strangers, since a lot of them are good people writing good software, and the Open Source culture is more effective in most cases at generating the level of functionality that users actually want (witness Linux versus Windows).

Conclusions

Engineering is an old field, and no matter whether one is building software, hardware, or railroad bridges, the elements of the engineering process are essentially the same:

- Identify a requirement, and its requirers.
- Design a solution that meets the requirement.
- Modularize the design; plan the implementation.
- Build it; test it; deliver it; support it.

Some fields put greater emphasis on some phases. For example, railroad bridge builders don't usually have to put a lot of thought into an MRD, the implementation process, or support—but they have to pay very close attention to the SDD and DDD and of course QA.

The seminal moment in the conversion of a "programmer" into a "software engineer" is that instant when they realize that engineering is a field and that they are able to enter that field but that it will require a fundamentally different mindset—and a lot more work. Open Source developers often succeed for years before the difference between programming and software engineering finally catches up to them, simply because Open Source projects take longer to suffer from the lack of engineering rigor.

This chapter has given a very shallow overview of software engineering, and hopefully provided some motivation and context for Open Source programmers to consider entering that field. Remember that the future is always a hybrid of all the best of what has gone into the past and present. Software engineering isn't just for the slide rule and pocket protector set—it's a rich field with a lot of proven techniques for building high-quality systems, especially high-quality systems that aren't amenable to the "one smart programmer" approach common to Open Source projects.

The Linux Edge

Linus Torvalds

Linux today has millions of users, thousands of developers, and a growing market. It is used in embedded systems; it is used to control robotic devices; it has flown on the space shuttle. I'd like to say that I knew this would happen, that it's all part of the plan for world domination. But honestly this has all taken me a bit by surprise. I was much more aware of the transition from one Linux user to one hundred Linux users than the transition from one hundred to one million users.

Linux has succeeded not because the original goal was to make it widely portable and widely available, but because it was based on good design principles and a good development model. This strong foundation made portability and availability easier to achieve.

Contrast Linux for a moment with ventures that have had strong commercial backing, like Java or Windows NT. The excitement about Java has convinced many people that "write once, run anywhere" is a worthy goal. We're moving into a time when a wider and wider range of hardware is being used for computing, so indeed this is an important value. Sun didn't invent the idea of "write once, run anywhere," however. Portability has long been a holy grail of the computer industry. Microsoft, for example, originally hoped that Windows NT would be a portable operating system, one that could run on Intel machines, but also on RISC machines common in the workstation environment. Linux never had such an ambitious original goal. It's ironic, then, that Linux has become such a successful medium for cross-platform code.

Originally Linux was targeted at only one architecture: the Intel 386. Today Linux runs on everything from PalmPilots to Alpha workstations; it is the most widely ported operating system available for PCs. If you write a program to run on Linux, then, for a wide range of machines, that program can be "write once, run anywhere." It's interesting to look at the decisions that went into the design of Linux, and how the Linux development effort evolved, to see how Linux managed to become something that was not at all part of the original vision.

Amiga and the Motorola Port

Linux is a Unix-like operating system, but not a version of Unix. This gives Linux a different heritage than, for example, Free BSD. What I mean is this: the creators of Free BSD started with the source code to Berkeley Unix, and their kernel is directly descended from that source code. So Free BSD is a version of Unix; it's in the Unix family tree. Linux, on the other hand, aims to provide an interface that is compatible with Unix, but the kernel was written from scratch, without reference to Unix source code. So Linux itself is not a port of Unix. It's a new operating system.

Porting this new operating systems to other platforms was really not on my mind at the beginning. At first I just wanted something that would run on my 386.

A serious effort to make the Linux kernel code portable began with the effort to port Linux to DEC's Alpha machine. The Alpha port was not the first port, however.

The first port came from a team who ported the Linux kernel to the Motorola 68K series, which was the chip in the early Sun, Apple, and Amiga computers. The programmers behind the Motorola port really wanted to do something low-level and in Europe you had a number of people who were in the Amiga community who were especially disenchanted with the idea of using DOS or Windows.

While the Amiga people did get a system running on the 68K, I don't really think of this as a successful port of Linux. They took the same kind of approach I had taken when writing Linux in the first place: writing code from scratch targeted to support a certain kind of interface. So that first 68K port could be considered a Linux-like operating system, and a fork off the original codebase.

In one sense this first 68K Linux was not helpful in creating a portable Linux, but in another sense it was. When I started thinking about the Alpha port I had to think about the 68K experience. If we took the same approach with Alpha, then I would have three different code bases to support in order to maintain Linux. Even if this had been feasible in terms of coding, it wasn't feasible in terms of management. I couldn't manage the development of Linux if it meant keeping track of an entirely new code base every time someone wanted Linux on a new architecture. Instead, I wanted to do a system where I have an Alpha specific tree, a 68K specific tree, and an x86 specific tree, but all in a common code base.

So the kernel underwent a major rewrite at this time. But that rewrite was motivated by how to work with a growing community of developers.

Microkernels

When I began to write the Linux kernel, there was an accepted school of thought about how to write a portable system. The conventional wisdom was that you had to use a microkernel-style architecture.

With a monolithic kernel such as the Linux kernel, memory is divided into user space and kernel space. Kernel space is where the actual kernel code is loaded, and where memory is allocated for kernel-level operations. Kernel operations include scheduling, process management, signaling, device I/O, paging, and swapping: the core operations that other programs rely on to be taken care of. Because the kernel code includes low-level interaction with the hardware, monolithic kernels appear to be specific to a particular architecture.

A microkernel performs a much smaller set of operations, and in more limited form: interprocess communication, limited process management and scheduling, and some low-level I/O. Microkernels appear to be less hardware-specific because many of the system specifics are pushed into user space. A microkernel architecture is basically a way of abstracting the details of process control, memory allocation, and resource allocation so that a port to another chipset would require minimal changes.

So at the time I started work on Linux in 1991, people assumed portability would come from a microkernel approach. You see, this was sort of the research darling at the time for computer scientists. However, I am a pragmatic person, and at the time I felt that microkernels (a) were experimental, (b) were obviously more complex than monolithic Kernels, and (c) executed notably slower than monolithic kernels. Speed matters a lot in a real-world operating system, and so a lot of the research dollars at the time were spent on examining optimization for microkernels to make it so they could run as fast as a normal kernel. The funny thing is if you actually read those papers, you find that, while the researchers were applying their optimizational tricks on a microkernel, in fact those same tricks could just as easily be applied to traditional kernels to accelerate their execution.

In fact, this made me think that the microkernel approach was essentially a dishonest approach aimed at receiving more dollars for research. I don't necessarily think these researchers were knowingly dishonest. Perhaps they were simply stupid. Or deluded. I mean this in a very real sense. The dishonesty comes from the intense pressure in the research community at that time to pursue the microkernel topic. In a computer science research lab, you were studying microkernels or you weren't studying kernels at all. So everyone was pressured into this dishonesty, even the people designing Windows NT. While the NT team knew the final result wouldn't approach a microkernel, they knew they had to pay lip service to the idea.

Fortunately I never felt much pressure to pursue microkernels. The University of Helsinki had been doing operating system research from the late 60s on, and people there didn't see the operating system kernel as much of a research topic anymore. In a way they were right: the basics of operating systems, and by extension the Linux kernel, were well understood by the early 70s; anything after that has been to some degree an exercise in self-gratification.

If you want code to be portable, you shouldn't necessarily create an abstraction layer to achieve portability. Instead you should just program intelligently. Essentially, trying to make microkernels portable is a waste of time. It's like building an exceptionally fast car and putting square tires on it. The idea of abstracting away the one thing that must be blindingly fast—the kernel—is inherently counter-productive.

Of course there's a bit more to microkernel research than that. But a big part of the problem is a difference in goals. The aim of much of the microkernel research was to design for a theoretical ideal, to come up with a design that would be as portable as possible across any conceivable architecture. With Linux I didn't have to aim for such a lofty goal. I was interested in portability between real world systems, not theoretical systems.

From Alpha to Portability

The Alpha port started in 1993, and took about a year to complete. The port wasn't entirely done after a year, but the basics were there. While this first port was difficult, it established some design principles that Linux has followed since, and that have made other ports easier.

The Linux kernel isn't written to be portable to any architecture. I decided that if a target architecture is fundamentally sane enough, and follows some basic rules then Linux would fundamentally support that kind of model. For example, memory management can be very different from one machine to another. I read up on the 68K, the Sparc, the Alpha, and the PowerPC memory management documents, and found that while there are differences in the details, there was a lot in common in the use of paging, caching, and so on. The Linux kernel memory management could be written to a common denominator among these architectures, and then it would not be so hard to modify the memory management code for the details of a specific architecture.

A few assumptions simplify the porting problem a lot. For example, if you say that a CPU must have paging, then it must by extension have some kind of translation lookup buffer (TLB), which tells the CPU how to map the virtual memory for use by the CPU. Of course, what form the TLB takes you aren't sure. But really, the only thing you need to know is how to fill it and how to flush it when you decide it has to go away. So in this sane architecture you know you need to have a few machine-specific parts in the kernel, but most of the code is based on the general mechanisms by which something like the TLB works.

Another rule of thumb that I follow is that it is always better to use a compile time constant rather than using a variable, and often by following this rule, the compiler will do a lot better job at code optimization. This is obviously wise, because you can set up your code so as to be flexibly defined, but easily optimized.

What's interesting about this approach—the approach of trying to define a sane common architecture—is that by doing this you can present a better architecture to the OS than is really available on the actual hardware platform. This sounds counterintuitive, but it's important. The generalizations you're looking for when surveying systems are frequently the same as the optimizations you'd like to make to improve the kernel's performance.

You see, when you do a large enough survey of things like page table implementation and you make a decision based on your observations—say, that the page tree should be only three deep—you find later that you could only have done it that way if you were truly interested in having high performance. In other words, if you had not been thinking about portability as a design goal, but had just been thinking about optimization of the kernel on a particular architecture, you would frequently reach the same conclusion—say, that the optimal depth for the kernel to represent the page tree is three deep.

This isn't just luck. Often when an architecture deviates from a sane general design in some of its details that's because it's a bad design. So the same principles that make you write around the design specifics to achieve portability also make you write around the bad design features and stick to a more optimized general design. Basically I have tried to reach middle ground by mixing the best of theory into the realistic facts of life on today's computer architectures.

Kernel Space and User Space

With a monolithic kernel such as the Linux kernel, it's important to be very cautious about allowing new code and new features into the kernel. These decisions can affect a number of things later on in the development cycle beyond the core kernel work.

The first very basic rule is to avoid interfaces. If someone wants to add something that involves a new system interface you need to be exceptionally careful. Once you give an interface to users they will start coding to it and once somebody starts coding to it you are stuck with it. Do you want to support the exact same interface for the rest of your system's life?

Other code is not so problematic. If it doesn't have an interface, say a disk driver, there isn't much to think about; you can just add a new disk driver with little risk. If Linux didn't have that driver before, adding it doesn't hurt anyone already using Linux, and opens Linux to some new users.

When it comes to other things, you have to balance. Is this a good implementation? Is this really adding a feature that is good? Sometimes even when the feature is good, it turns out that either the interface is bad or the implementation of that feature kind of implies that you can never do something else, now or in the future.

For example—though this is sort of an interface issue—suppose somebody has some stupid implementation of a filesystem where names can be no longer than 14 characters. The thing you really want to avoid having these limitations in an interface that is set in stone. Otherwise when you look to extend the filesystem, you are screwed because you have to find a way to fit within this lesser interface that was locked in before. Worse than that, every program that requests a filename may only have space in a variable for, say, 13 characters, so if you were to pass them a longer filename it would crash them.

Right now the only vendor that does such a stupid thing is Microsoft. Essentially, in order to read DOS/Windows files you have this ridiculous interface where all files had eleven characters, eight plus three. With NT, which allowed long filenames, they had to add a complete set of new routines to do the same things the other routines did, except that this set can also handle larger filenames. So this is an example of a bad interface polluting future works.

Another example of this happened in the Plan 9 operating system. They had this really cool system call to do a better process fork—a simple way for a program to split itself into two and continue processing along both forks. This new fork, which Plan 9 called R-Fork (and SGI later called S-Proc) essentially creates two separate process spaces that share an address space. This is helpful for threading especially.

Linux does this too with its clone system call, but it was implemented properly. However, with the SGI and Plan9 routines they decided that programs with two branches can share the same address space but use separate stacks. Normally when you use the same address in both threads, you get the same memory location. But you have a stack segment that is specific, so if you use a stack-based memory address you actually get two different memory locations that can share a stack pointer without overriding the other stack.

While this is a clever feat, the downside is that the overhead in maintaining the stacks makes this in practice really stupid to do. They found out too late that the performance went to hell. Since they had programs which used the interface they could not fix it. Instead they had to introduce an additional properly-written interface so that they could do what was wise with the stack space.

While a proprietary vendor can sometimes try to push the design flaw onto the architecture, in the case of Linux we do not have the latitude to do this.

This is another case where managing the development of Linux and making design decisions about Linux dictate the same approach. From a practical point of view, I couldn't manage lots of developers contributing interfaces to the kernel. I would not have been able to keep control over the kernel. But from a design point of view this is also the right thing to do: keep the kernel relatively small, and keep the number of interfaces and other constraints on future development to a minimum.

Of course Linux is not completely clean in this respect. Linux has inherited a number of terrible interfaces from previous implementations of Unix. So in some cases I would have been happier if I did not have to maintain the same interface as Unix. But Linux is about as clean as a system can be without starting completely from scratch. And if you want the benefit of being able to run Unix applications, then you get some of the Unix baggage as a consequence. Being able to run those applications has been vital to Linux's popularity, so the tradeoff is worth it.

GCC

Unix itself is a great success story in terms of portability. The Unix kernel, like many kernels, counts on the existence of C to give it the majority of the portability it needs. Likewise for Linux. For Unix the wide availability of C compilers on many architectures made it possible to port Unix to those architectures.

So Unix underscores how important compilers are. The importance of compilers was one reason I chose to license Linux under the GNU Public License (GPL). The GPL was the license for the GCC compiler. I think that all the other projects from the GNU group are for Linux insignificant in comparison. GCC is the only one that I really care about. A number of them I hate with a passion; the Emacs editor is horrible, for example. While Linux is larger than Emacs, at least Linux has the excuse that it needs to be.

But basically compilers are really a fundamental need.

Now that the Linux kernel follows a generally portable design, at least for reasonably sane architectures, portability should be possible as long as a reasonably good compiler is available. For the upcoming chips I don't worry much about architectural portability when it comes to the kernel anymore; I worry about the compilers. Intel's 64-bit chip, the Merced, is an obvious example, because Merced is very different for a compiler.

So the portability of Linux is very much tied to the fact that GCC is ported to major chip architectures.

Kernel Modules

With the Linux kernel it became clear very quickly that we want to have a system which is as modular as possible. The open-source development model really requires this, because otherwise you can't easily have people working in parallel. It's too painful when you have people working on the same part of the kernel and they clash.

Without modularity I would have to check every file that changed, which would be a lot, to make sure nothing was changed that would effect anything else. With modularity, when someone sends me patches to do a new filesystem and I don't necessarily trust the patches *per se*, I can still trust the fact that if nobody's using this filesystem, it's not going to impact anything else.

For example, Hans Reiser is working on a new filesystem, and he just got it working. I don't think it's worth trying to get into the 2.2 kernel at this point. But because of the modularity of the kernel I could if I really wanted to, and it wouldn't be too difficult. The key is to keep people from stepping on each other's toes.

With the 2.0 kernel Linux really grew up a lot. This was the point that we added loadable kernel modules. This obviously improved modularity by making an explicit structure for writing modules. Programmers could work on different modules without risk of interference. I could keep control over what was written into the kernel proper. So once again managing people and managing code led to the same design decision. To keep the number of people working on Linux coordinated, we needed something like kernel modules. But from a design point of view, it was also the right thing to do.

The other part of modularity is less obvious, and more problematic. This is the runtime loading part, which everyone agrees is a good thing, but leads to new problems. The first problem is technical, but technical problems are (almost) always the easiest to solve. The more important problem is the non-technical issues. For example, at which point is a module a derived work of Linux, and therefore under the GPL?

When the first module interface was done, there were people that had written drivers for SCO, and they weren't willing to release the source, as required by the GPL, but they were willing to recompile to provide binaries for Linux. At that point, for moral reasons, I decided I couldn't apply the GPL in this kind of situation.

The GPL requires that works "derived from" a work licensed under the GPL also be licensed under the GPL. Unfortunately what counts as a derived work can be a bit vague. As soon as you try to draw the line at derived works, the problem immediately becomes one of where do you draw the line?

We ended up deciding (or maybe I ended up decreeing) that system calls would not be considered to be linking against the kernel. That is, any program running on top of Linux would not be considered covered by the GPL. This decision was made very early on and I even added a special read-me file (see Appendix B) to make sure everyone knew about it. Because of this commercial vendors can write programs for Linux without having to worry about the GPL.

The result for module makers was that you could write a proprietary module if you only used the normal interface for loading. This is still a gray area of the kernel though. These gray areas leave holes for people to take advantage of things, perhaps, and it's partly because the GPL really isn't clear about things like module interface. If anyone were to abuse the guidelines by using the exported symbols in such a way that they are doing it just to circumvent the GPL, then I feel there would be a case for suing that person. But I don't think anyone wants to misuse the kernel; those who have shown commercial interest in the kernel have done so because they are interested in the benefits of the development model.

The power of Linux is as much about the community of cooperation behind it as the code itself. If Linux were hijacked—if someone attempted to make and distribute a proprietary version—the appeal of Linux, which is essentially the open-source development model, would be lost for that proprietary version.

Portability Today

Linux today has achieved many of the design goals that people originally assumed only a microkernel architecture could achieve.

By constructing a general kernel model drawn from elements common across typical architecture, the Linux kernel gets many of the portability benefits that otherwise require an abstraction layer, without paying the performance penalty paid by microkernels.

By allowing for kernel modules, hardware-specific code can often be confined to a module, keeping the core kernel highly portable. Device drivers are a good example of effective use of kernel modules to keep hardware specifics in the modules. This is a good middle ground between putting all the hardware specifics in the core kernel, which makes for a fast but unportable kernel, and putting all the hardware specifics in user space, which results in a system that is either slow, unstable, or both.

But Linux's approach to portability has been good for the development community surrounding Linux as well. The decisions that motivate portability also enable a large group to work simultaneously on parts of Linux without the kernel getting beyond my control. The architecture generalizations on which Linux is based give me a frame of reference to check kernel changes against, and provide enough abstraction that I don't have to keep completely separate forks of the code for separate architectures. So even though a large number of people work on Linux, the core kernel remains something I can keep track of. And the kernel modules provide an obvious way for programmers to work independently on parts of the system that really should be independent.

The Future of Linux

I'm sure we made the right decision with Linux to do as little as possible in the kernel space. At this point the honest truth is I don't envision major updates to the kernel. A successful software project should mature at some point, and then the pace of changes slows down. There aren't a lot of major new innovations in store for the kernel. It's more a question of supporting a wider range of systems than anything else: taking advantage of Linux's portability to bring it to new systems.

There will be new interfaces, but I think those will come partly from supporting the wider range of systems. For example, when you start doing clustering, suddenly you want to tell the scheduler to schedule certain groups of processes as gang scheduling and things like that. But at the same time, I don't want everybody just focusing on clustering and super-computing, because a lot of the future may be with laptops, or cards that you plug in wherever you go, or something similar, so I'd like Linux to go in that direction too.

And then there are the embedded systems were there is no user interface at all, really. You only access the system to upgrade the kernel perhaps, but otherwise they just sit there. So that's another direction for Linux. I don't think Java or Inferno (Lucent's embedded operating system) are going to succeed for embedded devices. They have missed the significance of Moore's Law. At first it sounds good to design an optimized system specific for a particular embedded device, but by the time you have a workable design, Moore's Law will have brought the price of more powerful hardware within range, undermining the value of designing for a specific device. Everything is getting so cheap that you might as well have the same system on your desktop as in your embedded device. It will make everyone's life easier.

Symmetric Multi-Processing (SMP) is one area that will be developed. The 2.2 Linux kernel will handle four processors pretty well, and we'll develop it up to eight or sixteen processors. The support for more than four processors is already there, but not really. If you have more than four processors now, it's like throwing money at a dead horse. So that will certainly be improved.

But, if people want sixty-four processors they'll have to use a special version of the kernel, because to put that support in the regular kernel would cause performance decreases for the normal users.

Some particular application areas will continue to drive kernel development. Web serving has always been an interesting problem, because it's the one real application that is really kernel-intensive. In a way, web serving has been dangerous for me, because I get so much feedback from the community using Linux as a web-serving platform that I could easily end up optimizing only for web serving. I have to keep in mind that web serving is an important application but not everything.

Of course Linux isn't being used to its full potential even by today's web servers. Apache itself doesn't do the right thing with threads, for example.

This kind of optimization has been slowed down by the limits in network bandwidth. At present, you saturate ten-megabit networks so easily that there's no reason to optimize more. The only way to not saturate ten-megabit networks is to have lots and lots of heavy duty CGIs. But that's not what the kernel can help with. What the kernel could potentially do is directly answer requests for static pages, and pass the more complicate requests to Apache. Once faster networking is more commonplace, this will be more intriguing. But right now we don't have the critical mass of hardware to test and develop it.

The lesson from all these possible future directions is that I want Linux to be on the cutting edge, and even a bit past the edge, because what's past the edge today is what's on your desktop tomorrow.

But the most exciting developments for Linux will happen in user space, not kernel space. The changes in the kernel will seem small compared to what's happening further out in the system. From this perspective, where the Linux kernel will be isn't as interesting a question as what features will be in Red Hat 17.5 or where Wine (the Windows emulator) is going to be in a few years.

In fifteen years, I expect somebody else to come along and say, hey, I can do everything that Linux can do but I can be lean and mean about it because my system won't have twenty years of baggage holding it back. They'll say Linux was designed for the 386 and the new CPUs are doing the really interesting things differently. Let's drop this old Linux stuff. This is essentially what I did when creating Linux. And in the future, they'll be able to look at our code, and use our interfaces, and provide binary compatibility, and if all that happens I'll be happy.

Giving It Away
How Red Hat Software Stumbled Across a New Economic Model and Helped Improve an Industry

Robert Young

As a founder of one of the leading commercial companies offering open-source software, anything I say is tainted for the purpose of objective academic research or analysis. The skeptical reader will not view this is a definitive paper on this topic, but simply a collection of interesting, enlightening, or just plain curious stories of the moments and events that have influenced the progress of Red Hat Software, Inc.

Where Did Red Hat Come From?

In the early days of the Linux OS (1993), we were a small software distribution company. We offered Unix applications, books, and low-cost CD-ROMs from vendors like Walnut Creek and Infomagic. In addition to conventional Unix offerings, these vendors were beginning to offer a new line: Linux CD-ROMs. The Linux CDs were becoming bestsellers for us. When we'd ask where this Linux stuff was coming from, we'd get answers like, "It's from the programmers according to their skill to the users according to their needs."

If the collapse of the Berlin Wall had taught us anything, it was that socialism alone was not a sustainable economic model. Hopeful slogans aside, human activities did not replicate themselves without a good economic model driving the effort. Linux seemed to lack such a model. We reasoned, therefore, that the whole Linux thing was a big fluke. A fluke that was generating enough cash to keep our little business and a number of other small businesses in the black, but a fluke nonetheless.

However, we found that instead of this bizarre Linux OS effort collapsing, it continued to improve. The number of users continued to grow and the applications they were putting it to were growing in sophistication.

So we began to study the OS development more carefully. We spoke to the key developers and the largest users. The more we studied, the more of a solid, albeit unusual, economic model we saw.

This economic model was effective. More importantly, our sales of Linux compared to our sales of other Unixes were sufficient to convince us that this was a real technology with a real future. At this point (fall of 94) we were looking for Linux products that we could sell into CompUSA and other leading retail distribution outlets. So Marc Ewing and I hooked up to create Red Hat Software, Inc. in January of 1995, and the rest of this chapter is devoted to the trials and errors of developing a business plan that was compatible with the bizarre economic model. Bizarre as it was, this model was producing a remarkable OS, providing value to our customers, and providing profit for our shareholders.

At Red Hat, our role is to work with all the development teams across the Internet to take some four hundred software packages and assemble them into a useful operating system. We operate much like a car assembly plant—we test the finished product and offer support and services for the users of the Red Hat Linux OS.

The "unique value proposition" of our business plan was, and continues to be, to cater to our customers' need to gain control over the operating system they were using by delivering the technical benefits of freely-redistributable software (source code and a free license) to technically-oriented OS consumers.

How Do You Make Money in Free Software?

That question assumes that it is easy, or at least easier, to make money selling proprietary binary-only software.

This is a mistake. Most software ventures, whether based on free or proprietary software, fail. Given that until very recently all software ventures were of the proprietary binary-only kind, it is therefore safe to say that the IP (Intellectual Property) model of software development and marketing is a very difficult way to make a living. Of course so was panning for gold during the gold rushes of the 19th century. But when software companies strike it rich they generate a lot of money, just like past gold rushes, so lots of people are willing to assume the risks in order to have an opportunity to "strike gold."

No one expects it to be easy to make money in free software. While making money with free software is a challenge, the challenge is not necessarily greater than with proprietary software. In fact you make money in free software exactly the same way you do it in proprietary software: by building a great product, marketing it with skill and imagination, looking after your customers, and thereby building a brand that stands for quality and customer service.

Marketing with skill and imagination, particularly in highly competitive markets, requires that you offer solutions to your customers that others cannot or will not match. To that end Open Source is not a liability but a competitive advantage. The Open Source development model produces software that is stable, flexible, and highly customizable. So the vendor of open-source software starts with a quality product. The trick is to devise an effective way to make money delivering the benefits of open-source software to you clients.

Inventing new economic models is not a trivial task, and the innovations that Red Hat has stumbled upon certainly do not apply to everyone or every product. But there are some principles that should apply to many software ventures, and to many Open Source ventures.

Many companies attempt a partially open-source approach to the market. Most commonly they will adopt a license that allows for free distribution of their software if the user is not using the software for a commercial purpose, but if he is he must pay the publisher a license fee or royalty. Open Source is defined as software that includes source code and a free license—these partially open-source companies provide source code but without a free license.

And remember, we're in the very early days of the deployment and growth of market share for free software. If you aren't making money today it may be simply because the market for your product is still small. While we are pleased with the growth of the Linux OS, estimates being as high as 10 million users today (1998), you need to remember that there are some 230 million DOS/Windows users.

We Are in the Commodity Product Business

If we do not own intellectual property the way almost all of today's software companies do, and if those companies insist that their most valuable asset is the intellectual property represented by the source code to the software they own, then it is safe to say that Red Hat is not in the Software Business. Red Hat is not licensing intellectual property over which it has ownership. That's not the economic model that will support our customers, staff, and shareholders. So the question became: What business are we in?

The answer was to look around at other industries and try and find one that matched. We wanted an industry where the basic ingredients were free, or at least freely available. We looked at the legal industry; you cannot trademark or patent legal arguments. If a lawyer wins a case in front of the Supreme Court, other lawyers are allowed to use those arguments without requesting permission. In effect, the arguments have become public domain.

We looked at the car industry; you can get parts from a large number of suppliers. No one drives a car—we all drive Hondas or Fords or any of several hundred alternative models of cars assembled from the collective parts available in that industry. Few people have the technical ability to assemble their own car. Those who do seldom have the time or inclination. Assembly and service form the core of the automotive business model.

We looked at the commodity industries and began to recognize some ideas. All leading companies selling commodity products, including bottled water (Perrier or Evian), the soap business (Tide), or the tomato paste business (Heinz), base their marketing strategies on building strong brands. These brands must stand for quality, consistency, and reliability. We saw something in the brand management of these commodity products that we thought we could emulate.

Ketchup is nothing more than flavored tomato paste. Something that looks and tastes a lot like Heinz Ketchup can be made in your kitchen sink without so much as bending a copyright rule. It is effectively all freely-redistributable objects: tomatoes, vinegar, salt, and spices. So why don't we, as consumers, make ketchup in our kitchen sink, and how does Heinz have 80% of the ketchup market?

We don't make ketchup because it is cheaper and much more convenient to buy ketchup from Heinz, Hunts, or Del Monte than it is to make it. But convenience is only part of the story. Convenience alone would suggest that Heinz, Hunts, and Del Monte share the market equally because they offer roughly equivalent convenience. In fact, Heinz owns 80% of the market.

Heinz owns 80% of the market not because Heinz tastes better. If you go to the Third World and find 100 people who have never tasted ketchup before, you find out two things: one is that people don't actually like tomato ketchup, the other is that they dislike all ketchups equally.

Heinz has 80% of the ketchup market because they have been able to define the taste of ketchup in the mind of ketchup consumers. Now the Heinz Ketchup brand is so effective that as consumers we think that ketchup that will not come out of the bottle is somehow better than ketchup that pours easily!

This was Red Hat's opportunity: to offer convenience, to offer quality, and most importantly to help define, in the minds of our customers, what an operating system can be. At Red Hat, if we do a good job of supplying and supporting a consistently high-quality product, we have a great opportunity to establish a brand that Linux OS customers simply prefer.

But how do we reconcile our need to create more Linux users with our need to ensure that those Linux users use Red Hat? We looked at industries where the participants benefit because of, not despite, the activities of the other participants.

Drinking water can be had in most industrial countries simply by turning on the nearest tap, so why does Evian sell millions of dollars of French tap water into those markets? It boils down to a largely irrational fear that the water coming from your tap is not to be trusted.

This is the same reason that many people prefer to purchase "Official" Red Hat Linux in a box for $50 when they could download it for free or buy unofficial CD-ROM copies of Red Hat for as little as $2. Evian does have the advantage that most of humanity drinks water—we still have to create a lot of Linux consumers in order to have a market to sell our brand into.

The challenge is to focus on market size, not just market share. When consumer demand for bottled water grows, Evian benefits, even though many of those consumers start with a bottle other than Evian. Red Hat, like Evian, benefits when other Linux suppliers do a great job building a taste for the product. The more Linux users there are overall, the more potential customers Red Hat has for our flavor.

The power of brands translate very effectively into the technology business. We have evidence of this in the Venture Capital investors who have recently invested in several Open Source software companies. The one common denominator between all of the investments to date have been that the companies or their products have great name recognition, and are recognized as being quality products. In other words, they have successfully established a brand.

The Strategic Appeal of This Model to the Corporate Computing Industry

Much of brand management comes down to market positioning. Consider the challenges that a new OS faces in trying to gain significant marketshare. The current OS market is crowded, and dominated by a definite market favorite from a brilliant marketing organization. Positioning a competing product correctly is crucial to competitive success.

Linux fills this role naturally and extremely well. The primary complaint about the market leader is the control that vendor has over the industry. A new OS must deliver control over the OS platform to its user and not become just another proprietary binary-only OS whose owner would then gain the same dominant market position that consumers are currently complaining about.

Consider that Linux is not really an OS. It has come to describe a whole collection of open-source components much like the term "car" describes an industry better than the thing we drive on the highway. We don't drive cars—we drive Ford Tauruses or Honda Accords. Red Hat is the equivalent of an OS assembly plant of the Free Software operating system industry. Red Hat succeeds when customers perceive themselves not as purchasing an operating system, or even purchasing Linux, but purchasing Red Hat first and foremost.

Honda buys tires from Michelin, airbags from TRW, and paint from Dupont and assembles these diverse pieces into an Accord that comes with certification, warranties, and a network of Honda and independent repair shops.

Red Hat takes compilers from Cygnus, web servers from Apache, an X Window System from the X Consortium (who built it with support from Digital, HP, IBM, Sun, and others), and assembles these into a certifiable, warranted, and award-winning Red Hat Linux OS.

Much like the car industry, it is Red Hat's job to take what it considers the best of the available open-source components to build the best OS we can. But control over the OS is not held by Red Hat or anyone else. If a Red Hat customer disagrees with our choice of Sendmail and want to use Qmail or some other solution, they continue to have the control that enables them to do this. In much the same way, someone buying a Ford Taurus may want a higher performance manifold installed on the engine in place of the one that was shipped from the factory. Because the Taurus owner can open the hood of the car they have control over the car. Similarly, Red Hat users have control over the Linux OS they use, because they have license to open and modify the source code.

You can't compete with a monopoly by playing the game by the monopolist's rules. The monopoly has the resources, the distribution channels, the R&D resources; in short, they just have too many strengths. You compete with a monopoly by changing the rules of the game into a set that favors your strengths.

At the end of the 19th century, the big American monopoly concern was not operating systems, but railroads. The major railroads held effective monopolies on transportation between major cities. Indeed, major American cities, like Chicago, had grown up around the central railway terminals owned by the railroad companies.

These monopolies were not overcome by building new railroads and charging several fewer dollars. They were overcome with the building of the interstate highway system and the benefit of door-to-door delivery that the trucking companies could offer over the more limited point-to-point delivery that the railroad model previously offered.

Today the owners of the existing proprietary OSes own a technology that is much like owning the railway system. The APIs of a proprietary OS are much like the routes and timetables of a railroad. The OS vendors can charge whatever toll they like. They can also control and change the "route" the APIs take through the OS to suit the needs of the applications they sell, without regard to the needs of the applications that their competitors sell. These OS vendors' biggest competitive advantage is that they control access to the source code that both their applications and the Independent Software Vendors (ISVs) applications must run on.

To escape the confines of this model, ISVs need an OS model where the vendor of that OS (Linux) does not control the OS; where the supplier of the OS is responsible for the maintenance of the OS only; and where the ISV can sell his application secure in the knowledge that the OS vendor is not his biggest competitive threat. The appeal of this OS model has begun to take hold in the software world. This is a big part of the reasoning behind Corel's port of WordPerfect to Linux, behind Oracle's port of their database software to Linux, and behind IBM's support for Apache.

The benefit an open-source OS offers over the proprietary binary-only OSes is the control the users gain over the technology they are using. The proprietary OS vendors, with their huge investment in the proprietary software that their products consist of, would be crazy to try and match the benefit we are offering their customers, as we generate a fraction of the revenue per user that the current proprietary OS vendors rely on.

Of course if our technology model becomes accepted by a large enough group of computer users, the existing OS vendors are going to have to react somehow. But that's still several years in the future. If they do react by "freeing" their code the way Netscape "freed" the code to the Navigator browser, it would result in better products at dramatically lower cost. The industry at large will be well served if that were the only result of our efforts. Of course it is not Red Hat's goal to stop there.

As an illustration of the importance of the "control" benefit of the Linux OS, it is interesting to note Fermilab's experience. Fermilab is the big particle accelerator research laboratory outside Chicago. They employ over a thousand high-level physics engineers who need state-of-the-art technology that they can customize to the needs of the projects they are working on. An example of the benefit of Linux is its ability to be used in cluster farms to build massively parallel super-computers. Fermilab needs this feature, as they are proposing to increase the performance of their accelerator. As a result of this performance increase, they expect to need to analyze almost 10 times more data per second than they have been. Their budgets simply will not enable them to acquire the computing power they need from the existing super-computer suppliers.

For this and other reasons Fermilab wanted something Open Source. They recognized that Red Hat Linux was one of the more popular Open Source choices, so they called us. In fact they called us six times in the four months during the system selection phase of the project, and we did not respond even once to their inquiries. Nonetheless the result of their study was to select Red Hat Linux as an officially supported OS at Fermilab. The moral here is that (a) we need to learn how to answer our phones better (we have), and (b) that Fermilab was able to recognize that our business model was delivering them the control over the Red Hat Linux OS they were intending to use—whether or not Red Hat Software, Inc. was in position to support them.

So whether it is the large computer consuming organizations, or the large computer technology suppliers (ISVs), the Linux OS provides benefits and is free from the major limitations of all the proprietary binary-only OSes available today. Careful brand management of Red Hat Linux among Linux distributions, and careful market position of Linux among OS alternatives, enables Red Hat to enjoy the growth and success we have today.

Licensing, Open Source, or Free Software

The benefit to using Linux is not the high reliability, ease of use, robustness, or the tools included with the Linux OS. It is the benefit of *control* that results from the two distinctive features of this OS; namely, that it ships with complete source code, and that you can use this source code for whatever you chose—without so much as asking our permission.

NASA, the outfit that rockets people off into outer space for a living, has an expression: "Software is not software without source code."

To the engineers at NASA, high reliability is not good enough. Extremely high reliability it not good enough. NASA need perfect reliability. They cannot afford to suffer the "blue screen of death" with twelve trusting souls rocketing at a thousand miles an hour around the earth, depending on their systems to keep them alive.

NASA needs access to the source code of the software they are using to build these systems. And they need that software to come with a license that allows them to modify it to meet their needs. Now I'll admit that the average dental office billing system does not need the standards of reliability that NASA astronauts depend on to bill patients for their annual teeth cleaning, but the principle remains the same.

And unlike proprietary binary-only OSes, with Linux our users can modify the product to meet the needs of the application they are building. This is the *unique value proposition* that Red Hat offers our customers. This is the proposition that none of our much bigger competitors are willing or able to offer.

This is a value proposition that overturns usual notions of intellectual property. Rather than using a license to lock customers in and wall them off from the source code, Red Hat needs a license that embodies the very idea of access to and control over source code. So what is an acceptable license for the purpose of delivering this unique value proposition? Reasonable people in the Open Source community can and do differ in how they answer this question. But at Red Hat we do have our current opinions on the subject and here they are:

The General Public License from the Free Software Foundation is in the spirit of Open Source and, because it ensures that the modifications and improvements made to the OS remain public, most effective for managing a cooperative development project.

Our definition of "effective" goes back to the old days of Unix development. Prior to 1984, AT&T used to share the source code to the Unix OS with any team who could help them improve it. When AT&T was broken up, the resulting AT&T was no longer restricted to being a telephone company. It decided to try and make money selling licenses to the Unix OS. All the universities and research groups who had helped build Unix suddenly found themselves having to pay for licenses for an OS that they had helped build. They were not happy, but could not do much about it—after all, AT&T owned the copyright to Unix. The other development teams had been helping AT&T at AT&T's discretion.

Our concern is the same. If Red Hat builds an innovation that our competitors are able to use, the least we can demand is that the innovations our competitors build are available to our engineering teams as well. And the GPL is the most effective license for ensuring that this forced cooperation among the various team members continues to occur regardless of the competitive environment at the time.

Keep in mind that one of the great strengths of the Linux OS is that it is a highly modular technology. When we ship a version of Red Hat Linux we are shipping over 435 separate packages. So licensing also has a practical dimension to it. A license that enables Red Hat to ship the software but not make modifications to it creates problems because users cannot correct or modify the software to their needs. A less restrictive license that requires that the user ask the permission of the original author before making changes still burdens Red Hat and our users with too many restrictions. Having to ask possibly 435 different authors or development teams for permission to make modifications is simply not practical.

But we are not ideological about licenses. We are comfortable with any license that provides us with control over the software we are using, because that in turn enables us to deliver the benefit of control to our customers and users, whether they are NASA engineers or application programmers working on a dental office billing system.

The Economic Engine Behind Development of Open Source Software

The interesting stories of where Linux comes from helps illustrate the strong economic model that is driving the development of this OS.

The Open Source community has had to overcome the stereotype of the hobbyist hacker. According to this stereotype, Linux, for example, is built by fourteen-year-old hackers in their bedrooms. We see here an example of the Fear, Uncertainty, and Doubt (FUD) foisted on the software industry by vendors of proprietary systems. After all, who wants to trust their mission-critical enterprise applications to software written by a fourteen-year-old in his spare time?

The reality, of course, is very different from this stereotype. While the "lone hacker" is a valuable and important part of the development process, such programmers account for a minority of the code that make up the Linux OS. Linux's creator, Linus Torvalds, began work on Linux while he was a student, and much of the code in the Linux OS is built by professional software developers at major software, engineering, and research organizations.

A few examples include the GNU C and C++ compilers that come from Cygnus Solutions Inc. of Sunnyvale, California. The X Window System originally came from the X Consortium (made up of support from IBM, HP, Digital, and Sun). A number of ethernet drivers are now largely the responsibility of engineers at NASA. Device drivers are now coming frequently from the device manufacturers themselves. In short, building open-source software is often not so different from building conventional software, and the talent behind Open Source is by and large the same talent that is behind conventional software.

Grant Guenther, at the time a member of Empress Software's database development team, wanted to enable his co-workers to work on projects from home. They needed a secure method of moving large files from their office to home and back. They were using Linux on PCs and using Zip drives. The only problem was that at the time (1996), good Zip drive support was not available in Linux.

So Grant had a choice: throw out the Linux solution and purchase a much more expensive proprietary solution, or stop what he was doing and spend a couple of days writing a decent Zip drive driver. He wrote one, and worked with other Zip drive users across the Internet to test and refine the driver.

Consider the cost to Red Hat, or any other software company, of having to pay Empress and Grant to develop that driver. Safe to say the cost would have been in the tens of thousands of dollars, and yet Grant chose to "give away" his work. In return, instead of money he received the use of a great solution for his problem of enabling Empress programmers to work from home, at a fraction of the cost of the alternatives. This is the kind of win-win proposition offered by cooperative models like the Open Source development model.

Unique Benefits

It's easy to confuse features with benefits. The Open Source model in general and Linux in particular certainly have some unique features, and it's tempting to say that those features are the reason that the world is adopting Linux with such enthusiasm. As hundreds of MIS managers have commented to me, "Why would anyone want source code to their OS?" The point is no one wants source code. No one needs a Free Software license. Those are simply features of the OS. But a feature is not necessarily a benefit. So what's the benefit associated with that feature?

To the ongoing disappointment of the technical computing community, the best technology seldom wins in even the most technical markets. Building a better mouse-trap does not assure you of success. Linux is not going to be successful because it can be installed on a machine with less memory than alternative OSes, or because it costs less than other OSes, or because it is more reliable. Those are all just features that make Linux arguably a better mousetrap than NT or OS/2.

The forces that will ultimately drive the success or failure of the Linux OS work at a different level. In effect those factors are lumped generally under the topic of "market positioning." As a senior executive at Lotus asked us recently, "Why does the world need another OS?" Linux will succeed only if it is not "just another OS." In other words, does Linux represent a new model for the development and deployment of OSes or is it "just another OS"?

That is the question. And the answer is: Linux and the whole Open Source movement represent a revolution in software development that will profoundly improve the computing systems we are building now and in the future.

Open-source code is a feature. Control is the benefit. Every company wants control over their software, and the feature of Open Source is the best way the industry has found so far to achieve that benefit.

The Great Unix Flaw

The best example I know of to illustrate that the Linux model is a profoundly different approach to building OSes is to look at what many people are convinced is the ultimate outcome of this OS effort, namely that Linux will balkanize the same way all the Unixes have. There are apparently thirty different, largely incompatible, versions of the Unix OS available today.

But the forces that drive the various Unixes apart are working to unify the various Linuxes.

The primary difference between Unix and Linux is not the kernel, or the Apache server, or any other set of features. The primary difference between the two is that Unix is just another proprietary binary-only or IP-based OS. The problem with a proprietary binary-only OS that is available from multiple suppliers is that those suppliers have short-term marketing pressures to keep whatever innovations they make to the OS to themselves for the benefit of their customers exclusively. Over time these "proprietary innovations" to each version of the Unix OS cause the various Unixes to differ substantially from each other. This occurs when the other vendors do not have access to the source code of the innovation and the license the Unix vendors use prohibit the use of that innovation even if everyone else involved in Unix wanted to use the same innovation.

In Linux the pressures are the reverse. If one Linux supplier adopts an innovation that becomes popular in the market, the other Linux vendors will immediately adopt that innovation. This is because they have access to the source code of that innovation and it comes under a license that allows them to use it.

An example of how this works is the very example that all the Linux skeptics have been using to predict the downfall of the OS, namely the debate in 1997 between the older libc C libraries and the new glibc libraries. Red Hat adopted the newer glibc libraries for strong technical reasons. There were popular versions of Linux that stuck with the older libc libraries. The debate raged for all of six months. Yet as 1998 drew to a close all the popular Linux distributions had either switched or announced plans to switch to the newer, more stable, more secure, and higher performance glibc libraries.

That is part of the power of Open Source: it creates this kind of unifying pressure to conform to a common reference point—in effect, an open standard—and it removes the intellectual property barriers that would otherwise inhibit this convergence.

It's Your Choice

Whenever a revolutionary new practice comes along there are always skeptics who predict its inevitable downfall, pointing out all the obstacles the new model must overcome before it can be called a success. There are also the ideologues who insist that it is only the purest implementation of the new model that can possibly succeed. And then there are the rest of us who are just plugging away, testing, innovating, and using the new technology model for those applications where the new model works better than the old one.

The primary benefit of this new technology model can be seen in the birth of the PC. When IBM published the specs to its PC in 1981, why did the world adopt the PC computing model with such enthusiasm? It was not that the IBM PC was a better mousetrap. The original 8086-based PCs shipped with 64K (yes, K) bytes of main memory. They had an upper memory limit of 640K. No one could imagine that a single user would need more that 640K on their individual machine. A tape cassette recorder was available for data back-up.

What drove the PC revolution was that it provided its users with control over their computing platform. They could buy their first PC from IBM, their second from Compaq, and their third from HP. They could buy memory or hard drives from one of a hundred suppliers, and they could get an almost infinite range of peripheral equipment for almost any purpose or application.

This new model introduced a huge number of inconsistencies, incompatibilities, and confusion, between technologies, products, and suppliers. But as the world now knows, consumers *love* choice. Consumers will put up with a measure of confusion and inconsistency in order to have choice—choice and control.

Notice also that the PC hardware business did not fragment. Specifications have generally remained open, and there is strong pressure to conform to standards to preserve interoperability. No one has a sufficiently better mousetrap with which to entice users and then hold them hostage by going proprietary. Instead innovations—better mousetraps—accrue to the community at large.

The Linux OS gives consumers choice over the technology that comes with their computers at the operating system level. Does it require a whole new level of responsibility and an expertise on the part of the user? Certainly.

Will that user prefer to go back to the old model of being forced to trust his proprietary binary-only OS supplier once he has experienced the choice and freedom of the new model? Not likely.

Critics will continue to look for, and occasionally find, serious problems with Linux technology. But consumers love choice, and the huge Internet-based open-source software development marketplace is going to figure out ways to solve all of them.

Diligence, Patience, and Humility

Larry Wall

We have a fondness for sayings in the Perl community. One of them is "There's more than one way to do it." This is true in Perl. It's also true of Perl. And it's true of the Open Source community, as the essays in this volume illustrate. I won't tell you everything about how Open Source works; that would be like trying to explain why English works. But I can say something about the state of Perl, and where it's going.

Here's another saying: Three great virtues of programming are laziness, impatience, and hubris. Great Perl programmers embrace those virtues. So do Open Source developers. But here I'm going to talk about some other virtues: diligence, patience, and humility. If you think these sound like the opposite, you're right. If you think a single community can't embrace opposing values, then you should spend more time with Perl. After all, there's more than one way to do it.

Written languages probably began with impatience. Or laziness. Without written language, you had to meet another person face to face to communicate with them, or you had to persuade another person to convey your message for you. And there was no way to know what had previously been said except to remember it. But written language gave people symbols, symbols that could stand for things—if the community could agree on what the symbols stood for. So language requires consensus. It's something a group can agree on. It is, in short, a symbol that ties a community together. Most symbols work that way.

So let's look at some symbols:

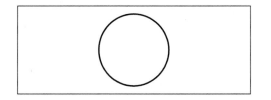

Study it carefully. It's called a circle. It's a very nice circle, as circles go. Very pretty. Very symmetrical. Very simple.

Now if you're a reductionist, you'll say it's only a circle, and nothing more. Well, actually, if you're really a reductionist, you'll say it's a just bunch of photons, but we won't go there, because it wouldn't shed any light on the subject.

If you're not a reductionist, then the circle you see here does not exist in isolation. It exists in relationship to many other things, and in fact takes its meaning from them. In order to understand this simple circle, you have to understand its context, which means you have to understand something about reality.

So here's a picture of reality:

As we all know, reality is a mess.

This is a picture of many things. It's a picture of air molecules bouncing around. It's a picture of the economy. It's a picture of all the relationships of the people in this room. It's a picture of what the typical human language looks like. It's a picture of your company's information systems. It's a picture of the World Wide Web. It's a picture of chaos, and of complexity.

It's certainly a picture of how Perl is organized, since Perl is modeled on human languages. And the reason human languages are complex is because they have to deal with reality.

We all have to deal with reality one way or another. So we simplify. Often we over-simplify.

Our ancestors oversimplified. They fooled themselves into thinking that God only created circles and spheres. They thought God would always prefer simplicity over complexity. When they discovered that reality was more complicated than they thought, they just swept the complexity under a carpet of epicycles. That is, they created unnecessary complexity. This is an important point. The universe is complex, but it's usefully complex.

Evidence abounds that people continue to oversimplify today. Some people prefer to oversimplify their cosmology. Others prefer to oversimplify their theology. Many computer language designers oversimplify their languages, and end up sweeping the universe's complexity under the carpet of the programmer.

It's a natural human trait to look for patterns in the noise, but when we look for those patterns, sometimes we see patterns that aren't really there. But that doesn't mean there aren't real patterns. If we can find a magic wand to suppress the noise, then the signal pops right out. Abracadabra . . . Here is the shape of the big bang, and of stars, and of soap bubbles:

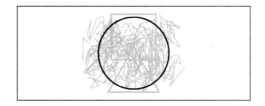

Here is the shape of dimensionality, of salt crystals, and the spaces between tree trunks:

Here is the shape of an anthill, or a Christmas tree. Or the shape of a trinity:

And, of course, once you know the patterns are there, you can pick out the simple figures without the extra chromatic help:

Our brains are built to do that.

Now, you may be wondering what all this has to do with Perl. The fact is, your brain is built to do Perl programming. You have a deep desire to turn the complex into the simple, and Perl is just another tool to help you do that—just as I am using English right now to try to simplify reality. I can use English for that because English is a mess.

This is important, and a little hard to understand. English is useful because it's a mess. Since English is a mess, it maps well onto the problem space, which is also a mess, which we call reality. Similarly, Perl was designed to be a mess (though in the nicest of possible ways).

This is counterintuitive, so let me explain. If you've been educated as any kind of an engineer, it has been pounded into your skull that great engineering is simple engineering. We are taught to admire suspension bridges more than railroad trestles. We are taught to value simplicity and beauty. That's nice. I like circles too.

However, complexity is not always the enemy. What's important is not simplicity or complexity, but how you bridge the two.

You need a certain amount of complexity to do any particular job. A Saturn V rocket is said to have had seven million parts, all of which had to work. But that's not entirely true. Many of those parts were redundant. But that redundancy was absolutely necessary to achieve the goal of putting someone on the moon in 1969. So if some of those rocket parts had the job of being redundant, then each of those parts still had to do their part. So to speak. They also serve who only stand and wait.

We betray ourselves when we say "That's redundant," meaning "That's useless." Redundancy is not always "redundant," whether you're talking about rockets or human languages or computer languages. In short, simplicity is often the enemy of success.

Suppose I want to take over the world. Simplicity says I should just take over the world by myself. But the reality of the situation is that I need your help to take over the world, and you're all very complex. I actually consider that a feature. Your relationships are even more complex. I usually think of those as features. But sometimes they're bugs. We can debug relationships, but it's always good policy to consider the people themselves to be features. People get annoyed when you try to debug them.

We mentioned that some complexity is useless, and some is useful. Here's another example of useful complexity:

Now, most of you sitting here are probably prejudiced in favor of western writing systems, and so you think an ideographic writing system is needlessly complex. You may even be thinking that this picture is as complicated as the previous one. But again, it's a kind of engineering tradeoff. In this case, the Chinese have traded learnability for portability. Does that sound familiar?

Chinese is not, in fact, a single language. It's about five major languages, any of which are mutually unintelligible. And yet, you can write Chinese in one language and read it in another. That's what I call a portable language. By choosing a higher level of abstraction, the Chinese writing system optimizes for communication rather than for simplicity. There are a billion people in China who can't all talk to each other, but at least they can pass notes to each other.

Computers also like to pass notes to each other. Only we call it networking.

A lot of my thinking this year has been influenced by working with Unicode and with XML. Ten years ago, Perl was good at text processing. It's even better at it now, for the old definition of text. But the definition of "text" has been changing out from under Perl over those ten years.

You can blame it all on the Internet.

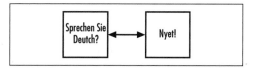

It seems that when you click buttons on your browser, it makes computers want to pass notes to each other. And they want to pass these notes over cultural boundaries. Just as you want to understand what pops up on your screen, your computer wants to understand what it's about to pop up on your screen, because, believe it or not, the computer would actually like to do it right. Computers may be stupid, but they're always obedient. Well, almost always.

That's where Unicode and XML come in. Unicode is just a set of universal ideographs so that the world's computers can pass notes around to each other, and have some chance of doing the right thing with them. Some of the ideographs in Unicode happen to match up with various national character sets such as ASCII, but nobody in the world will ever learn all of those languages. Nobody is expecting you to learn all those languages. That's not the point.

Here's the point. Last month I was working on my church's web page. Our church has just started a Chinese congregation, so it now has two names, one of which can be represented in ASCII, and one of which cannot. Here's what the page looks like:

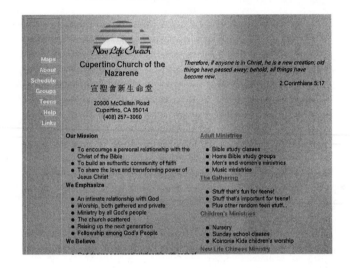

If your browser is fairly recent, and if you have a Unicode font loaded, then this is what you see. There's something important I want you to notice here.

If I'd done this a year ago, this block of Chinese characters would probably have been a GIF image. But there's a problem with images. You can't cut and paste characters from a GIF image. I've tried it often enough to know, and I'm sure you have too. If I'd done this a year ago, I'd also have had to add another layer of complexity to the page. I'd need something like a CGI script to detect whether the browser supports Unicode, because if it doesn't, these characters splatter garbage all over the page. Garbage is usually construed as useless complexity.

Anyway, back to simplicity:

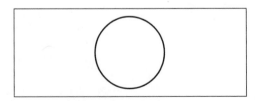

We use circles to represent many things. Our circle of friends. A hug, when written on the back of an envelope. The circle of a wedding ring, which stands for unending love.

Proceeding from the sublime to the ridiculous, we also have the round file, which is a kind of hell for dead paperwork.

Spheres of light. Black holes. Or at least their event horizons.

One ring to rule them all, and in the darkness bind them.

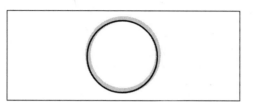

Crystal balls. Pearls.

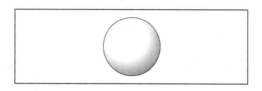

Onions. Pearl onions.

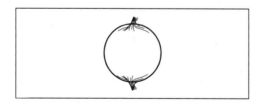

Circles figure heavily in our symbology. And in particular, by adding various appurtenances to circles, we sometimes represent some rather complicated notions with simple symbols. These symbols are the bridges between simplicity and complexity.

Here's a real Zen diagram:

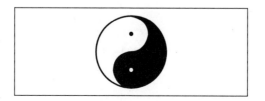

Well, actually, it's not. In fact, the yinyang comes from the Tao, or Dao if you can't pronounce an unaspirated "t". The Tao is an ancient oriental philosophy, and predates Zen by more than a millennium.

Anyway, back to yins and yangs.

The yinyang represents a dualistic philosophy, much like The Force in *Star Wars*. You know, how is The Force like duct tape? Answer: it has a light side, a dark side, and it holds the universe together. I'm not a dualist myself, because I believe the light is stronger than the darkness. Nevertheless, the concept of balanced forces is useful at times, especially to engineers. When an engineer wants to balance forces, and wants them to stay balanced, he reaches for the duct tape.

When I made this yinyang, I wondered whether I was doing it right. It'd be a shame to get it backwards, or sideways, or something.

Well, you know, sometimes that sort of thing matters. It matters a lot to organic chemists, who call it chirality—if you take a molecule of spearmint flavor and flip it left for right, you end up with a molecule of caraway flavor. Yuck. I used to think I hated rye bread, till I discovered it was the caraway seeds they put in that I didn't like.

Now, which of those flavors you prefer is just a matter of taste, but doctors and organic chemists will tell you that there are times when chirality is a matter of life and death. Or of deformed limbs, in the case of Thalidomide. It was the "wrong" kind of Thalidomide that actually caused the problems. Dyslexics will tell you that chirality matters a lot in visual symbols. This talk is brought to you by the letters "b" and "d". And "p" and "q". And the number 6. Not to mention the number 9. You can see a 6 and a 9 in the yinyang, in this orientation.

In short, I wondered whether the yinyang is like a swastika, where which way you make it determines who gets mad at you.

So I did some research, on the Web, of course. The fact is, the Web is the perfect example of TMTOWTDI—there's more than one way to do it. In this case, there's every way to do it. You can find the yinyang in every possible orientation. I still don't know whether any of them is more right than the others.

A TYEDYE WORLD is some folks on the Web who sell tie-dyed tee shirts. I guess they'd be Tao-dyed in this case. They think it looks like this:

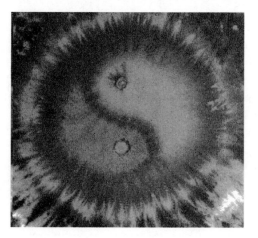

I suppose if you want it the other way you just put the shirt on inside-out. Putting it on upside-down is going to get you stared at.

The folks at the Unicode consortium think it looks like this. I don't know if they're right, but if they're not, it doesn't matter. They published it this way, and now it's right by definition.

Of course, my dictionary has it upside from that:

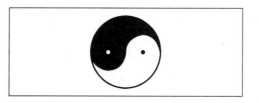

Well, back to Unicode. Unicode is full of circles. Many national scripts within Unicode make use of the circle, and in most of those, it represents the digit 0. Here is Unicode number 3007 (hex). It's the ideographic symbol for 0:

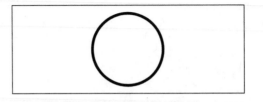

Surprise, surprise. It looks like our 0. Chalk one up for cultural imperialism. In English, of course, we tend to squish our 0 sideways to distinguish it from the letter O.

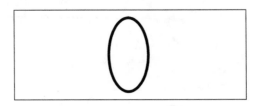

In Bengali, they squish it the other way, but for similar reasons:

I find it interesting that the world has so many different representations for nothing. One could make endless jokes on it: Much ado about nothing, or Nothing can stop an idea whose time has come. Here's something related to nothing:

This is the universal "prohibited" symbol. In Unicode, it's classified as a combining character.

Of course, in Perl culture, almost nothing is prohibited. My feeling is that the rest of the world already has plenty of perfectly good prohibitions, so why invent more? That applies not just to programming, but also to interpersonal relationships, by the way. I have upon more than one occasion been requested to eject someone from the Perl community, generally for being offensive in some fashion or other. So far I have consistently refused. I believe this is the right policy. At least, it's worked so far, on a practical level. Either the offensive person has left eventually of their own accord, or they've settled down and learned to deal with others more constructively. It's odd. People understand instinctively that the best way for computer programs to communicate with each other is for each of the them to be strict in what they emit, and liberal in what they accept. The odd thing is that people themselves are not willing to be strict in how they speak and liberal in how they listen. You'd think that would also be obvious. Instead, we're taught to express ourselves.

On the other hand, we try to encourage certain virtues in the Perl community. As the apostle Paul points out, nobody makes laws against love, joy, peace, patience, kindness, goodness, gentleness, meekness, or self-control. So rather than concentrating on forbidding evil, let's concentrate on promoting good. Here's the Unicode for that:

Of course, if you're a flower child, you might prefer this one:

Some of the positive Unicodes aren't so obvious.

Here's the symbol for a bilabial click, one of the symbols in the International Phonetic Alphabet. You may not know it, but many of you make this noise regularly. If you want to try doing one, here's how. You just kind of put your lips together, then make an affricated sort of noise with ingressive mouth air.

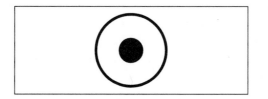

Of course, in English we write that with an X, to go with those O's on the back of the envelope. But you're witnessing the passing of an era. What with email taking over, sending hugs and kisses on the backs of envelopes is becoming a lost art. It just doesn't have quite the same effect as a header line in email. Content-type: text/hugs&kisses.

You know, it's also rather difficult to perfume an email message. Content-type: text/scented. The mind boggles.

Here are more simple circles that represent complicated things. Here's the symbol for earth:

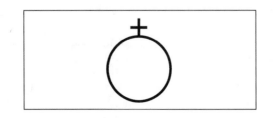

Here's the symbol for Mars:

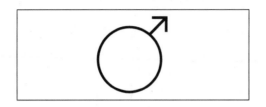

And here's the symbol for Venus:

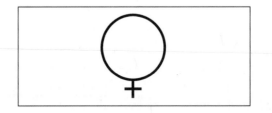

Now, I used to work at Jet Propulsion Laboratory, and I helped just a little to discover that Mars and Venus are pretty complicated. But as if things weren't complicated enough, the ancients complicated things further by overloading those symbols to represent male and female. Men are from Mars, women are from Venus, we are told, but that is not a new idea.

Here's some more history.

If you cut an onion, it looks like this. If we take this to be a picture of the world of Perl, then I must be that little bit of onion inside.

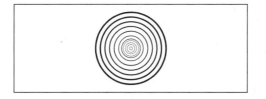

Around me are some of the early adopters of Perl, who are now revered as heroes of the revolution. As more people have joined the movement, new layers have been added. You can also picture this as an atom, with layers of electron shells. Of course, no atom we know of has quite that many electron shells. So stick with the onion.

Now the thing about the onion is that it teaches me something about my own importance, or lack thereof. Namely, that while I may have started all this, I'm still a little bit of the onion. Most of the mass is in the outer layers. (That's why I like to see grassroots movements like the Perl Mongers springing up.) But here I sit in the middle. I get a bit of honor for my historical significance, but in actual fact, most people see the outside of the onion, not the inside. Unless they make onion rings. But even then, the bigger rings have more to them than the smaller rings. Let that be a lesson to those of you who wish to be "inner ringers." That's not where the real power is. Not in this movement, anyway. I've tried to model the Perl movement on another movement I'm a member of, and the founder of that movement said, "He who wishes to be greatest among you must become the servant of all." Of his twelve inner ringers, one betrayed him, and ten of the other eleven went on to suffer a martyr's death. Not that I'm asking any of my friends to throw themselves to the lions just yet.

But back to growth patterns. Natural pearls grow in layers too, around a grain of sand that irritates the oyster in question, which forms layers of pretty stuff. This could be the cross-section of a pearl. People cut up onions frequently, but they almost never cut up pearls. So it's even truer of pearls than of onions. The outer layer is the most important. It's what people see. Or if the pearl is still growing, it's the layer that will support the layer after it. I realize that that classifies me as a mere irritant. I am content to be so classified.

Other things grow over time too. Perhaps if we change the picture to a set of tree rings, it'll be clearer:

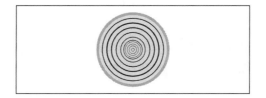

If you're familiar with a bit of physics, you know that a pipe is almost as strong as a solid bar of the same diameter, because most of the force is transmitted in the outer layers. The fact is, the center of the tree can rot, but the tree remains perfectly healthy. In a similar fashion, most of the health of Perl culture is in what is happening in the periphery, not in the center. People are saving themselves billions of dollars every year by programming in Perl, but most of those savings are happening out in the trenches. Even closer into the center, a lot more work is going into hooking Perl up to other things than into changing Perl itself. And I think this is as it should be. Core Perl is stabilizing somewhat. Even with core changes such as multithreading and Unicode support, we pretend that we're adding extension modules, because that's cleaner, and people don't have to invoke the new functionality if they don't want to.

All this stuff about growth rings is fine for talking about the past, but what about the future? I don't have a crystal ball. I do own two pairs of binoculars. Here's the typical symbol for that:

This is, of course, the usual cinematic device for indicating that someone is looking through binoculars. I don't know offhand what I should put for the field of view here, so let's see what's at the other end of the binoculars:

Of course, this can also be a picture of two tidally locked bodies rotating around each other:

Each of these planets is raising tides on the other one. People usually understand why there is a tidal bulge on the side facing the other planet. What they don't understand so easily is why there's a bulge on the other side of the planet. But it makes sense when you consider that the other planet is not only pulling the near bulge away from the center of the planet, but it's also pulling the center of the planet away from the far bulge.

This is a really good picture of the relationship of the free software community with the commercial software community. We might even label some of the extremes. Let's just make up some names. We could call the left extreme, um, "Richard." And we could call the right extreme something like, oh, "Bill."

The middle bulges are a little harder to name, but just for today we can call this one on the middle left "Larry," and that one on the middle right "Tim."

This is, of course, another oversimplification, because various people and organizations aren't at a single spot in the diagram, but tend to rattle around. Some people manage to oscillate back and forth from one bulge to the other. One moment they're in favor of more cooperation between the freeware and commercial communities, and the next moment they're vilifying anything commercial. At least our hypothetical Richard and Bill are consistent.

But the action is in the middle.

That's where everybody's been looking, to see what's going to happen. In fact, this is really last year's picture. This year it looks more like this:

Robert L. Forward has written a book, actually a series of books, about a place called Rocheworld. It's named after a fellow named Roche, surprise, surprise. He's the fellow who defined Roche's limit, which predicted that planets would break up if they got too close to each other. It turns out he oversimplified because his math wasn't powerful enough. If you allow your planets to deform into shapes like these, you can get them very much closer together, and keep them stable. Mind you, the net gravitational pull on these points is very low, but it's enough to keep the planets together.

In similar fashion, the freeware and commercial communities are much closer together this year than many people thought possible by the old calculations. In Rocheworld, the planets did not touch, but they shared atmospheres. If we fuzz things out a little with the magic of xpaint, then we kind of get the picture:

You see how you can fly from one planet to the other, but not walk. It's reminiscent of quantum mechanical tunneling, where you can't get from here to there but you do it anyway with a flying leap.

What we have flowing between the freeware and commercial communities is a lot of ideas. Together, these two inner lobes define what we're now calling the Open Source movement. What we have here is something brand new: former enemies agreeing on a common good that transcends any particular business model. And that common good is better software sooner. Here's what made it all possible. People realized the power of a simple idea. We don't need software patents or trade secrets. All we need another simple circle:

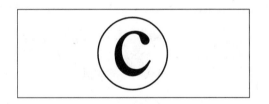

A circle with a "c" in it. Open Source lives or dies on copyright law. Our fond hope is that it lives. Please, let's all do our part to keep it that way. If you have a chance to plug copyrights over patents, please do so. I know many of you are already plugging copyrights over trade secrets. Let's also uphold copyright law by respecting the wishes of copyright holders, whether or not they are spelled out to the satisfaction of everyone's lawyer. The "c" in the circle should stand for civility.

When we think of civility, we think of cities, and of doing things fair and square. So here's the requisite square:

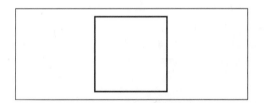

And indeed, cities are built on squares, and rectangles. We call them blocks. And if the city planners leave the buildings off of a block, we call it a square. Even if it isn't square. Go figure.

Sometimes the buildings themselves are square:

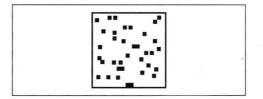

But often they're not. Similarly, if you look through the Unicode book, there are not nearly so many squares as there are circles. I think there's a fundamental underlying reason for that. When we build buildings, and when we write characters, we install them into a rectilinear framework. In terms of writing, we write left-to-right, or right-to-left, or top-to-bottom. The abstract cells into which we install the characters or buildings are squarish. But both buildings and characters tend to disappear visually if they follow the same lines as the overall text. So most characters tend to contain lines at odd angles, just as many modern skyscrapers are designed to avoid looking like boxes. Nobody really likes the skyscrapers of the 1960s, because they're too boxy. People like things to be visually distinct from their surroundings.

That is also why the various classes of operators and variables in Perl are visually distinct from each other. It's just sound human engineering, as far as I'm concerned. I don't like the fact that all the operators look the same in Lisp. I don't like the fact that most the street signs look alike in Europe. And I applaud the decision of Germany to make their stop signs look different from all the other signs. Of course, it's also helpful to us ignorant Americans that they made them look like American stop signs. Chalk up another one for cultural imperialism.

However, in repentance for American cultural imperialism, let me point out another advantage of the ideographic system of writing. Because ideographs are written into square cells, they can just as easily be written horizontally as vertically. Or vice versa. Our variable-width characters do not have that nice property. Especially in a font like Helvetica, where you have trouble telling i's and l's apart even when they're next to each other. Put one above the other and it'd just look like a dotted line. Chalk one up for the Chinese, the Japanese, and the Koreans.

To wrap up, I'd like to talk about triangles. Here's a sample:

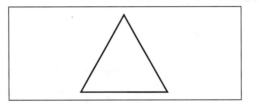

Triangles are related to circles in the same way that arrowheads are related to targets. Here's a target:

I know I got this one right. I looked it up on the Web. More importantly, I stopped as soon as I found the first one.

Actually, this is the Unicode character named "bulls-eye."

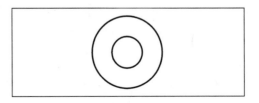

I'm not quite sure what it's supposed to mean. But that's never stopped me before. I'll make it mean something.

I've shot a lot of arrows in this essay, and I don't know whether I've hit any bulls-eyes yet. We put triangles on the front of arrows because they're sharp. Triangles are associated with pain, especially if you step on one. The angles of the triangle tend to suggest the hard work of climbing a mountain:

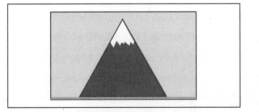

On the other hand, looks can be deceiving. A triangle also represents a flat road stretching to the horizon:

It's all a matter of perspective. You can choose your view by choosing where to stand. I can't predict whether Perl's road ahead will be bumpy or smooth, but I can predict that the more perspectives we can see things from, the easier it will be to choose the perspectives we like. And this is, after all, the job of a language designer, to survey the problem from many perspectives, to be just a little bit omniscient, so that other people can benefit. I do a little triangulation, and I map the territory. That's my job. If my map gets you where you're going, I'm happy.

If you take a section out of the Perl onion, it looks kind of like a triangle. Put in on its side and you have a growth chart for Perl over the last ten years:

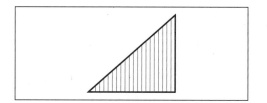

All fine and dandy. This chart is notional, of course. I have no way of measuring Perl's actual growth. But obviously it is still growing. We're doing a lot of things right, and by and large we should keep doing just what we're doing.

Now suppose we shrink this triangle and extend the chart to show the whole lifetime of Perl. We really don't know how long it might last.

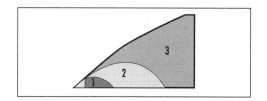

It's hard to say what will make the difference here. But I have to tell you that I don't evaluate the success of Perl in terms of how many people like me. When I integrate these curves, I count the number of people I've helped get their job done.

I can tell you that I think the difference between curve 1 and curve 2 might depend on adding in all the potential Windows users, and all the problems they need to solve. Which are many. It's no accident that we've just put out a Win32 Perl Resource Kit.

And I can tell you that the difference between curve 2 and curve 3 may depend on adding in all the international users that could benefit from Perl. It's no accident that the latest development version of Perl lets you name your variables with any characters that are considered to be alphanumeric in Unicode. That includes ideographs. There are a billion people in China. And I want them to be able to pass notes to each other written in Perl. I want them to be able to write poetry in Perl.

That is my vision of the future. My chosen perspective.

I began by talking about the virtues of a programmer: laziness, impatience, and hubris.

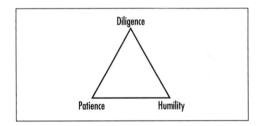

These are virtues of passion. They are also virtues of an individual. They are not, however, virtues of community. The virtues of community sound like their opposites: diligence, patience, and humility.

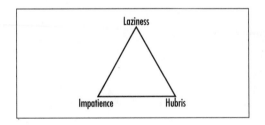

They're not really opposites, because you can do them all at the same time. It's another matter of perspective. These are the virtues that have brought us this far. These are the virtues that will carry our community into the future, if we do not abandon them.

Basically, we just have to stay the course. Friedrich Nietzsche called it a "long obedience in the same direction," which is a good snappy slogan. But I like the full quote too:

> The essential thing "in heaven and earth" is . . . that there should be long obedience in the same direction; there thereby results, and has always resulted in the long run, something which has made life worth living.

And now we've come full circle, back to the circle. Here is the front door of Bilbo Baggins' house. There's a road that goes from that door, and Bilbo wrote a poem about it.

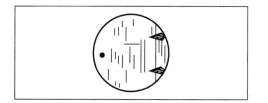

The Road goes ever on and on,
Down from the door where it began.
Now far ahead the Road has gone,
And I must follow, if I can,
Pursuing it with eager feet,
Until it joins some larger way
Where many paths and errands meet.
And whither then? I cannot say.

—*J.R.R. Tolkien, The Hobbit*

Open Source as a Business Strategy

Brian Behlendorf

Over 1997 and 1998, open-source software such as Linux, FreeBSD, Apache, and Perl started to attract widespread attention from a new audience: engineering managers, executives, industry analysts, and investors.

Most of the developers of such software welcomed this attention: not only does it boost the pride of developers, it also allows them to justify their efforts (now increasingly related to their salaried positions) to upper management and their peers.

But this new audience has hard questions:

- Is this really a new way of building software?

- Are each of the successes in open-source software a fluke of circumstance, or is there a repeatable methodology to all this?

- Why on earth would I allocate scarce financial resources to a project where my competitor would get to use the same code, for free?

- How reliant is this whole development model upon the hobbyist hacker or computer science student who just happens to put the right bits together to make something work well?

- Does this threaten or obsolesce my company's current methods for building software and doing business?

I suggest that the open-source model is indeed a reliable model for conducting software development for commercial purposes. I will attempt to lay out the preconditions for such a project, what types of projects make sense to pursue in this model, and the steps a company should go through to launch such a project. This essay is intended for companies who either release, sell, and support software commercially, or for technology companies that use a given piece of software as a core component to their business processes.

It's All About Platforms

While I'm indeed a big fan of the open-source approach to software development, there are definitely situations where an open-source approach would not benefit the parties involved. There are strong tradeoffs to this model, and returns are never guaranteed. A proper analysis requires asking yourself what your goals as a company are in the long term, as well as what your competitive advantages are today.

Let's start first with a discussion about Application Programming Interfaces (APIs), platforms, and standards. For the purposes of this essay, I'll wrap APIs (such as the Apache server API for building custom modules), on-the-wire protocols like HTTP, and operating system conventions (such as the way Linux organizes system files, or NT servers are administered) into the generic term "platform."

Win32, the collection of routines and facilities provided and defined by Microsoft for all Windows 95 and NT application developers, is a platform. If you intend to write an application for people to use on Windows, you must use this API. If you intend, as IBM once did with OS/2, to write an operating system which can run programs intended for MSWindows, you must implement the Win32 API in its entirety, as that's what Windows applications expect to be able to use.

Likewise, the Common Gateway Interface, or "CGI," is a platform. The CGI specification allows web server developers to write scripts and programs that run behind a web server. CGI is a much much simpler platform than Win32, and of course does much less, but its existence was important to the web server market because it allowed application developers to write portable code, programs that would run behind any web server. Besides a few orders of magnitude in complexity, a key difference between CGI and Win32 was that no one really owned the CGI specification; it was simply something the major web servers implemented so that they could run each others' CGI scripts. Only after several years of use was it deemed worthwhile to define the CGI specification as an informational Request for Comments (RFCs) at the Internet Engineering Task Force (IETF).

A platform is what essentially defines a piece of software, any software, be it a web browser like Netscape, or be it Apache. Platforms enable people to build or use one piece of software on top of another, and are thus essential not just for the Internet space, where common platforms like HTTP and TCP/IP are what really facilitated the Internet's explosive growth, but are becoming more and more essential to consider within a computer environment, both in a server context and in an end-user client context.

In the Apache project, we were fortunate in that early on we developed an internal API to allow us to distinguish between the core server functionality (that of handling the TCP connections, child process management, and basic HTTP request handling) and almost all other higher-level functionality like logging, a module for CGI, server-side includes, security configuration, etc. Having a really powerful API has also allowed us to hand off other big pieces of functionality, such as mod_perl (an Apache module that bundles a Perl interpreter into Apache) and mod_jserv (which implements the Java Servlet API), to separate groups of committed developers. This freed the core development group from having to worry about building a "monster" to support these large efforts in addition to maintaining and improving the core of the server.

There are businesses built upon the model of owning software platforms. Such a business can charge for all use of this platform, whether on a standard software installation basis, or a pay-per-use basis, or perhaps some other model. Sometimes platforms are enforced by copyright; other times platforms are obfuscated by the lack of a written description for public consumption; other times they are evolved so quickly, sometimes other than for technical reasons, that others who attempt to provide such a platform fail to keep up and are perceived by the market as "behind" technologically speaking, even though it's not a matter of programming.

Such a business model, while potentially beneficial in the short term for the company who owns such a platform, works against the interests of every other company in the industry, and against the overall rate of technological evolution. Competitors might have better technology, better services, or lower costs, but are unable to use those benefits because they don't have access to the platform. On the flip side, customers can become reliant upon a platform and, when prices rise, be forced to decide between paying a little more in the short run to stick with the platform, or spending a large quantity of money to change to a different platform, which may save them money in the long run.

Computers and automation have become so ingrained and essential to day-to-day business that a sensible business should not rely on a single vendor to provide essential services. Having a choice of service means not just having the freedom to choose; a choice must also be affordable. The switching cost is an important aspect to this freedom to choose. Switching costs can be minimized if switching software does not necessitate switching platforms. Thus it is always in a customers' interests to demand that the software they deploy be based on non-proprietary platforms.

This is difficult to visualize for many people because classic economics, the supply and demand curves we were all taught in high school, are based on the notion that products for sale have a relatively scalable cost—that to sell ten times as much product, the cost of raw goods to a vendor typically rises somewhere on the order of ten times as well. No one could have foreseen the dramatic economy of scale that software exhibits, the almost complete lack of any direct correlation between the amount of effort it takes to produce a software product and the number of people who can thus purchase and use it.

A reference body of open-source software that implements a wire protocol or API is more important to the long-term health of that platform than even two or three independent non-open-source implementations. Why is this? Because a commercial implementation can always be bought by a competitor, removing it from the market as an alternative, and thus destroying the notion that the standard was independent. It can also serve as an academic frame of reference for comparing implementations and behaviors.

There are organizations like the IETF and the W3C who do a more-or-less excellent job of providing a forum for multiparty standards development. They are, overall, effective in producing high-quality architectures for the way things should work over the Internet. However, the long-term success of a given standard, and the widespread use of such a standard, are outside of their jurisdiction. They have no power to force member organizations to create software that implements the protocols they define faithfully. Sometimes, the only recourse is a body of work that shows why a specific implementation is correct.

For example, in December of 1996, AOL made a slight change to their custom HTTP proxy servers their customers use to access web sites. This "upgrade" had a cute little political twist to it: when AOL users accessed a web site using the Apache 1.2 server, at that time only a few months old and implementing the new HTTP/1.1 specification, they were welcomed with this rather informative message:

UNSUPPORTED WEB VERSION

The Web address you requested is not available in a version supported by AOL. This is an issue with the Web site, and not with AOL. The owner of this site is using an unsupported HTTP language. If you receive this message frequently, you may want to set your web graphics preferences to COMPRESSED at Keyword: PREFERENCES

Alarmed at this "upgrade," Apache core developers circled the wagons and analyzed the situation. A query to AOL's technical team came back with the following explanation:

New HTTP/1.1 web servers are starting to generate HTTP/1.1 responses to HTTP/1.0 requests when they should be generating only HTTP/1.0 responses. We wanted to stem the tide of those faults proliferating and becoming a de facto standard by blocking them now. Hopefully the authors of those web servers will change their software to only generate HTTP/1.1 responses when an HTTP/1.1 request is submitted.

Unfortunately AOL engineers were under the mistaken assumption that HTTP/1.1 responses were not backward-compatible with HTTP/1.0 clients or proxies. They are; HTTP was designed to be backward-compatible within minor-number revisions. But the specification for HTTP/1.1 is so complex that a less than thorough reading may lead one to have concluded this was not the case, especially with the HTTP/1.1 document that existed at the end of 1996.

So we Apache developers had a choice—we could back down and give HTTP/1.0 responses to HTTP/1.0 requests, or we could follow the specification. Roy Fielding, the "HTTP cop" in the group, was able to clearly show us how the software's behavior at the time was correct and beneficial; there would be cases where HTTP/1.0 clients may wish to upgrade to an HTTP/1.1 conversation upon discovering that a server supported 1.1. It was also important to tell proxy servers that even if the first request they proxied to an origin server they saw was 1.0, the origin server could also support 1.1.

It was decided that we'd stick to our guns and ask AOL to fix their software. We suspected that the HTTP/1.1 response was actually causing a problem with their software that was due more to sloppy programming practices on their part than to bad protocol design. We had the science behind our decision. What mattered most was that Apache was at that point on 40% of the web servers on the Net, and Apache 1.2 was on a very healthy portion of those, so they had to decide whether it was easier to fix their programming mistakes or to tell their users that some 20% or more of the web sites on the Internet were inaccessible through their proxies. On December 26th, we published a web page detailing the dispute, and publicized its existence not just to our own user base, but to several major news outlets as well, such as C|Net and *Wired*, to justify our actions.

AOL decided to fix their software. Around the same time, we announced the availability of a "patch" for sites that wanted to work around the AOL problem until it was rectified, a patch that degraded responses to HTTP/1.0 for AOL. We were resolute that this was to remain an "unofficial" patch, with no support, and that it would not be made a default setting in the official distribution.

There have been several other instances where vendors of other HTTP products (including both Netscape and Microsoft) had interoperability issues with Apache; in many of those cases, there was a choice the vendor had to make between expending the effort to fix their bug, or writing off any sites which would become inoperable because of it. In many cases a vendor would implement the protocol improperly but consistently on their clients and servers. The result was an implementation that worked fine for them, but imperfectly at best with either a client or server from another vendor. This is much more subtle than even the AOL situation, as the bug may not be apparent or even significant to the majority of people using this software—and thus the long-term ramifications of such a bug (or additional bugs compounding the problem) may not be seen until it's too late.

Were there not an open-source and widely used reference web server like Apache, it's entirely conceivable that these subtle incompatibilities could have grown and built upon each other, covered up by mutual blame or Jedi mind tricks ("We can't repeat that in the lab. . . ."), where the response to "I'm having problem when I connect vendor X browser to vendor Y server" is, "Well, use vendor Y client and it'll be all better." At the end of this process we would have ended up with two (or more) World Wide Webs—one that was built on vendor X web servers, the other on vendor Y servers, and each would only work with their respective vendors' clients. There is ample historic precedence for this type of anti-standard activity, a policy ("locking in") which is encoded as a basic business practice of many software companies.

Of course this would have been a disaster for everyone else out there—the content providers, service providers, software developers, and everyone who needed to use HTTP to communicate would have had to maintain two separate servers for their offerings. While there may have been technical customer pressure to "get along together," the contrary marketing pressure to "innovate, differentiate, lead the industry, define the platform" would have kept either party from attempting to commodify their protocols.

We did, in fact, see such a disaster with client-side JavaScript. There was such a big difference in behavior between different browsers, even within different beta versions of the same browser, that developers had to create code that would detect different revisions and give different behavior—something that added significantly more development time to interactive pages using JavaScript. It wasn't until the W3C stepped in and laid the groundwork for a Document Object Model (DOM) that we actually saw a serious attempt at creating a multiparty standard around JavaScript.

There are natural forces in today's business world that drive for deviation when a specification is implemented by closed software. Even an accidental misreading of a common specification can cause a deviation if not corrected quickly.

Thus, I argue that building your services or products on top of a standards-based platform is good for the stability of your business processes. The success of the Internet has not only shown how common platforms help facilitate communication, it has also forced companies to think more about how to create value in what gets communicated, rather than trying to take value out of the network itself.

Analyzing Your Goals for an Open-Source Project

What you need to ask yourself, as a company, is to what degree your products implement a new platform, and to what extent is it in your business interests to maintain ownership of that platform. How much of your overall product and service set, and thus how much of your revenue, is above that platform, or below it? This is probably something you can even apply numbers to.

Let's say you're a database company. You sell a database that runs on multiple OSes; you separately sell packages for graphical administration, rapid development tools, a library of common stored procedures people can use, etc. You sell support on a yearly basis. Upgrades require a new purchase. You also offer classes. And finally, you've got a growing but healthy consulting group who implement your database for customers.

Let's say your revenue balance looks something like this:

- 40%—Sales of the database software
- 15%—Support
- 10%—Consulting work
- 10%—Rapid development tools
- 10%—Graphical administration tools
- 10%—Library of stored procedures/applications on top of this DB
- 5%—Manuals/classes

At first glance, the suggestion that you give away your database software for free would be ludicrous. That's 40% of your revenue gone. If you're lucky as a company you're profitable, and if you're even luckier you've got maybe a 20% profit margin. 40% wipes that out completely.

This of course assumes nothing else changes in the equation. But the chances are, if you pull this off right, things will change. Databases are the type of application that companies don't just pull off the shelf at CompUSA, throw the CD into their machine, and then forget about. All of the other categories of revenue are still valid and necessary no matter how much was charged for the OS. In fact, there is now more freedom to charge more for these other services than before, when the cost of the software ate up the bulk of what a customer typically paid for when they bought database software.

So very superficially speaking, if the free or low-cost nature of the database were to cause it to be used on twice as many systems, and users were as equally motivated as before to purchase consulting and support and development tools and libraries and such from your company, you'd see a 20% gain in the overall amount of revenue. What's more likely is that three to four times as many new users are introduced to your software, and while the take-up rate of your other services is lower (either because people are happy just using the free version, or you have competitors now offering these services for your product), so long as that take-up rate doesn't go too low, you've probably increased overall revenue into the company.

Furthermore, depending on the license applied, you may see lower costs involved in development of your software. You're likely to see bugs fixed by motivated customers, for example. You're also likely to see new innovations in your software by customers who contribute their code to the project because they want to see it maintained as a standard part of the overall distribution. So overall, your development costs could go down.

It's also likely that, given a product/services mix like the above example, releasing this product for free does little to help your competitors compete against you in your other revenue spaces. There are probably already consultants who do integration work with your tools; already independent authors of books; already libraries of code you've encouraged other companies to build. The availability of source code will marginally help competitors be able to provide support for your code, but as the original developers, you'll have a cache to your brand that the others will have to compete against.

Not all is wine and roses, of course. There are costs involved in this process that are going to be difficult to tie to revenue directly. For example, the cost of infrastructure to support such an endeavor, while not significant, can consume systems administration and support staff. There's also the cost of having developers communicating with others outside the company, and the extra overhead of developing the code in a public way. There may be significant cost involved in preparing the source code for public inspection. And after all this work, there may simply not be the "market need" for your product as freeware. I'll address all these points in the rest of this essay.

Evaluating the Market Need for Your Project

It may be very tempting for a company to look to Open Source as a way to save a particular project, to gain notoriety, or to simply have a good story to end a product category. These are not good reasons to launch an open-source project. If a company is serious about pursuing this model, it needs to do its research in determining exactly what the product needs to be for an open-source strategy to be successful.

The first step is to conduct a competitive analysis of the space, both for the commercial competitors and the freeware competitors, no matter how small. Be very careful to determine exactly what your product offers by componentizing your offering into separable "chunks" that could be potentially bundled or sold or open-sourced separately. Similarly, don't exclude combinations of freeware and commercialware that offer the same functionality.

Let's continue with the database vendor example above. Let's say there are actually three components to the vendor's database product: a core SQL server, a backup/transaction logging manager, and a developer library. Such a vendor should not only compare their product's offering to the big guys like Oracle and Sybase, not only to the smaller but growing commercial competitors like Solid and Velocis, but also to the free databases like MySQL and Postgres. Such an analysis may conclude that the company's core SQL server provides only a little more functionality than MySQL, and in an area that was never considered a competitive advantage but merely a necessary feature to keep up with the other DB vendors. The backup/transaction logging manager has no freeware competition, and the developer library is surpassed by the Perl DBI utilities but has little Java or C competition.

This company could then consider the following strategies:

1. Replace the core SQL server with MySQL, and then package up the core SQL server functionality and backup/transaction logging manager, and sell Java/C libraries while providing and supporting the free Perl library. This would ride upon the momentum generated by the MySQL package, and the incredible library of add-on code and plug-in modules out there for it; it would also allow you to keep private any pieces of code you may believe have patents or patentable code, or code you simply think is cool enough that it's a competitive advantage. Market yourself as a company that can scale MySQL up to larger deployments.

2. Contribute the "extra core SQL server functionality" to MySQL, then design the backup/transaction logger to be sold as a separate product that works with a wider variety of databases, with a clear preference for MySQL. This has smaller revenue potential, but allows you as a company to be more focused and potentially reach a broader base of customers. Such a product may be easier to support as well.

3. Go in the other direction: stick with a commercial product strategy for the core SQL server and libraries, but open-source the backup/transaction logger as a general utility for a wide array of databases. This would cut down on your development costs for this component, and be a marketing lead generator for your commercial database. It would also remove a competitive advantage some of your commercial competitors would have over open source, even though it would also remove some of yours too.

All of these are valid approaches to take. Another approach:

4. Open-source the entire core server as its own product, separate from MySQL or Postgres or any of the other existing packages, and provide commercial support for it. Sell as standard non-open-source the backup/logging tool, but open-source the development libraries to encourage new users. Such a strategy carries more risk, as a popular package like MySQL or Postgres tends to have been around for quite some time, and there's inherently much developer aversion to swapping out a database if their current one is working fine. To do this, you'd have to prove *significant* benefit over what people are currently using. Either it has to be dramatically faster, more flexible, easier to administer or program with, or contain sufficiently new features that users are motivated to try it out. You also have to spend much more time soliciting interest in the project, and you probably will have to find a way to pull developers away from competing products.

I wouldn't advocate the fourth approach in this exact circumstance, as MySQL actually has a very healthy head start here, lots and lots of add-on programs, and a rather large existing user base.

However, from time to time an open source project loses momentum, either because the core development team is not actively doing development, or the software runs into core architectural challenges that keep it from meeting new demands, or the environment that created this demand simply dries up or changes focus. When that happens, and it becomes clear people are looking for alternatives, there is the possibility of introducing a replacement that will attract attention, even if it does not immediately present a significant advance over the status quo.

Analyzing demand is essential. In fact, it's demand that usually creates new open-source projects. Apache started with a group of webmasters sharing patches to the NCSA web server, deciding that swapping patches like so many baseball cards was inefficient and error-prone, and electing to do a separate distribution of the NCSA server with their patches built in. None of the principals involved in the early days got involved because they wanted to sell a commercial server with Apache as its base, though that's certainly a valid reason for being involved.

So an analysis of the market demand for a particular open-source project also involves joining relevant mailing lists and discussion forums, cruising discussion archives, and interviewing your customers and their peers; only then can you realistically determine if there are people out there willing to help make the project bear fruit.

Going back to Apache's early days: those of us who were sharing patches around were also sending them back to NCSA, hoping they'd be incorporated, or at the very least acknowledged, so that we could be somewhat assured that we could upgrade easily when the next release came out. NCSA had been hit when the previous server programmers had been snatched away by Netscape, and the flood of email was too much for the remaining developers. So building our own server was more an act of self-preservation than an attempt to build the next great web server. It's important to start out with limited goals that can be accomplished quite easily, and not have to rely upon your project dominating a market before you realize benefits from the approach.

Open Source's Position in the Spectrum of Software

To determine which parts of your product line or components of a given product to open-source, it may be helpful to conduct a simple exercise. First, draw a line representing a spectrum. On the left hand side, put "Infrastructural," representing software that implements frameworks and platforms, all the way down to TCP/IP and the kernel and even hardware. On the right hand side, put "End-user applications," representing the tools and applications that the average, non-technical user will use. Along this line, place dots representing, in relative terms, where you think each of the components of your product offering lie. From the above example, the GUI front-ends and administrative tools lie on the far right-hand side, while code that manages backups is off to the far left. Development libraries are somewhat to the right of center, while the core SQL facilities are somewhat to the left. Then, you may want to throw in your competitors' products as well, also separating them out by component, and if you're really creative, using a different color pen to distinguish the free offerings from the commercial offerings. What you are likely to find is that the free offerings tend to clump towards the left-hand side, and the commercial offerings towards the right.

Open-source software has tended to be slanted towards the infrastructural/back-end side of the software spectrum represented here. There are several reasons for this:

- End-user applications are hard to write, not only because a programmer has to deal with a graphical, windowed environment which is constantly changing, nonstandard, and buggy simply because of its complexity, but also because most programmers are not good graphical interface designers, with notable exceptions.

- Culturally, open-source software has been conducted in the networking code and operating system space for years.

- Open-source tends to thrive where incremental change is rewarded, and historically that has meant back-end systems more than front-ends.

- Much open-source software was written by engineers to solve a task they had to do while developing commercial software or services; so the primary audience was, early on, other engineers.

This is why we see solid open-source offerings in the operating system and network services space, but very few offerings in the desktop application space.

There are certainly counterexamples to this. A great example is the GIMP, or GNU Image Manipulation Program, an X11 program comparable in feature set to Adobe Photoshop. Yet in some ways, this product is also an "infrastructure" tool, a platform, since it owes its success to its wonderful plug-in architecture, and the dozens and dozens of plug-ins that have been developed that allow it to import and export many different file formats and which implement hundreds of filter effects.

Look again at the spectrum you've drawn out. At some point, you can look at your offering in the context of these competitors, and draw a vertical line. This line denotes the separation between what you open-source and what you may choose to keep proprietary. That line itself represents your true platform, your interface between the public code you're trying to establish as a standard on the left, and your private code you want to drive demand for on the right.

Nature Abhors a Vacuum

Any commercial-software gaps in an otherwise open-source infrastructural framework are a strong motivating force for redevelopment in the public space. Like some force of nature, when a commercial wall exists between two strong pieces of open-source software, there's pressure to bridge that gap with a public solution. This is because every gap can be crossed given enough resources, and if that gap is small enough for your company to cross with your own development team, it's likely to be small enough for a set of motivated developers to also cross.

Let's return to the database example: say you decide to open-source your core SQL server (or your advanced code on top of MySQL), but decide to make money by building a commercial, non-source-available driver for plugging that database into a web server to create dynamic content. You decide the database will be a loss leader for this product, and therefore you'll charge far higher than normal margins on this component.

Since hooking up databases to web servers is a very common and desirable thing, developers will either have to go through you, or find another way to access the database from the web site. Each developer will be motivated by the idea of saving the money they'd otherwise have to pay you. If enough developers pool their resources to make it worth their while, or a single talented individual simply can't pay for the plug-in but still wants to use that database, it's possible you could wake up one morning to find an open-source competitor to your commercial offering, completely eliminating the advantage of having the only solution for that task.

This is a piece of a larger picture: relying upon proprietary source code in strategic places as your way of making money has become a risky business venture. If you can make money by supporting the web server + plug-in + database combination, or by providing an interface to managing that system as a whole, you can protect yourself against these types of surprises.

Not all commercial software has this vulnerability—it is specifically a characteristic of commercial software that tries to slot itself into a niche directly between two well-established open-source offerings. Putting your commercial offering as an addition to the current set of open-source offerings is a more solid strategy.

Donate, or Go It Alone? ·

Open-source software exists in many of the standard software categories, particularly those focused on the server side. Obviously we have operating systems; web servers;

mail (SMTP, POP, IMAP), news (NNTP), and DNS servers; programming languages (the "glue" for dynamic content on the Web); databases; networking code of all kinds. On the desktop you have text editors like Emacs, Nedit, and Jove; windowing systems like Gnome and KDE; web browsers like Mozilla; and screen savers, calculators, checkbook programs, PIMs, mail clients, image tools—the list goes on. While not every category has category-killers like Apache or Bind, there are probably very few commercial niches that don't have at least the beginnings of a decent open source alternative available. This is much less true for the Win32 platform than for the Unix or Mac platforms, primarily because the open-source culture has not adopted the Win32 platform as "open" enough to really build upon.

There is a compelling argument for taking advantage of whatever momentum an existing open-source package has in a category that overlaps with your potential offering, by contributing your additional code or enhancements to the existing project and then aiming for a return in the form of higher-quality code overall, marketing lead generation, or common platform establishment. In evaluating whether this is an acceptable strategy, one needs to look at licensing terms:

- Are the terms on the existing package copacetic to your long-term goals?
- Can you legally contribute your code under that license?
- Does it incent future developers sufficiently? If not, would the developers be willing to accommodate you by changing the license?
- Are your contributions general enough that they would be of value to the developers and users of the existing project? If all they do is implement an API to your proprietary code, they probably won't be accepted.
- If your contributions are hefty, can you have "peer" status with the other developers, so that you can directly apply bug fixes and enhancements you make later?
- Are the other developers people you can actually work with?
- Are your developers people who can work with others in a collaborative setting?

Satisfying developers is probably the biggest challenge to the open-source development model, one which no amount of technology or even money can really address. Each developer has to feel like they are making a positive contribution to the project, that their concerns are being addressed, their comments on architecture and design questions acknowledged and respected, and their code efforts rewarded with integration into the distribution or a really good reason why not.

People mistakenly say "open-source software works because the whole Internet becomes your R&D and QA departments!" In fact, the amount of talented programmer effort available for a given set of tasks is usually limited. Thus, it is usually to everyone's interests if parallel development efforts are not undertaken simply because of semantic disputes between developers. On the other hand, evolution works best when alternatives compete for resources, so it's not a bad thing to have two competing solutions in the same niche if there's enough talent pool for critical mass—some real innovation may be tried in one that wasn't considered in the other.

There is strong evidence for competition as a healthy trait in the SMTP server space. For a long time, Eric Allman's "Sendmail" program was the standard SMTP daemon every OS shipped with. There were other open-source competitors that came up, like Smail or Zmailer, but the first to really crack the usage base was Dan Bernstein's Qmail package. When Qmail came on the scene, Sendmail was 20 years old, and had started to show its age; it was also not designed for the Internet of the late 90s, where buffer overflows and denial of service attacks are as common as rainfall in Seattle. Qmail was a radical break in many ways—program design, administration, even in its definition of what good "network behavior" for an SMTP server is. It was an evolution that would have been exceedingly unlikely to have been made within Allman's Sendmail package. Not because Allman and his team weren't good programmers or because there weren't motivated third-party contributors; it's just that sometimes a radical departure is needed to really try something new and see if it works. For similar reasons, IBM funded the development of Weiste Venema's "SecureMailer" SMTP daemon, which as of this writing also appears to be likely to become rather popular. The SMTP daemon space is well-defined enough and important enough that it can support multiple open-source projects; time will tell which will survive.

Bootstrapping

Essential to the health of an open-source project is that the project have sufficient momentum to be able to evolve and respond to new challenges. Nothing is static in the software world, and each major component requires maintenance and new enhancements continually. One of the big selling points of this model is that it cuts down on the amount of development any single party must do, so for that theory to become fact, you need other active developers.

In the process of determining demand for your project, you probably ran into a set of other companies and individuals with enough interest here to form a core set of developers. Once you've decided on a strategy, shop it to this core set even more heavily; perhaps start a simple discussion mailing list for this purpose, with nothing set in stone. Chances are this group will have some significant ideas for how to make this a successful project, and list their own set of resources they could apply to make it happen.

For the simplest of projects, a commitment from this group that they'll give your product a try and if they're happy stay on the development mailing list is probably enough. However, for something more significant, you should try and size up just how big the total resource base is.

Here is what I would consider a minimum resource set for a project of moderate complexity, say a project to build a common shopping cart plug-in for a web server, or a new type of network daemon implementing a simple protocol. In the process I'll describe the various roles needed and the types of skills necessary to fill them.

- *Role 1: Infrastructure support*: Someone to set up and maintain the mailing list aliases, the web server, the CVS (Concurrent Versioning System) code server, the bug database, etc.

  Startup: 100 hours
  Maintenance: 20 hrs/week.

- *Role 2: Code "captain"*: Someone who watches all commits and has overall responsibility for the quality of the implemented code. Integrates patches contributed by third parties, fixing any bugs or incompatibilities in these contributions. This is outside of whatever new development work they are also responsible for.

  Startup: 40–200 hours (depends on how long it takes to clean up the code for public consumption!)
  Maintenance: 20 hrs/week

- *Role 3: Bug database maintenance*: While this is not free "support," it is important that the public have an organized way of communicating bug reports and issues to the server developers. In a free setting, the developers are of course not even obliged to answer all mail they get, but they should make reasonable efforts to respond to valid issues. The bug database maintainer would be the first line of support, someone who goes through the submissions on a regular basis and weeds out the simple questions, tosses the clueless ones, and forwards the real issues on to the developers.

  Startup: just enough to learn their way around the code
  Maintenance: 10–15 hrs/week

- *Role 4: Documentation/web site content maintenance*: This position is often left unattended in open-source projects and left to the engineers or to people who really want to contribute but aren't star programmers; all too often it's simply left undone. So long as we're going about this process deliberately, locating dedicated resources to make sure that non-technical people can understand and appreciate the tools they are deploying is essential to widespread usage. It helps cut down on having to answer bug reports which are really just misunderstandings, and it also helps encourage new people to learn their way around the code and become future contributors. A document that describes at a high level the internal architecture of the software is essential; documentation that explains major procedures or classes within the code is almost as important.

Startup: 60 hours (presuming little code has been documented)
Maintenance: 10 hrs/week

- Role 5: Cheerleader/zealot/evangelist/strategist: Someone who can work to build momentum for the project by finding other developers, push specific potential customers to give it a try, find other companies who could be candidates for adopting this new platform, etc. Not quite a marketer or salesperson, as they need to stay close to the technology; but the ability to clearly see the role of the project in a larger perspective is essential.

Startup: enough to learn the project
Maintenance: 20 hrs/week

So here we have five roles representing almost three full-time people. In reality, some of these roles get handled by groups of people sharing responsibility, and some projects can survive with the average core participant spending less than 5 hrs/week after the first set of release humps are passed. But for the early days of the project it is essential that developers have the time and focus they would if the project were a regular development effort at the company.

These five roles also do not cover any resources that could be put towards new development; this is purely maintenance. In the end, if you can not find enough resources from peers and partners to cover these bases *and* enough extra developers to do some basic new development (until new recruits are attracted), you may want to reconsider open-sourcing your project.

What License to Use?

Determining which license to use for your project can be a fairly complex task; it's the kind of task you probably don't enjoy but your legal team will. There are other papers and web sites that cover copyright issues in finer detail; I'll provide an overview, though, of what I see as the business considerations of each style of license.

The BSD-Style Copyright

This is the copyright used by Apache and by the BSD-based operating systems projects (FreeBSD, OpenBSD, NetBSD), and by and large it can be summed up as, "Here's this code, do what you like with it, we don't care, just give us credit if you try and sell it." Usually that credit is demanded in different forms—on advertising, or in a README file, or in the printed documentation, etc. It has been brought up that such a copyright may be inscalable—that is, if someone ever released a bundle of software that included 40 different open-source modules, all BSD-based, one might argue that there'd be 40 different copyright notices that would be necessary to display. In practice this has not been a problem, and in fact it's been seen as a positive force in spreading awareness of the use of open-source software.

From a business perspective, this is the best type of license for jumping into an existing project, as there are no worries about licenses or restrictions on future use or redistribution. You can mix and match this software with your own proprietary code, and only release what you feel might help the project and thus help you in return. This is one reason why we chose it for the Apache group—unlike many free software projects, Apache was started largely by commercial webmasters in search of a better web server for their own commercial needs. While probably none of the original team had a goal of creating a commercial server on top of Apache, none of us knew what our futures would hold, and felt that limiting our options at the beginning wasn't very smart.

This type of license is ideal for promoting the use of a reference body of code that implements a protocol or common service. This is another reason why we chose it for the Apache group—many of us wanted to see HTTP survive and become a true multiparty standard, and would not have minded in the slightest if Microsoft or Netscape chose to incorporate our HTTP engine or any other component of our code into their products, if it helped further the goal of keeping HTTP common.

This degree of openness has risks. No incentive is built into the license to encourage companies to contribute their code enhancements back to the project. There have certainly been cases in Apache's history where companies have developed technology around it that we would have like to have seen offered back to the project. But had we had a license which mandated that code enhancements be made available back to the project, such enhancements would perhaps never have been made in the first place.

All this means that, strategically speaking, the project needs to maintain sufficient momentum, and that participants realize greater value by contributing their code to the project, even code that would have had value if kept proprietary. This is a tricky ratio to maintain, particularly if one company decides to dramatically increase the amount of coding they do on a derivative project; and begins to doubt the potential return in proportion to their contribution to the project, e.g., "We're doing all this work, more than anyone else combined, why should we share it?" The author has no magic bullet for that scenario, other than to say that such a company probably has not figured out the best way to inspire contributions from third parties to help meet their engineering goals most efficiently.

The Mozilla Public License

The Mozilla Public License (MPL) was developed by the Netscape Mozilla team for use on their project. It was the first new license in several years when it was released, and really addressed some key issues not addressed by the BSD or GNU licenses. It is adjacent to the BSD-style license in the spectrum of open-source software licenses. It has two key differences:

It mandates that changes to the "distribution" also be released under the same copyright as the MPL, which thus makes it available back to the project. The "distribution" is defined as the files as distributed in the source code. This is important, because it allows a company to add an interface to a proprietary library of code without mandating that the other library of code also be made MPL—only the interface. Thus, this software can more or less be combined into a commercial software environment.

It has several provisions protecting both the project as a whole and its developers against patent issues in contributed code. It mandates that the company or individual contributing code back to the project release any and all claims to patent rights that may be exposed by the code.

This second provision is really important; it also, at the time of this writing, contains a big flaw.

Taking care of the patent issue is a Very Good Thing. There is always the risk that a company could innocently offer code to a project, and then once that code has been implemented thoroughly, try and demand some sort of patent fee for its use. Such a business strategy would be laughably bad PR and very ugly, but unfortunately not all companies see this yet. So, this second provision prevents the case of anyone surreptitiously providing code they know is patented and liable to cause headaches for everyone down the road.

Of course it doesn't block the possibility that someone *else* owns a patent that would apply; there is no legal instrument that does provide that type of protection. I would actually advocate that this is an appropriate service for the U.S. Patent and Trade Office to perform; they seem to have the authority to declare certain ideas or algorithms as property someone owns, so shouldn't they also be required to do the opposite and certify my submitted code as patent-free, granting me some protection from patent lawsuits?

As I said earlier, though, there is a flaw in the current MPL, as of December 1998. In essence, Section 2.2 mandates (through its definition of "Contributor Version") that the contributor waive patent claims on *any* part of Mozilla, not just on the code they contribute. Maybe that doesn't seem like a bug. It would be nice to get the whole package waived by a number of large companies.

Unfortunately, a certain large company with one of the world's largest patent portfolios has a rather specific, large issue with this quirk. Not because they intend to go after Mozilla some day and demand royalties—that would be foolhardy. They are concerned because there are parts of Mozilla that implement processes they have patents on and receive rather large numbers of dollars for every year—and were they to waive patent claims over the Mozilla code, those companies who pay them dollars for those patents could simply take the code from Mozilla that implements those same patents and shove them into their own products, removing the need to license the patent from said large company. Were Section 2.2 to simply refer to the contributed patches rather than the whole browser when it comes to waiving patents, this would not be a problem.

Aside from this quirk, the MPL is a remarkably solid license. Mandating back the changes to the "core" means that essential bug fixes and portability enhancements will flow back to the project, while value-added features can still be developed by commercial entities. It is perhaps the best license to use to develop an end-user application, where patents are more likely to be an issue, and the drive to branch the project may be greater. In contrast, the BSD license is perhaps more ideal for projects intended to be "invisible" or essentially library functions, like an operating system or a web server.

The GNU Public License

While not obviously a business-friendly license, there are certain aspects of the GNU license which are attractive, believe it or not, for commercial purposes.

Fundamentally, the GPL mandates that enhancements, derivatives, and even code that incorporates GPL'd code are also themselves released as source code under the GPL. This "viral" behavior has been trumpeted widely by open-source advocates as a way to ensure that code that begins free remains free—that there is no chance of a commercial interest forking their own development version from the available code and committing resources that are not made public. In the eyes of those who put a GPL on their software, they would much rather have no contribution than have a contribution they couldn't use as freely as the original. There is an academic appeal to this, of course, and there are advocates who claim that Linux would have never gotten as large as it has unless it was GPL'd, as the lure of forking for commercial purposes would have been too great, keeping the critical mass of unified development effort from being reached.

So at first glance, it may appear that the GPL would not have a happy co-existence with a commercial intent related to open-source software. The traditional models of making money through software value-add are not really possible here. However, the

GPL could be an extraordinarily effective means to establish a platform that discourages competitive platforms from being created, and which protects your claim to fame as the "premier" provider of products and services that sit upon this platform.

An example of this is Cygnus and GCC. Cygnus makes a very healthy chunk of change every year by porting GCC to various different types of hardware, and maintaining those ports. The vast majority of that work, in compliance with the GPL, gets contributed to the GCC distribution, and made available for free. Cygnus charges for the effort involved in the port and maintenance, not for the code itself. Cygnus's history and leadership in this space make it the reference company to approach for this type of service.

If a competitor were to start up and compete against Cygnus, it too would be forced to redistribute their changes under the GPL. This means that there is no chance for a competitor to find a commercial technical niche on top of the GCC framework that could be exploited, without giving Cygnus the same opportunity to also take advantage of that technology. Cygnus has created a situation where competitors can't compete on technology differentiation, unless a competitor were to spend a very large amount of time and money and use a platform other than GCC altogether.

Another way in which the GPL could be used for business purposes is as a technology "sentinel," with a non-GPL'd version of the same code available for a price. For example, you may have a great program for encrypting TCP/IP connections over the Internet. You don't care if people use it non-commercially, or even commercially—your interest is in getting the people who want to embed it in a product or redistribute it for profit to pay you for the right to do that. If you put a GPL license on the code, this second group of users can't do what they want, without making their entire product GPL as well, something many of them may be unwilling to do. However, if you maintain a separate branch of your project, one which is *not* under the GPL, you can commercially license the separate branch of code any way you like. You have to be very careful, though, to make sure that any code volunteered to you by third parties is explicitly available for this non-free branch; you ensure this by either declaring that only you (or people employed by you) will write code for this project, or that (in addition) you'll get explicit clearance from each contributor to take whatever they contribute into a non-free version.

There are companies for whom this is a viable business model—an example is Transvirtual in Berkeley, who are applying this model to a commercial lightweight Java virtual machine and class library project. Some may claim that the number of contributors who would be turned off by such a model would be high, and that the GPL and non-GPL versions may branch; I would claim that if you treat your contributors right, perhaps even offer them money or other compensation for their contributions (it is, after all, helping your commercial bottom line), this model could work.

The open-source license space is sure to evolve over the next few years as people discover what does and does not work. The simple fact is that you are free to invent a new license that exactly describes where on the spectrum (represented by BSD on the right and GPL on the left) you wish to place it. Just remember, the more freedoms you grant those who use and extend your code, the more incented they will be to contribute.

Tools for Launching Open Source Projects

We have a nice set of available, well-maintained tools used in the Apache Project for allowing our distributed development process to work.

Most important among these is CVS, or Concurrent Versioning System. It is a collection of programs that implement a shared code repository, maintaining a database of changes with names and dates attached to each change. It is extremely effective for being able to allow multiple people to simultaneously be the "authors" of a program without stepping over each others' toes. It also helps in the debugging process, as it is possible to roll back changes one by one to find out exactly where a certain bug may have been introduced. There are clients for every major platform, and it works just fine over dial-up lines or across long-distance connections. It can also be secured by tunneling it over an encrypted connection using SSH.

The Apache project uses CVS not just for maintaining the actual software, but also for maintaining our "STATUS" file, in which we place all major outstanding issues, with comments, opinions, and even votes attached to each issue. We also use it to register votes for decisions we make as a group, maintain our web site documents with it, manage development documents, etc. In short it is the asset and knowledge management software for the project. Its simplicity may seem like a drawback—most software in this space is expensive and full-featured—but in reality simplicity is a very strong virtue of CVS. Every component of CVS is free—the server and the clients.

Another essential element to an open-source project is a solid set of discussion forums for developers and for users. The software to use here is largely inconsequential—we use Majordomo, but ezmlm or Smartlist or any of the others would probably be fine. The important thing is to give each development effort their own list, so that developers can self-select their interests and reasonably keep up with development. It's also smart to create a separate list for each project to which the CVS server emails changes that get made to the CVS repository, to allow for a type of passive peer review of changes. Such a model is actually very effective in maintaining code standards and discovering bugs. It may also make sense to have different lists for users and developers, and perhaps even distinguish between *all* developers and *core* developers if your project is large enough. Finally, it is important to have archives of the lists publicly available so that new users can search to see if a particular issue has been brought up in the past, or how something was addressed in the past.

Bug and issue tracking is also essential to a well-run project. On the Apache Project we use a GNU tool called GNATS, which has served us very well through 3,000+ bug reports. You want to find a tool that allows multiple people to answer bug reports, allows people to specialize on bugs in one particular component of the project, and allows people to read bug reports by email and reply to them by email rather than exclusively by a web form. The overriding goal for the bug database is that it should be as easy and automated as possible both for developers to answer bugs (because this is really a chore to most developers), and to search to see if a particular bug has already been reported. In essence, your bug database will become your repository for anecdotal knowledge about the project and its capabilities. Why is a particular behavior a feature and not a bug? Is anyone addressing a known problem? These are the types of questions a good bug database should seek to answer.

The open-source approach is *not* a magic bullet for every type of software development project. Not only do the conditions have to be right for conducting such a project, but there is a tremendous amount of real work that has to go into launching a successful project that has a life of its own. In many ways you, as the advocate for a new project, have to act a little like Dr. Frankenstein, mixing chemicals here, applying voltage there, to bring your monster to life. Good luck.

The Open Source Definition

Bruce Perens

The typical computer user owns lots of software that he bought years ago and no longer uses today. He may have upgraded his computer or changed brands, and then the program wouldn't work any longer. The software might have become obsolete. The program may simply not do what he needs. He may have bought two or more computers, and doesn't want to pay for a second copy of the software. Whatever the reason, the software that he paid for years ago isn't up to the task today. Does that really need to happen?

What if you had the right to get a free upgrade whenever your software needed it? What if, when you switched from a Mac to a PC, you could switch software versions for free? What if, when the software doesn't work or isn't powerful enough, you can have it improved or even fix it yourself? What if the software was still maintained even if the company that produced it went out of business? What if you could use your software on your office workstation, and your home desktop computer, and your portable laptop, instead of just one computer? You'd probably still be using the software you paid for years ago. These are some of the rights that Open Source gives you.

The Open Source Definition is a bill of rights for the computer user. It defines certain rights that a software license must grant you to be certified as Open Source. Those who don't make their programs Open Source are finding it difficult to compete with those who do, as users gain a new appreciation of rights they always should have had. Programs like the Linux operating system and Netscape's web browser have become extremely popular, displacing other software that has more restrictive licenses. Companies that use open-source software have the advantage of its very rapid development, often by several collaborating companies, and much of it contributed by individuals who simply need an improvement to serve their own needs.

The volunteers who made products like Linux possible are only there, and the companies are only able to cooperate, because of the rights that come with Open Source. The average computer programmer would feel stupid if he put lots of work into a program, only to have the owner of the program sell his improvement without giving anything back. Those same programmers feel comfortable contributing to Open Source because they are assured of these rights:

- The right to make copies of the program, and distribute those copies.

- The right to have access to the software's source code, a necessary preliminary before you can change it.

- The right to make improvements to the program.

These rights are important to the software contributor because they keep all contributors at the same level relative to each other. Everyone who wants to is allowed to sell an Open Source program, so prices will be low and development to reach new markets will be rapid. Anyone who invests the time to build knowledge in an Open Source program can support it, and this provides users with the option of providing their own support, or the economy of a number of competing support providers. Any programmer can tailor an Open Source program to specific markets in order to reach new customers. People who do these things aren't compelled to pay royalties or license fees.

The reason for the success of this somewhat communist-sounding strategy, while the failure of communism itself is visible around the world, is that the economics of information are fundamentally different from those of other products. There is very little cost associated with copying a piece of information like a computer program. The electricity involved costs less than a penny, and the use of the equipment not much more. In comparison, you can't copy a loaf of bread without a pound of flour.

History

The concept of free software is an old one. When computers first reached universities, they were research tools. Software was freely passed around, and programmers were paid for the act of programming, not for the programs themselves. Only later on, when computers reached the business world, did programmers begin to support themselves by restricting the rights to their software and charging fees for each copy. Free Software as a *political* idea has been popularized by Richard Stallman since 1984, when he formed the Free Software Foundation and its GNU Project. Stallman's premise is that people should have more freedom, and should appreciate their freedom. He designed a set of rights that he felt all users should have, and codified them in the GNU General Public License or GPL. Stallman punningly christened his license the copyleft because it leaves the right to copy in place. Stallman himself developed seminal works of free software such as the GNU C Compiler, and GNU

Emacs, an editor so alluring to some that it is spoken of as it were a religion. His work inspired many others to contribute free software under the GPL. Although it is not promoted with the same libertarian fervor, the Open Source Definition includes many of Stallman's ideas, and can be considered a derivative of his work.

The Open Source Definition started life as a policy document of the Debian GNU/Linux Distribution. Debian, an early Linux system and one still popular today, was built entirely of free software. However, since there were other licenses than the copyleft that purported to be free, Debian had some problem defining what was free, and they had never made their free software policy clear to the rest of the world. I was the leader of the Debian project, at that time, and I addressed these problems by proposing a Debian Social Contract and the Debian Free Software Guidelines in July 1997. Many Debian developers had criticisms and improvements that I incorporated into the documents. The Social Contract documented Debian's intent to compose their system entirely of free software, and the Free Software Guidelines made it possible to classify software into free and non-free easily, by comparing the software license to the guidelines.

Debian's guidelines were lauded in the free software community, especially among Linux developers, who were working their own free software revolution at the time in developing the first practical free operating system. When Netscape decided to make their web browser free software, they contacted Eric Raymond. Raymond is the Margaret Meade of free software: he has written several anthropological articles explaining the free software phenomenon and the culture that has grown around it, works that are the first of their kind and have shown a spotlight on this formerly little-known phenomenon. Netscape management was impressed with Raymond's essay "The Cathedral and the Bazaar," a chronicle of a successful free software development using unpaid volunteer contributors, and asked him to consult, under a non-disclosure agreement, while they developed a license for their free software. Raymond insisted that Netscape's license comply with Debian's guidelines for it to be taken seriously as free software.

Raymond and I had met occasionally at the Hacker's Conference, an invitation-only gathering of creative and unconventional programmers. We had corresponded on various subjects via email. He contacted me in February of 1997 with the idea for Open Source. Raymond was concerned that conservative business people were put off by Stallman's freedom pitch, which was, in contrast, very popular among the more liberal programmers. He felt this was stifling the development of Linux in the business world while it flourished in research. He met with business people in the fledgling Linux industry, and together they conceived of a program to market the free software concept to people who wore ties. Larry Augustin of VA Research and Sam Ockman (who later left VA to form Penguin Computing) were involved, as well as others who aren't known to me.

Some months before Open Source, I had conceived of the idea of Open Hardware, a similar concept but for hardware devices and their interfaces rather than software programs. Open Hardware has not been as successful as Open Source to date, but it is still operating and you can find information on it at *http://www.openhardware.org/*.

Raymond felt that the Debian Free Software Guidelines were the right document to define Open Source, but that they needed a more general name and the removal of Debian-specific references. I edited the Guidelines to form the Open Source Definition. I had formed a corporation for Debian called Software in the Public Interest, and I offered to register a trademark for Open Source so that we could couple its use to the definition. Raymond agreed, and I registered a certification mark, a special form of trademark meant to be applied to other people's products, on the term. About a month after I registered the mark, it became clear that Software in the Public Interest might not be the best home of the Open Source mark, and I transferred ownership of the mark to Raymond. Raymond and I have since formed the Open Source Initiative, an organization exclusively for managing the Open Source campaign and its certification mark. At this writing, the Open Source Initiative is governed by a six-person board chosen from well-known free software contributors, and seeks to expand its board to about ten people.

At the time of its conception there was much criticism for the Open Source campaign, even among the Linux contingent who had already bought-in to the free software concept. Many pointed to the existing use of the term "Open Source" in the political intelligence industry. Others felt the term "Open" was already overused. Many simply preferred the established name Free Software. I contended that the overuse of "Open" could never be as bad as the dual meaning of "Free" in the English language—either *liberty* or *price*, with price being the most oft-used meaning in the commercial world of computers and software. Richard Stallman later took exception to the campaign's lack of an emphasis on freedom, and the fact that as Open Source became more popular, his role in the genesis of free software, and that of his Free Software Foundation, were being ignored—he complained of being "written out of history." This situation was made worse by a tendency for people in the industry to compare Raymond and Stallman as if they were proponents of competing philosophies rather than people who were using different methods to market the same concept. I probably exacerbated the situation by pitting Stallman and Raymond against each other in debates at Linux Expo and Open Source Expo. It became so popular to type-cast the two as adversaries that an email debate, never intended for publication, appeared the online journal *Salon*. At that point, I asked Raymond to tone down a dialogue that it had never been his intent to enter.

When the Open Source Definition was written, there were already a large number of products that fit the definition. The problem was with programs that did not meet the definition, yet were seductive to users.

KDE, Qt, and Troll Tech

The case of KDE, Qt, and Troll Tech is relevant to this essay because the KDE group and Troll Tech tried to place a *non-Open-Source* product in the infrastructure of Linux, and met with unexpected resistance. Public outcry and the threat of a fully open-source replacement for their product eventually convinced Troll to switch to a fully Open Source license. It's an interesting example of the community's enthusiastic acceptance of the Open Source Definition that Troll Tech *had* to make its license comply, if their product was to succeed.

KDE was the first attempt at a free graphical desktop for Linux. The KDE applications were themselves under the GPL, but they depended on a proprietary graphical library called Qt, from Troll Tech. Qt's license terms prohibited modification or use with any display software other than the senescent X Window System. Other use required a $1,500 developer's license. Troll Tech provided versions of Qt for Microsoft Windows and the Macintosh, and this was its main revenue source. The pseudo-free license for X systems was meant to leverage the contributions of Linux developers into demos, examples, and accessories for their pricey Windows and Mac products.

Although the problems with the Qt license were clear, the prospect of a graphical desktop for Linux was so attractive that many users were willing to overlook its non-Open-Source nature. Open Source proponents found KDE objectionable because they perceived that the KDE developers were trying to blur the definition of what free software was to include partially-free items like Qt. The KDE developers contended that their programs were Open Source, even though there were no runnable versions of the programs that did not require a non-Open-Source library. I, and others, asserted that KDE applications were only Open Source fragments of non-Open-Source programs, and that an Open Source version of Qt would be necessary before KDE could be referred to as Open Source.

The KDE developers attempted to partially address the problem of Qt's license by negotiating a KDE Free Qt Foundation agreement with Troll Tech, in which Troll and KDE would jointly control releases of the free version of Qt, and Troll Tech would release Qt under an Open-Source-complaint license if the company was ever purchased or went out of business.

Another group initiated the GNOME project, a fully Open Source competitor of KDE that aimed to provide more features and sophistication, and a separate group initiated a Harmony project to produce a fully Open Source clone of Qt that would support KDE. As GNOME was being demonstrated to accolades and Harmony was about to become useful, Troll Tech realized Qt would not be successful in the Linux market without a change in license. Troll Tech released a fully Open Source license for Qt, defusing the conflict and removing the motivation for the Harmony project.

The GNOME project continues, and now aims to best KDE in terms of functionality and sophistication rather than in terms of its license.

Before they released their new Open Source license, Troll Tech provided me with a copy for auditing, with the request that it be kept confidential until they could announce it. In my enthusiasm to make peace with the KDE group and in an embarrassing feat of self-deception, I pre-announced their license eight hours early on a KDE mailing list. That email was almost immediately picked up by *Slashdot* and other online news magazines, to my chagrin.

Troll Tech's new license is notable in that it takes advantage of a loophole in the Open Source Definition that allows patch files to be treated differently from other software. I would like to address this loophole in a future revision of the Open Source Definition, but the new text should not place Qt outside of Open Source.

At this writing, proponents of Open Source are increasing exponentially. The recent Open Source contributions of IBM and Ericsson have been in the headlines. Two Linux distributions, Yggdrasil and Debian, are distributing complete Linux system distributions, including many applications, that are entirely Open Source, and several others, including Red Hat, are very close. With the completion of the GNOME system, an Open Source GUI desktop OS capable of competing with Microsoft NT will have been realized.

Analysis of the Open Source Definition

In this section, I'll present the entire text of the Open Source Definition, with commentary (in italic). You can find the canonical version of the Open Source Definition at *http://www.opensource.org/osd.html*.

Pedants have pointed out minor ambiguities in the Open Source Definition. I've held off revising it as it's little more than a year old and I'd like people to consider it *stable*. The future will bring slight language changes, but only the most minor of changes in the *intent* of the document.

The Open Source Definition (Version 1.0)

Open source doesn't just mean access to the source code. The distribution terms of an open-source program must comply with the following criteria:

Note that the Open Source Definition is not itself a software license. It is a specification of what is permissible in a software license for that software to be referred to as Open Source. The Open Source Definition was not intended to be a legal document. The inclusion of the Open Source Definition in software licenses, such as a proposed license of the Linux Documentation Project, has tempted me to write a more rigorous version that would be appropriate for that use.

To be Open Source, all of the terms below must be applied together, and in all cases. For example, they must be applied to derived versions of a program as well as the original program. It's not sufficient to apply some and not others, and it's not sufficient for the terms to only apply some of the time. After working through some particularly naive interpretations of the Open Source Definition, I feel tempted to add: this means you!

1. Free Redistribution

   The license may not restrict any party from selling or giving away the software as a component of an aggregate software distribution containing programs from several different sources. The license may not require a royalty or other fee for such sale.

   This means that you can make any number of copies of the software, and sell or give them away, and you don't have to pay anyone for that privilege.

   The "aggregate software distribution containing programs from several different sources" was intended to fit a loophole in the Artistic License, a rather sloppy license in my opinion, originally designed for Perl. Today, almost all programs that use the Artistic License are also available under the GPL. That provision is thus no longer necessary, and may be removed from a future version of the Open Source Definition.

2. Source Code

   The program must include source code, and must allow distribution in source code as well as compiled form. Where some form of a product is not distributed with source code, there must be a well-publicized means of downloading the source code, without charge, via the Internet. The source code must be the preferred form in which a programmer would modify the program. Deliberately obfuscated source code is not allowed. Intermediate forms such as the output of a preprocessor or translator are not allowed.

   Source code is a necessary preliminary for the repair or modification of a program. The intent here is for source code to be distributed with the initial work, and all derived works.

3. Derived Works

   The license must allow modifications and derived works, and must allow them to be distributed under the same terms as the license of the original software.

   Software has little use if you can't maintain it (fix bugs, port to new systems, make improvements), and modification is necessary for maintenance. The intent here is for modification of any sort to be allowed. It must be allowed for a modified work to be distributed under the same license terms as the original work. However, it is not required that any producer of a derived work must use the same license terms, only that the option to do so be open to them. Various licenses speak differently on this subject—the BSD license allows you to take modifications private, while the GPL does not.

A concern among some software authors is that this provision could allow unscrupulous people to modify their software in ways that would embarrass the original author. They fear someone deliberately making the software perform incorrectly in a way that would make it look as if the author was a poor programmer. Others are concerned that software could be modified for criminal use, by the addition of Trojan horse functions or locally-banned technologies such as cryptography. All of these actions, however, are covered by criminal law. A common misunderstanding about software licenses is that they must specify everything, including things like "don't use this software to commit a crime." However, no license has any valid existence outside of the body of civil and criminal law. Considering a license as something apart from the body of applicable law is as silly as considering an English-language document as being apart from the dictionary, in which case none of the words would have any defined meaning.

4. Integrity of the Author's Source Code

The license may restrict source code from being distributed in modified form only if the license allows the distribution of "patch files" with the source code for the purpose of modifying the program at build time.

Some authors were afraid that others would distribute source code with modifications that would be perceived as the work of the original author, and would reflect poorly on that author. This gives them a way to enforce a separation between modifications and their own work without prohibiting modifications. Some consider it un-aesthetic that modifications might have to be distributed in a separate "patch" file from the source code, even though Linux distributions like Debian and Red Hat use this procedure for all of the modifications they make to the programs they distribute. There are programs that automatically merge patches into the main source, and one can have these programs run automatically when extracting a source package. Thus, this provision should cause little or no hardship.

Note also that this provision says that in the case of patch files, the modification takes place at build-time. This loophole is employed in the Qt Public License to mandate a different, though less restrictive, license for the patch files, in contradiction of Section 3 of the Open Source Definition. There is a proposal to clean up this loophole in the definition while keeping Qt within Open Source.

The license must explicitly permit distribution of software built from modified source code. The license may require derived works to carry a different name or version number from the original software.

This means that Netscape, for example, can insist that only they can name a version of the program Netscape Navigator(tm) while all free versions of the program must be called Mozilla or something else.

5. No Discrimination Against Persons or Groups

The license must not discriminate against any person or group of persons.

A license provided by the Regents of the University of California, Berkeley, prohibited an electronic design program from being used by the police of South Africa. While this was a laudable sentiment in the time of apartheid, it makes little sense today. Some people are still stuck with software that they acquired under that license, and their derived versions must carry the same restriction. Open Source licenses may not contain such provisions, no matter how laudable their intent.

6. No Discrimination Against Fields of Endeavor

The license must not restrict anyone from making use of the program in a specific field of endeavor. For example, it may not restrict the program from being used in a business, or from being used for genetic research.

Your software must be equally usable in an abortion clinic, or by an anti-abortion organization. These political arguments belong on the floor of Congress, not in software licenses. Some people find this lack of discrimination extremely offensive!

7. Distribution of License

The rights attached to the program must apply to all to whom the program is redistributed without the need for execution of an additional license by those parties.

The license must be automatic, no signature required. Unfortunately, there has not been a good court test in the U.S. of the power of a no-signature-required license when it is passed from a second party to a third. However, this argument considers the license in the body of contract law, while some argue that it should be considered as copyright law, where there is more precedent for no-signature licenses. A good court test will no doubt happen in the next few years, given the popularity of this sort of license and the booming nature of Open Source.

8. License Must Not Be Specific to a Product

The rights attached to the program must not depend on the program's being part of a particular software distribution. If the program is extracted from that distribution and used or distributed within the terms of the program's license, all parties to whom the program is redistributed should have the same rights as those that are granted in conjunction with the original software distribution.

This means you can't restrict a product that is identified as Open Source to be free only if you use it with a particular brand of Linux distribution, etc. It must remain free if you separate it from the software distribution it came with.

9. License Must Not Contaminate Other Software

The license must not place restrictions on other software that is distributed along with the licensed software. For example, the license must not insist that all other programs distributed on the same medium must be open-source software.

A version of GhostScript (a PostScript-rendering program) requires that the media on which it is distributed contain only free software programs. This isn't permissible for Open Source licenses. Fortunately, the GhostScript author distributes another (somewhat older) version of the program with a true Open Source license.

*Note that there is a difference between **derivation** and **aggregation**. Derivation is when a program actually incorporates part of another program into itself. Aggregation is when you include two programs on the same CD-ROM. This section of the Open Source Definition is concerned with aggregation, **not** derivation. Section 4 is concerned with derivation.*

10. Example Licenses

The GNU GPL, BSD, X Consortium, and Artistic licenses are examples of licenses that we consider conformant to the Open Source Definition. So is the MPL.

This would get us in trouble if any of these licenses are ever changed to be non-Open-Source—we'd have to issue a revision of the Open Source Definition immediately. It really belongs in explanatory text, not in the Open Source Definition itself.

Analysis of Licenses and Their Open Source Compliance

To understand the Open Source Definition, we need to look at some common licensing practices as they relate to Open Source.

Public Domain

A common misconception is that much free software is *public-domain*. This happens simply because the idea of free software or Open Source is confusing to many people, and they mistakenly describe these programs as public-domain because that's the closest concept that they understand. The programs, however, are clearly copyrighted and covered by a license, just a license that gives people more rights than they are used to.

A public-domain program is one upon which the author has deliberately surrendered his copyright rights. It can't really be said to come with a license; it's your personal property to use as you see fit. Because you can treat it as your personal property, you can do what you want with a public-domain program. You can even re-license a public-domain program, removing that version from the public domain, or you can remove the author's name and treat it as your own work.

If you are doing a lot of work on a public-domain program, consider applying your own copyright to the program and re-licensing it. For example, if you don't want a third party to make their own modifications that they then keep private, apply the GPL or a similar license to your version of the program. The version that you started with will still be in the public domain, but your version will be under a license that others must heed if they use it or derive from it.

You can easily take a public-domain program private, by declaring a copyright and applying your own license to it or simply declaring "All Rights Reserved."

Free Software Licenses in General

If you have a free software collection like a Linux disk, you may believe the programs on that disk are your property. That's not entirely true. Copyrighted programs are the property of the copyright holder, even when they have an Open Source license like the GPL. The program's license grants you some rights, and you have other rights under the definition of *fair use* in copyright law.

It's important to note that an author does not have to issue a program with just one license. You can GPL a program, and also sell a version of the same program with a commercial, non-Open-Source license. This exact strategy is used by many people who want to make a program Open Source and still make some money from it. Those who do not want an Open Source license may pay for the privilege, providing a revenue stream for the author.

All of the licenses we will examine have a common feature: they each disclaim all warranties. The intent is to protect the software owner from any liability connected with the program. Since the program is often being given away at no cost, this is a reasonable requirement—the author doesn't have a sufficient revenue stream from the program to fund liability insurance and legal fees.

If free-software authors lose the right to disclaim all warranties and find themselves getting sued over the performance of the programs that they've written, they'll stop contributing free software to the world. It's to our advantage as users to help the author protect this right.

The GNU General Public License

Please see Appendix B for the full text of the GPL. The GPL is a political manifesto as well as a software license, and much of its text is concerned with explaining the rationale behind the license. This political dialogue has put some people off, and thus provided some of the reason that people have written other free software licenses. However, the GPL was assembled with the assistance of law professors, and is much better written than most of its ilk. I'd strongly urge that you use the GPL, or its library variant the LGPL, if you can. If you choose another license, or write your own, be sure about your reasons. People who write their own licenses should consider that this is not a step to be taken lightly. The unexpected complications of an ill-considered license can create a decades-long burden for software users.

The text of the GPL is not itself under the GPL. Its license is simple: *Everyone is permitted to copy and distribute verbatim copies of this license document, but changing it is not allowed*. An important point here is that the text of the licenses of Open Source software are generally *not* themselves Open Source. Obviously, a license would offer no protection if anyone could change it.

The provisions of the GPL satisfy the Open Source Definition. The GPL does not require any of the provisions permitted by paragraph 4 of the Open Source Definition, *Integrity of the Author's Source Code*.

The GPL does not allow you to *take modifications private*. Your modifications must be distributed under the GPL. Thus, the author of a GPL-ed program is likely to receive improvements from others, including commercial companies who modify his software for their own purposes.

The GPL doesn't allow the incorporation of a GPL-ed program into a proprietary program. The GPL's definition of a proprietary program is any program with a license that doesn't give you as many rights as the GPL.

There are a few loopholes in the GPL that allow it to be used in programs that are not entirely Open Source. Software libraries that are normally distributed with the compiler or operating system you are using may be linked with GPL-ed software; the result is a partially-free program. The copyright holder (generally the author of the program) is the person who places the GPL on the program and has the right to violate his own license. This was used by the KDE authors to distribute their programs with Qt before Troll Tech placed an Open Source license on Qt. However, this right does not extend to any third parties who redistribute the program—they must follow all of the terms of the license, even the ones that the copyright holder violates, and thus it's problematical to redistribute a GPL-ed program containing Qt. The KDE developers appear to be addressing this problem by applying the LGPL, rather than the GPL, to their software.

The political rhetoric in the GPL puts some people off. Some of them have chosen a less appropriate license for their software simply because they eschew Richard Stallman's ideas and don't want to see them repeated in their own software packages.

The GNU Library General Public License

The LGPL is a derivative of the GPL that was designed for software libraries. Unlike the GPL, a LGPL-ed program can be incorporated into a proprietary program. The C-language library provided with Linux systems is an example of LGPL-ed software—it can be used to build proprietary programs, otherwise Linux would only be useful for free software authors.

An instance of an LGPL-ed program can be converted into a GPL-ed one at any time. Once that happens, you can't convert that instance, or anything derived from it, back into an LGPL-ed program.

The rest of the provisions of the LGPL are similar to those in the GPL—in fact, it includes the GPL by reference.

The X, BSD, and Apache Licenses

The X license and its relatives the BSD and Apache licenses are very different from the GPL and LGPL. These licenses let you do nearly anything with the software licensed under them. This is because the software that the X and BSD licenses originally covered was funded by monetary grants of the U.S. Government. Since the U.S. citizens had already paid for the software with their taxes, they were granted permission to make use of that software as they pleased.

The most important permission, and one missing from the GPL, is that you can take X-licensed modifications private. In other words, you can get the source code for a X-licensed program, modify it, and then sell binary versions of the program without distributing the source code of your modifications, and without applying the X license to those modifications. This is still Open Source, however, as the Open Source Definition does not require that modifications always carry the original license.

Many other developers have adopted the X license and its variants, including the BSD (Berkeley System Distribution) and the Apache web server project. An annoying feature of the BSD license is a provision that requires you to mention (generally in a footnote) that the software was developed at the University of California any time you mention a feature of a BSD-licensed program in advertising. Keeping track of which software is BSD-licensed in something huge like a Linux distribution, and then remembering to mention the University whenever any of those programs are mentioned in advertising, is somewhat of a headache for business people. At this writing, the Debian GNU/Linux distribution contains over 2,500 software packages, and if even a fraction of them were BSD-licensed, advertising for a Linux system like Debian might contain many pages of footnotes! However, the X Consortium license does not have that advertising provision. If you are considering using a BSD-style license, use the X license instead.

The Artistic License

Although this license was originally developed for Perl, it's since been used for other software. It is, in my opinion, a sloppily-worded license, in that it makes requirements and then gives you loopholes that make it easy to bypass the requirements. Perhaps that's why almost all Artistic-license software is now dual-licensed, offering the choice of the Artistic License or the GPL.

Section 5 of the Artistic License prohibits sale of the software, yet allows an aggregate software distribution of more than one program to be sold. So, if you bundle an Artistic-licensed program with a five-line hello-world.c, you can sell the bundle. This feature of the Artistic License was the sole cause of the "aggregate" loophole in paragraph 1 of the Open Source Definition. As use of the Artistic License wanes, we are considering removing the loophole. That would make the Artistic a non-Open-Source license. This isn't a step we would take lightly, and there will probably be more than a year of consideration and debate before it happens.

The Artistic License requires you to make modifications free, but then gives you a loophole (in Section 7) that allows you to take modifications private or even place parts of the Artistic-licensed program in the public domain!

The Netscape Public License and the Mozilla Public License

NPL was developed by Netscape when they made their product Netscape Navigator Open Source. Actually, the Open-Source version is called Mozilla; Netscape reserves the trademark Navigator for their own product. Eric Raymond and I acted as unpaid consultants during the development of this license. I tried, unsuccessfully, to persuade Netscape to use the GPL, and when they declined, I helped them compose a license that would comply with the Open Source Definition.

An important feature of the NPL is that it contains special privileges that apply to Netscape and nobody else. It gives Netscape the privilege of re-licensing modifications that you've made to their software. They can take those modifications private, improve them, and refuse to give you the result. This provision was necessary because when Netscape decided to go Open Source, it had contracts with other companies that committed it to provide Navigator to them under a non-Open-Source license.

Netscape created the MPL, or Mozilla Public License, to address this concern. The MPL is much like the NPL, but does not contain the clause that allows Netscape to re-license your modifications.

The NPL and MPL allow you to take modifications private.

Many companies have adopted a variation of the MPL for their own programs. This is unfortunate, because the NPL was designed for the specific business situation that Netscape was in at the time it was written, and is not necessarily appropriate for others to use. It should remain the license of Netscape and Mozilla, and others should use the GPL or the or X licenses.

Choosing a License

Do not write a new license if it is possible to use one of the ones listed here. The propagation of many different and incompatible licenses works to the detriment of Open Source software because fragments of one program cannot be used in another program with an incompatible license.

Steer clear of the Artistic License unless you are willing to study it carefully and edit out its loopholes. Then, make a few decisions:

1. Do you want people to be able to *take modifications private* or not? If you want to get the source code for modifications back from the people who make them, apply a license that mandates this. The GPL and LGPL would be good choices. If you don't mind people taking modifications private, use the X or Apache license.

2. Do you want to allow someone to merge your program with their own proprietary software? If so, use the LGPL, which explicitly allows this without allowing people to make modifications to your own code private, or use the X or Apache licenses, which do allow modifications to be kept private.

3. Do you want some people to be able to buy commercial-licensed versions of your program that are not Open Source? If so, dual-license your software. I recommend the GPL as the Open Source license; you can find a commercial license appropriate for you to use in books like *Copyright Your Software* from Nolo Press.

4. Do you want *everyone* who uses your program to pay for the privilege? If so, perhaps Open Source isn't for you. If you're satisfied with having only some people pay you, you can work that and keep your program Open Source. Most of the Open Source authors consider their programs to be contributions to the public good, and don't care if they are paid at all.

The table below gives a comparison of licensing practices:

License	Can be mixed with non-free software	Modifications can be taken private and not returned to you	Can be re-licensed by anyone	Contains special privileges for the original copyright holder over your modifications
GPL				
LGPL	✓			
BSD	✓	✓		
NPL	✓	✓		✓
MPL	✓	✓		
Public Domain	✓	✓	✓	

The Future

As this essay went to press, IBM joined the Open Source world, and the venture capital community is discovering Open Source. Intel and Netscape have invested in Red Hat, a Linux distributor. VA Research, an integrator of Linux server and workstation hardware, has announced an outside investor. Sendmail Inc., created to commercialize the ubiquitous Sendmail e mail delivery program, has announced six million dollars in funding. IBM's Postfix secure mailer has an Open Source license, and another IBM product, the Jikes Java compiler, has a license that, at this writing, tries but doesn't quite meet the intent of the Open Source Definition. IBM appears to be willing to modify the Jikes license to be fully Open Source, and is collecting comments from the community as I write this.

Two internal Microsoft memos, referred to as the Halloween Documents, were leaked to the online public. These memos clearly document that Microsoft is threatened by Open Source and Linux, and that MS will launch an offensive against them to protect its markets. Obviously, we are in for some interesting times. I think we'll see Microsoft use two main strategies: *copyrighted interfaces* and *patents*. Microsoft will extend networking protocols, including Microsoft-specific features in them that will not be made available to free software. They, and other companies, will aggressively research new directions in computer science and will patent whatever they can before we can first use those techniques in free software, and then they'll lock us out with patent royalty fees. I've written an essay for the webzine *Linux World* on how to fight Open Source's enemies on the patent front.

The good news is that Microsoft is scared! In the second Halloween document, a Microsoft staffer writes about the exhilarating feeling that he could easily change part of the Linux system to do exactly what he wanted, and that it was so much easier to do this on Linux than it was for a Microsoft employee to change NT!

Efforts to hurt us from inside are the most dangerous. I think we'll also see more attempts to dilute the definition of Open Source to include partially-free products, as we saw with the Qt library in KDE before Troll Tech saw the light and released an Open Source license. Microsoft and others could hurt us by releasing a lot of software that's just free enough to attract users without having the full freedoms of Open Source. It's conceivable that they could kill off development of some categories of Open Source software by releasing a "good enough," "almost-free-enough" solution. However, the strong reaction against the KDE project before the Qt library went fully Open Source bodes poorly for similar efforts by MS and its ilk.

We've escaped Trojan horses so far. Suppose that someone who doesn't like us contributes software that contains Trojan horse, a hidden way to defeat the security of a Linux system. Suppose, then, that this person waits for the Trojan-horse software to be widely distributed, and then publicizes its vulnerability to security exploits. The public will then have seen that our Open Source system may leave us more vulnerable to this sort of exploit than the closed system of Microsoft, and this may reduce the public's trust in Open Source software. We can argue that Microsoft has its share of security bugs even if they don't allow outsiders to insert them, and that the disclosed source-code model of Open Source makes these bugs easier to find. Any bug like this that comes up on Linux will be fixed the day after it's announced, while a similar bug in Windows might go undetected or unrepaired for years. But we still need to beef up our defense against Trojan horses. Having good identification of the people who submit software and modifications is our best defense, as it allows us to use criminal law against the perpetrators of Trojan horses. While I was manager of the Debian GNU/Linux distribution, we instituted a system for all of our software maintainers to be reliably identified, and for them to participate in a public-key cryptography network that would allow us to verify whom our software came from. This sort of system has to be expanded to include all Open Source developers.

We have tremendous improvements to make before Linux is ready for the average person to use. The graphical user interface is an obvious deficit, and the KDE and GNOME projects are addressing this. System administration is the next frontier: while *linuxconf* partially addresses this issue, if falls far short of being a comprehensive system-administration tool for the naive user. If Caldera's COAS system is successful, it could become the basis of a full solution to the system administration problem. However, Caldera has had trouble keeping sufficient resources allocated to COAS to finish its development, and other participants have dropped off the bandwagon due to the lack of progress.

The plethora of Linux distributions appear to be going through a shake-out, with Red Hat as the perceived winner and Caldera coming in second. Red Hat has shown a solid commitment to the concept of Open Source so far, but a new president and rumors of an Initial Public Offering (IPO) could mean a weakening of this commitment, especially if competitors like Caldera, who are not nearly as concerned about Open Source, make inroads into Red Hat's markets. If the commitment of commercial Linux distributions to Open Source became a problem, that would probably spawn an effort to replace them with pure Open Source efforts similar to Debian GNU/Linux, but ones more directed to the commercial market than Debian has been.

Despite these challenges, I predict that Open Source *will* win. Linux has become the testbed of computer science students, and they will carry those systems with them into the workplace as they graduate. Research laboratories have adopted the Open Source model because the sharing of information is essential to the scientific method, and Open Source allows software to be shared easily. Businesses are adopting the Open Source model because it allows groups of companies to collaborate in solving a problem without the threat of an anti-trust lawsuit, and because of the leverage they gain when the computer-programming public contributes free improvements to their software. Some large corporations have adopted Open Source as a strategy to combat Microsoft and to assure that another Microsoft does not come to dominate the computer industry. But the most reliable indication of the future of Open Source is its past: in just a few years, we have gone from nothing to a robust body of software that solves many different problems and is reaching the million-user count. There's no reason for us to slow down now.

Hardware, Software, and Infoware

Tim O'Reilly

I was talking with some friends recently, friends who don't own a computer. They were thinking of getting one so they could use Amazon.com to buy books and CDs. Not to use "the Internet," not to use "the Web," but to use Amazon.com.

Now, that's the classic definition of a "killer application": one that makes someone go out and buy a computer.

What's interesting is that the killer application is no longer a desktop productivity application or even a back-office enterprise software system, but an individual web site. And once you start thinking of web sites as applications, you soon come to realize that they represent an entirely new breed, something you might call an "information application," or perhaps even "infoware."

Information applications are used to computerize tasks that just couldn't be handled in the old computing model. A few years ago, if you wanted to search a database of a million books, you talked to a librarian, who knew the arcane search syntax of the available computerized search tools and might be able to find what you wanted. If you wanted to buy a book, you went to a bookstore, and looked through its relatively small selection. Now, tens of thousands of people with no specialized training find and buy books online from that million-record database every day.

The secret is that computers have come one step closer to the way that people communicate with each other. Web-based applications use plain English to build their interface—words and pictures, not specialized little controls that acquire meaning only as you learn the software.

Traditional software embeds small amounts of information in a lot of software; infoware embeds small amounts of software in a lot of information. The "actions" in an infoware product are generally fairly simple: make a choice, buy or sell, enter a small amount of data, and get back a customized result.

These actions are often accomplished by scripts attached to a hypertext link using an interface specification called CGI (the Common Gateway Interface). CGI defines a way for a web server to call any external program and return the output of that program as a web page. CGI programs may simply be small scripts that perform a simple calculation, or they may connect to a full-fledged back-end database server. But even when there's a heavy-duty software engine behind a site, the user interface itself is not composed of traditional software. The interface consists of web pages (which may well have been created by a writer, editor, or designer rather than by a programmer).

Information interfaces are typically dynamic. For example, Amazon.com's presentation of books is driven by sales rankings that are updated every hour. Customers can add comments and ratings on the fly, which then become a key part of the information-rich decision-support interface for purchasers. A site designed to help someone buy or sell stocks online needs to not only present updated share prices, but also the latest relevant news stories, insider trading information, analyst recommendations, and perhaps even user discussion groups. The information interface thus typically consists of a rich mix of hand-crafted documents, program-generated data, and links to specialized application servers (such as email, chat, or conferencing).

Information interfaces are not as efficient for tasks that you do over and over as pure software interfaces, but they are far better for tasks you do only rarely, or differently each time. In particular, they are good for interfaces in which you make choices based on information presented to you. Whether you're buying a book or CD at Amazon.com, or a stock at E*Trade, the actual purchase is a fairly trivial part of the interaction. It's the quality of the information provided to help you make a decision that forms the heart of the application you interact with.

The way the Web is transforming the whole computing paradigm was never clearer to me than back in 1994, before Microsoft had gotten the Web religion, and I shared the stage (via satellite) with Microsoft VP Craig Mundie at an NTT event in Japan. Mundie was demonstrating the planned interface for Microsoft's "Tiger" server, which was supposed to enable video on demand. The interface emulated Windows, with cascading menus responding to a kind of virtual remote control channel clicker.

It was pretty obvious to those of us who were involved in the Web that the right interface for video on demand, when and if it comes, will be a Web-like information interface. It's ironic that even then, Microsoft had the perfect interface for video-on-demand: its own CD-ROM-based movie encyclopedia, Cinemania. What better way to choose what movie to watch than to search by category, read a few reviews, watch a few film clips, and then, homework done, click on a hypertext link to start the movie? Cinemania has it all but the last step. It's not until hypertext-based information products are connected to network servers that their real power becomes apparent. Suddenly, information is not an end in itself, but an interface that allows a user to control an application space far too complex for a traditional software application.

(Amazon.com clearly knows this: their purchase of the Internet Movie Database, a collection of user reviews and other information about movies, will put them in pole position not only for selling videotapes online, but as a future gateway for video-on-demand services.)

Information interfaces are particularly appropriate for decision-support applications, but they also make sense for one-time tasks. In a sense, the use of "wizards" for software installation is an example of the same trend.

There are also information applications that use a simpler, more software-like interface for user interaction, but provide dynamic information output. My favorite example is something that would have been virtually unthinkable as an application only a few years ago: getting maps and directions. A mapping site like *maps.yahoo.com* lets you type in two addresses, and get back a map and a set of directions showing how to get to one from the other.

So what does all this have to do with Open Source software?

There's an obvious answer: most of the technologies that make the Web possible are Open Source.

The Internet itself—features like the TCP/IP network protocol and key infrastructure elements such as the Domain Name System (DNS) were developed through the open-source process. It's easy to argue that the open-source BIND (Berkeley Internet Name Daemon) program that runs the DNS is the single most mission-critical Internet application. Even though most web browsing is done with proprietary products (Netscape's Navigator and Microsoft's Internet Explorer), both are outgrowths of Tim Berners-Lee's original open-source web implementation and open protocol specification. According to the automated Netcraft web server survey (*http://www.netcraft.co. uk/survey*), more than 50% of all visible web sites are served by the open-source Apache web server. The majority of web-based dynamic content is generated by open-source scripting languages such as Perl, Python, and Tcl.

But this obvious answer is only part of the story. After all, why is it the Web and not some proprietary technology that is the basis for the networked information applications of the future?

Microsoft actually was ahead of the curve in realizing the power of online multimedia. In 1994, when the Web started to take off, Microsoft's CD-ROM products like Encarta, their online encyclopedia, and Cinemania, their online movie reference, were ahead of the Web in providing online hyperlinked documents with rich multimedia capabilities. Microsoft even realized that it was important to provide information resources via online networks.

There was only one problem with Microsoft's vision of the Microsoft Network: barriers to entry were high. Publishers were expected to use proprietary Microsoft tools, to apply and be approved by Microsoft, and to pay to play. By contrast, anyone could start a web site. The software you needed was free. The specifications for creating documents and dynamic content were simple, open, and clearly documented.

Perhaps even more important, both the technology and the Internet ethic made it legitimate to copy features from other people's web sites. The HTML (HyperText Markup Language) pages that were used to implement various features on a web site could be easily saved and imitated. Even the CGI scripts used to create dynamic content were available for copying. Although traditional computer languages like C run faster, Perl became the dominant language for CGI because it was more accessible. While Perl is powerful enough to write major applications, it is possible for amateurs to write small scripts to accomplish specialized tasks. Even more important, because Perl is not a compiled language, the scripts that are used on web pages can be viewed, copied, and modified by users. In addition, archives of useful Perl scripts were set up and freely shared among web developers. The easy cloning of web sites built with the HTML+CGI+Perl combination meant that for the first time, powerful applications could be created by non-programmers.

In this regard, it's interesting to point out that the software industry's first attempts to improve on the web interface for active content—technologies like browser-side Java applets and Microsoft ActiveX controls—failed because they were aimed at professional programmers and could not easily be copied and implemented by the amateurs who were building the Web. Vendors viewed the Web in software terms, and didn't understand that the Web was changing not only what applications were being built but what tools their builders needed.

Industry analysts have been predicting for years that Perl and CGI will be eclipsed by newer software technologies. But even now, when major web sites employ large staffs of professional programmers, and newer technologies like Microsoft's Active Server Pages (ASP) and Sun's Java servlets are supplanting CGI for performance reasons, Perl continues to grow in popularity. Perl and other open-source scripting languages such as Python and Tcl remain central to web sites large and small because infoware applications are fundamentally different than software applications and require different tools.

If you look at a large web site like Yahoo!, you'll see that behind the scenes, an army of administrators and programmers are continually rebuilding the product. Dynamic content isn't just automatically generated, it is also often hand-tailored, typically using an array of quick and dirty scripting tools.

"We don't create content at Yahoo! We aggregate it," says Jeffrey Friedl, author of the book *Mastering Regular Expressions* and a full-time Perl programmer at Yahoo. "We have feeds from thousands of sources, each with its own format. We do massive amounts of 'feed processing' to clean this stuff up or to find out where to put it on

Yahoo!." For example, to link appropriate news stories to tickers at *quotes.yahoo.com*, Friedl needed to write a "name recognition" program able to search for more than 15,000 company names. Perl's ability to analyze free-form text with powerful regular expressions was what made that possible.

Perl is also a central component in the system administration infrastructure used to keep the site live and current. Vast numbers of Perl scripts are continually crawling the Yahoo! servers and their links to external sites, and paging the staff whenever a URL doesn't return the expected result. The best-known of these crawlers is referred to as "the Grim Reaper." If an automated connection to a URL fails more than the specified number of times, the page is removed from the Yahoo! directory.

Amazon.com is also a heavy user of Perl. The Amazon.com authoring environment demonstrates Perl's power to tie together disparate computing tools; it's a "glue language" par excellence. A user creates a new document with a form that calls up a Perl program, which generates a partially-completed SGML document, then launches either Microsoft Word or GNU Emacs (at the user's choice), but also integrates CVS (Concurrent Versioning System) and Amazon.com's homegrown SGML tools. The Amazon.com SGML classes are used to render different sections of the web site—for example, HTML with or without graphics—from the same source base. A Perl-based parser renders the SGML into HTML for approval before the author commits the changes.

Perl has been called "the duct tape of the Internet," and like duct tape, it is used in all kinds of unexpected ways. Like a movie set held together with duct tape, a web site is often put up and torn down in a day, and needs lightweight tools and quick but effective solutions.

Microsoft's failed attempt to turn infoware back into software with ActiveX is rooted in the way paradigms typically shift in the computer industry. As a particular market segment matures, the existing players have an enormous vested interest in things continuing the way they are. This makes it difficult for them to embrace anything really new, and allows—almost requires—that new players ("the barbarians," to use Philippe Kahn's phrase) come in to create the new markets.

Microsoft's ascendancy over IBM as the ruling power of the computer industry is a classic example of how this happened the last time around. IBM gave away the market to Microsoft because it didn't see that the shift of power was not only from the glass house to the desktop, but also from proprietary to commodity hardware and from hardware to software.

In the same way, despite its attempts to get into various information businesses, Microsoft still doesn't realize—perhaps can't realize and still be Microsoft—that software, as Microsoft has known it, is no longer the central driver of value creation in the computer business.

In the days of IBM's dominance, hardware was king, and the barriers to entry into the computer business were high. Most software was created by the hardware vendors, or by software vendors who were satellite to them.

The availability of the PC as a commodity platform (as well as the development of open systems platforms such as Unix) changed the rules in a fundamental way. Suddenly, the barriers to entry were low, and entrepreneurs such as Mitch Kapor of Lotus and Bill Gates took off.

If you look at the early history of the Web, you see a similar pattern. Microsoft's monopoly on desktop software had made the barriers to entry in the software business punishingly high. What's more, software applications had become increasingly complex, with Microsoft putting up deliberate barriers to entry against competitors. It was no longer possible for a single programmer in a garage (or a garret) to make an impact.

This is perhaps the most important point to make about open-source software: it lowers the barriers to entry into the software market. You can try a new product for free—and even more than that, you can build your own custom version of it, also for free. Source code is available for massive independent peer review. If someone doesn't like a feature, they can add to it, subtract from it, or reimplement it. If they give their fix back to the community, it can be adopted widely very quickly.

What's more, because developers (at least initially) aren't trying to compete on the business end, but instead focus simply on solving real problems, there is room for experimentation in a less punishing environment. As has often been said, open-source software "lets you scratch your own itch." Because of the distributed development paradigm, with new features being added by users, open-source programs "evolve" as much as they are designed.

Indeed, the evolutionary forces of the market are freer to operate as nature "intended" when unencumbered by marketing barriers or bundling deals, the equivalent of prosthetic devices that help the less-than-fit survive.

Evolution breeds not a single winner, but diversity.

It is precisely the idiosyncratic nature of many of the open-source programs that is their greatest strength. Again, it's instructive to look at the reasons for Perl's success.

Larry Wall originally created Perl to automate some repetitive system administration tasks he was faced with. After releasing the software to the Net, he found more and more applications, and the language grew, often in unexpected directions.

Perl has been described as a "kitchen sink language" because its features seem chaotic to the designers of more "orthogonal" computer languages. But chaos can often reveal rich structure. Chaos may also be required to model what is inherently complex. Human languages are complex because they model reality. As Wall says in his essay in this volume, "English is useful because it's a mess. Since English is a mess, it maps well onto the problem space, which is also a mess. . . . Similarly, Perl was designed to be a mess (though in the nicest of possible ways)."

The Open Source development paradigm is an incredibly efficient way of getting developers to work on features that matter. New software is developed in a tight feedback loop with customer demand, without distortions caused by marketing clout or top-down purchasing decisions. Bottom-up software development is ideal for solving bottom-up problems.

Using the open-source software at the heart of the Web, and its simpler development paradigm, entrepreneurs like Jerry Yang and David Filo were able to do just that. It's no accident that Yahoo!, the world's largest and most successful web site, is built around freely available open-source software: the FreeBSD operating system, Apache, and Perl.

Just as it was last time around, the key to the next stage of the computer industry is in fact the commoditization of the previous stage. As Bob Young of Red Hat, the leading Linux distributor, has noted, his goal is not to dethrone Microsoft at the top of the operating systems heap, but rather, to shrink the dollar value of the operating systems market.

The point is that open-source software doesn't need to beat Microsoft at its own game. Instead it is changing the nature of the game.

To be sure, for all their astronomical market capitalization, information-application providers such as Amazon.com and Yahoo! are still tiny compared to Microsoft. But the writing on the wall is clear. The edges of human-computer interaction, the opportunities for computerizing tasks that haven't been computerized before, are in infoware, not in software.

As the new "killer applications" emerge, the role of software will increasingly be as an enabler for infoware. There are enormous commercial opportunities to provide web servers, database backends and application servers, and network programming languages like Java, as long as these products fit themselves into the new model rather than trying to supplant it. Note that in the shift from a hardware-centric to a software-centric computer industry, hardware didn't go away. IBM still flourishes as a company (though most of its peers have down-sized or capsized). But other hardware players emerged who were suited to the new rules: Dell, Compaq, and especially Intel.

Intel realized that the real opportunity for them was not in winning the computer systems wars, but in being an arms supplier to the combatants.

The real challenge for open-source software is not whether it will replace Microsoft in dominating the desktop, but rather whether it can craft a business model that will help it to become the "Intel Inside" of the next generation of computer applications.

Otherwise, the Open Source pioneers will be shouldered aside just as Digital Research was in the PC operating system business by someone who understands precisely where the current opportunity lies.

But however that turns out, open-source software has already created a fork in the road. Just as the early microcomputer pioneers (in both hardware and software) set the stage for today's industry, open-source software has set the stage for the drama that is just now unfolding, and that will lead to a radical reshaping of the computer industry landscape over the next five to ten years.

Freeing the Source
The Story of Mozilla

Jim Hamerly and Tom Paquin
with Susan Walton

On January 23, 1998, Netscape made two announcements. The first, as reported by C|Net: "In an unprecedented move, Netscape Communications will give away its Navigator browser, confirming rumors over the last several weeks."

The second: "It also will give away the source code for the next generation of its Communicator suite."

The decision to give away the browser came as no surprise, but the release of the source code stunned the industry. It hit the pages of newspapers around the world, and even the Open Source community was surprised at the move. Never before had a major software company opened up its proprietary code. What was Netscape up to now?

We had decided to change the playing field, and not for the first time. Always known for thinking outside the box, this time Netscape was taking the commitment to building a better Internet to a new level. When Netscape initiated unrestricted distribution of early versions of its browser over the Internet in 1994, people said "That's crazy!" When Netscape said "Free Source Code" they said the same thing.

The discussion period leading up to the Open Source announcement moved like a runaway train. After months of deliberation about whether or not to release the binary for free, critical mass was reached in the decision to free the source in an unbelievable twenty-four hours.

As fast and surprising as the announcement seemed to both insiders and outsiders, it reflected several converging tracks of thought. Netscape executives were discussing a whitepaper by Frank Hecker that expressed a view coming to the forefront. In it he advocated that Netscape free its source. Frank had done his homework, citing Eric Raymond's paper, "The Cathedral and the Bazaar," and talking to people in departments throughout the organization—from engineering to marketing to management.

In a twenty-page opus that was widely circulated, he pled the case that was gaining momentum:

> When Netscape first made Navigator available for unrestricted download over the Internet, many saw this as flying in the face of conventional wisdom for the commercial software business, and questioned how we could possibly make money "giving our software away." Now of course this strategy is seen in retrospect as a successful innovation that was a key factor in Netscape's rapid growth, and rare is the software company today that does not emulate our strategy in one way or another. Among other things, this provokes the following question: What if we were to repeat this scenario, only this time with source code?

In the engineering pit there was a similar view. Many Netscape employees had experience working with Open Source. And since Communicator's code was so tightly integrated with Java and HTML, most recognized an emerging truth: It wasn't such a huge jump to make. The nature of Java invites a more open view of source distribution. Because it is cross-platform and can be compiled down to class files that are machine-independent executables, each binary is like a virtual machine. One effect of this is that programmers can decompile the executable and turn it back into source code. And the browser "view source" command made HTML a common vernacular. Rather than trying to block this, many believed Netscape should facilitate it, encourage it, and if possible, benefit from it.

The various grassroots schools of thoughts merged with unexpected suddenness. In meetings, reaction to the suggestion went from stunned shock to nods in minutes. Most of the discussions passed quickly from "should we?" to "when?" Most of the key people believed that we had to move fast, set a firm date, and make it happen. In January, Netscape made a promise to the Net: Communicator source will be released in the first calendar quarter of 1998. Netscape took this promise with deadly seriousness, and Project Source 331 came into being. This was the name for Netscape's all-out effort to have the source code out by March 31, 1998.

Then the reality set in.

Making It Happen

The body of Communicator source code at Netscape was called "Mozilla." Mozilla was a term initially created by Jamie Zawinsky and company during the development of Navigator. The team was working at a similarly frantic pace to create a beast vastly more powerful than Mosaic, and the word became the official code name for Navigator. Later the big green dinosaur became an inside joke, then a company mascot, and finally a public symbol. Now the name came into use as the generic term referring to the open-source web browsers derived from the source code of Netscape Navigator. The move was on to "Free the Lizard."

There was an amazing amount to be done to make the code ready for prime time. As issues surfaced, they separated themselves into categories and were claimed. The next three months were devoted to resolving issues at the fanatical pace that Netscapers knew well.

One of the largest issues was the disposition of the third-party modules included in the browser. Communicator contained over seventy-five third-party modules in its source, and all of the code owners needed to be approached. Teams of engineers and evangelists were organized to visit and sell each company on the concept of joining Netscape on the road to Open Source. All of them had heard Netscape's Open Source announcement, and now each company had a choice to make: their code could be removed or replaced, shipped as binary (kept in its compiled state), or shipped as source code along with Communicator. To complicate matters, many of the third-party contracts were unique and ran for different lengths of time. No one scenario would be appropriate as a solution for all situations.

Making the deadline for Project Source 331 was considered essential. And that required tough choices. This was surely the case when it came to the participation of the third-party developers. The rule was either you're in by February 24th, or your element will have to be scrubbed from the source. Those kinds of deadlines are not hard to set early on, but they became brutal when we hit the wall. When the time came, some code had to be removed.

Java was a proprietary language, so it had to be removed. Three engineers were assigned to perform a "Java-ectomy." The browser had to build, compile, and run— without Java. Since the overall code was so tightly integrated with Java, this was no small feat. The goal was to have the source code ready by March 15th so that the final two weeks could be devoted to testing. Engineers had to disentangle all Java code from the browser in an inconceivably short time.

Cleansing the code was a huge project. Early on, many felt it just couldn't be done in time for the deadline. But as steam gathered at meetings, strategies formed. The wheels began to turn. The Product Team dropped their entire workload (most were developing the next generation of the browser) and everyone got down to the business of surgery. Not only did the inclusion (or excision) of each third-party participant have to be resolved, all comments had to be edited from the code. Responsibility for each module was assigned to a team and they went in to scrub.

One of the great innovations that happened early on was the decision to use the Intranet bug-reporting system as a task manager. "Bugsplat" was the name for Scopus, a bug-reporting program fronted with an HTML interface. It was ideal as a workflow management system. New jobs were reported to the system as they came up, input in a simple HTML form. Just as with a bug that has been reported to the system, priorities were set, relevant participants were determined, and mailing lists grew up around each task. When the task (or bug) was resolved, all of the mailing lists and prioritization collapsed and disappeared from view. Engineers were able to track the progress of their modules and watch the project unfold by logging on to the Intranet.

The removal of the cryptographic modules was another tremendous task for the engineering team. Not only did the government insist that all cryptographic support had to be removed, but every hook that called it had to be redacted. One team's sole job was to keep in constant contact with the NSA and manage compliance issues.

Creating the License

Parallel to the Great Code Cleanup was the license effort. The first step was to resolve the big question: Would any of the existing licenses work with the open code? No one wanted to have to draft new licenses, but everyone realized it might be necessary to accommodate all of the third-party code and to make the project work on a corporate level. No existing proprietary software had ever been released under a free source license.

A group of Open Source community leaders, including Linus Torvalds, Eric Raymond, and Tim O'Reilly, were invited to visit the Mountain View campus. They spoke with audiences of executives, attorneys, and programmers about what they were in for, and met with small groups to talk about some of the issues they were likely to face. They spent a great deal of time with the Netscape legal team discussing the existing licenses—both their strengths and the problems they created. These advisors also acted as a sounding board for ideas.

One team dove into researching existing licensing agreements with the advice and guidance of the Netscape legal team, trying to determine whether one of them would work for Mozilla. Beginning with the GNU General Public License, the GNU Library General Public License (LGPL), and the BSD license, we took long looks to outline exactly what problems they solved and created. Unlike the code to which these agreements had been applied in the past, Netscape's existing code base presented unique circumstances. One of the thorniest issues was the private licensing agreements that governed many of the third-party components used in the code. The license needed to create an environment where these and other new commercial developers could contribute their code to Mozilla while protecting their business interests.

The more permissive BSD license, which only requires that the copyright holder be referenced in unlimited changes to code, was deemed insufficient for Mozilla development. It would leave developers open to the risk that modifications to their work would not be returned to them or to the rest of the community. This point alone was a big issue, since it was crucial to the long-term viability of open source development efforts.

On the other hand, the requirements of the GPL made it undesirable in this project. The GPL is "viral"; when applied to an original piece of code, any other code with which the original is compiled must also be covered under the GPL. This aspect made it untenable for commercial software developers. For instance, the GPL would require that third-party components compiled into branded versions of Communicator also be released under the GPL, something outside of Netscape's reach, as Netscape does not control these third parties. And Netscape itself uses a portion of the Communicator code in its other products (such as servers). Since Netscape has no immediate plans to release that source code, the GPL viral effect on these products would present the same problem for Netscape as for other companies. The more open and less restrictive LGPL, a modification of the GPL, came closest to meeting Netscape's needs for use with commercial development, but it still contained too many of the same commercial pitfalls as the GPL.

After a frenzied month of research, discussion, meetings with experts and advocates from the free software community, and amidst public speculation, the team decided that a new license had to be crafted for this unique situation. The Netscape Public License (NPL) broke new ground in attempting to strike a compromise between promoting free source development by commercial enterprises and protecting free source developers. The process of fashioning a next-generation Open Source license took over a month.

In another extraordinary move, when the first draft of the Netscape Public License (NPL) was complete it was beta-tested publicly. On March 5, a draft was posted in a new newsgroup called netscape.public.mozilla.license, and a request was made for public comment. It was met with cheers and jeers. One section of the license acted as a lightening rod, catching most of the flames: the portion of the NPL that granted Netscape special rights to use code covered by the NPL in other Netscape products without those products falling under the NPL. It also allowed Netscape to issue revised versions of the NPL, and most controversially, to re-license code covered by the NPL to third parties under terms different from the NPL. Some of the people providing feedback went so far as to suggest that this fact alone would make the NPL unacceptable to the Open Source development community.

On March 11th, a status report appeared on netscape.public.mozilla.license from jwz (Jamie Zawinsky). It read, in part:

> First of all, THANK YOU for the incredible amount of cogent feedback you've been giving! It has been incredibly helpful, and rest assured, the opinions expressed here are being taken very seriously.

Next week, you can expect to see a dramatically reworked section 5. I probably shouldn't comment on it too much (wouldn't want to set expectations incorrectly) but the message that most of you hate it as it stands now has been received loud and clear.

On March 21st, the revision was posted. This was unprecedented. The reaction was incredulous: "I told them it was awful and they listened! I can't believe it!" People realized that this was a true open-source project, in spite of its unlikely birthplace. The discussions going on in the newsgroups were helping to guide the process, rather than providing commentary on its results. The continuing discussions took on a new tone and spirits were high.

The community criticism of the beta of the NPL had sent the license team back to the drawing board. They sought a solution that would allow Netscape to balance the goals of engaging free source developers while continuing to meet business objectives. The result was the release of a second license to work with the NPL, the Mozilla Public License (MozPL). The two licenses are identical, except that the NPL includes amendments granting Netscape additional rights.

All of the code initially issued on March 31, 1998 was released under the NPL, and all modifications to that code must be released under the NPL. New code developed can be released under the MozPL or any other compatible license. Changes to files contained in the source code are considered modifications and are covered by the NPL. And to resolve much of the concern expressed on the Net: new files that do not contain any of the original code or subsequent modified code are not considered modifications and are not covered by the NPL. This resulting code can be covered by any compatible license. The GPL is not compatible with the Netscape Public License or the Mozilla Public License. The GPL is by design incompatible with all other licenses, since it prohibits the addition of any restrictions or further permissions to its boundaries. All code developed to work with GPL software must in turn be covered by the GPL. Another minor point is that the GPL insists that when you distribute code covered under its terms, it must be complete and entire. The NPL does not have this condition.

The discussions on the newsgroups had brought an important issue into sharp relief: developers needed Netscape to allow a distinction between bug fixes and new code. Clearly, it's one thing to say, "I'm making a bug fix, a small modification to your program," and quite another to realize "I'm adding a new feature to your program." They provoke different feelings. Most people feel all right about giving away a bug fix, and the value of making a contribution is its own reward. But new code is a different story. A developer who has done a lot of new work doesn't want to see somebody else use it to make money for themselves.

The NPL and the MozPL were designed to encourage open development on the Mozilla code base, but from the beginning there was also another goal in mind.

Netscape was willing to be the first large corporation to open up its proprietary source, because it wanted to foster wider corporate interest in development in open source environments. Creating an atmosphere that made it possible for large, profit-making organizations to adopt this model and participate in the movement was paramount. The legal infrastructure in most Open Source licensing is a big hurdle to corporate cooperation. With Mozilla, the license was a project unto itself.

By giving away the source code for future versions, we hoped to engage the entire Net community in creating new innovation in the browser market. The idea that there would be talented programmers worldwide hacking on our code, infusing the browser with their creative energy, motivated everyone to keep going even when the going got tough.

Mozilla.org

People who had been involved in open-source projects before realized that the code had to have a place to live. The night after Netscape announced that it would free the source, Jamie registered a new domain name with Internic and drew up a chart on how distributed development projects work. Mozilla.org was born.

There's a pattern that all successful open-source projects follow, not necessarily by design. There tends to be one person or group that does coordination. People work on whatever aspect of the code they care about, scratching their own itches. At the end of the day, they have something that works a little better for them. But what happens a month later when a new version of the software comes out? Their fix is gone, and they're back to square one—or worse, because the software may have changed.

The result is that developers want to get their patch included in the main distribution. And if there's just a pile of source code floating around and a bunch of people working on it, eventually someone will stand up and say, "I might as well collect a bunch of patches and do a release." When the next person comes along wondering how to get his patch into the next release, he'll say, "I don't know who else to give my patch to, so I'll give it to that guy. He seems to be doing a good job of it." And as time goes by, that person becomes the maintainer.

For this open-source project, the horse was put in front of the cart. Mozilla.org was conceived and designed to fill the role of maintainer from the outset. Since the role would be filled one way or another, we decided to create the infrastructure to become the clearinghouse.

In the next months, mozilla.org began to set up an organization, getting funding and machines, posting mailing lists, and developing the underpinnings necessary to make it work. The mission was simply to get the organization off the ground and functioning. It was crucial that there be a central depot in operation as soon as the source code was released. And if we weren't prepared, in six months time, we'd be watching someone else do it. Netscape is not known for sitting around and watching the other guy.

Giving away the source code meant Netscape was collaborating with the Net. And there was a crucial concept that had to be accepted: the Netscape Client Product Development Group and mozilla.org were not the same organization. Mozilla.org's goal is to act as the coordinator for all of the people worldwide working on the software. Product Development's purpose is to ship products—Netscape products based on the Mozilla code. Since both groups are working on the same product, interests can overlap. But the group behind mozilla.org knew that it would be disastrous for the Net to look at the organization and say, "These people only have Netscape's interests in mind and they're only about shipping Netscape products." This would mean that mozilla.org had failed in its goal to be a good maintainer. The separation had to be real and the Net had to know it.

Behind the Curtain

What happens when a developer makes a change and pipes up, "Hey, mozilla.org, please take this code?" One of mozilla.org's most important roles is to draw lines as to what code is accepted and what is not. We must factor in a number of issues. First and foremost is merit. Is it good? Second, is it under a license that is compatible with NPL? We decided not to accept contributions that were not under a license compatible with NPL. Otherwise there would have to be separate directories, Chinese walls, and lots and lots of legalese for everyone involved. The potential for error goes into the stratosphere.

Since Mozilla is a highly modular code base, each major module, such as the Image Library or the XML Parser, have a designated "owner." That person knows the code best and is the arbiter of what should go in to that module and what shouldn't.

Many module owners are Netscape engineers, but some are coming on board from the Net-at-large. When a module owner makes changes (for example, adding an API to the Image Library) the modifications are sent to mozilla.org for inclusion in distributions. If differences arise between a contributor and the module owner, mozilla.org performs as the arbitrator, making the final call—always aware that if it stops playing fair, it will be ignored and someone else will usurp the duties.

Mozilla.org had to contend with the fact that there would be both internal Netscape developers and people on the Net working on their code. The methods used to work on code internally had to accommodate the Web and be accessible on all platforms, in all time zones. This was done with "tree control" performed by the tools Bonsai and Tinderbox.

"Bonsai" is a tool that lets you perform queries on the contents of an archive. Like the front desk of a library, you can "check in" code you've worked on, or see what "checkins" have been made by others. In the background, it constantly runs the code, checking the code tree. If the tree breaks, it sends up a red flag, stopping further checkins until the problem can be identified. Logs can be pulled and problems traced to a particular time period. Previously used by Netscape developers in-house, it was erected on mozilla.org for use by developers around the world and could be used directly through the browser on any platform.

If you get more than ten developers together without tools, there is going to be an explosion. That's the theory behind "Tinderbox," a program that keeps this potentially explosive situation under control. Tinderbox is a detective tool. It allows you to see what is happening in the source tree. It shows who checked in what (by asking Bonsai), what platforms have built successfully, what platforms are broken, exactly how they are broken, and the state of the files that made up the build so you can track down who may have done the damage.

April Fool's Day, 1998

It was a week and a half before the end of March 1998, and the deadline was closing in fast. There was a general sense that there needed to be a party to celebrate the code release, but nothing had been done about it. In keeping with the rest of this project, the bash would become a groundbreaking event that invited the public into Netscape's world, shields down.

In a meeting Jamie laid out his plan to rent out a nightclub in San Francisco, invite the world, and broadcast it over the Net. "You mean invite non-employees to the party? But we've never done that before!" In character with the rest of the project, after a pause the reaction was . . . "Why not?"

The party will not soon be forgotten. Jamie rented out one of the biggest nightclubs in San Francisco, The Sound Factory, on the night of April 1st. DJs (including Apache founder Brian Behlendorf) gave away thousands of mozilla.org T-shirts, software, and items from NetObjects, Macromedia, Digital, Be, Wired, and unAmerican Activities.

When the doors opened for the "Mozilla Dot Party" at eight, there was already a line. An hour and a half later, the place was filled to its fire-code maximum of two thousand, and the line wrapped around the block. People were being waved in twenty at a time as others departed, and by the end of the night, over 3,500 had passed through the doors, including free software gurus like Brewster Kahle (founder of WAIS) and Eric Raymond. Hundreds more synched their watches and toasted Mozilla around the world. The virtual partygoers included a group of over a hundred at The Waag castle in Amsterdam, The Netherlands, and various individual groups in Norway, Montreal, Canada, Pennsylvania, North Carolina, Wisconsin, Colorado, and Alabama.

Inside, three projection screens scrolled the code at roughly sixty lines per second. (At that rate, the party would have had to linger more than seven hours to see the full million and a half lines of Mozilla code.) During the second of two sets played by the Kofy Brown Band (featuring a Netscape engineer), Eric Raymond, who had flown in from Philadelphia for the party, jumped on stage and surprised everyone with a flute solo. Toward the end of the night, a dozen CDs of the Mozilla Source Code, Signature Edition (CDs signed and numbered the night before by the Netscape Build Team and members of mozilla.org) were thrown to a lucky few in the crowd. The lizard was free!

The Revenge of the Hackers

Eric S. Raymond

I wrote the first version of "A Brief History of Hackerdom" in 1996 as a web resource. I had been fascinated by hacker culture *as* a culture for many years, since long before I edited the first edition of *The New Hacker's Dictionary* in 1990. By late 1993, many people (including myself) had come to think of me as the hacker culture's tribal historian and resident ethnographer. I was comfortable in that role.

At that time, I hadn't the faintest idea that my amateur anthropologizing could itself become a significant catalyst for change. I think nobody was more surprised than I when that happened. But the consequences of that surprise are still reverberating through the hacker culture and the technology and business worlds today.

In this essay, I'll recapitulate from my personal point of view the events that immediately led up to the January 1998 "shot heard 'round the world" of the open-source revolution. I'll reflect on the remarkable distance we've come since. Then I will tentatively offer some projections into the future.

Beyond Brooks's Law

My first encounter with Linux came in late 1993, via the pioneering Yggdrasil CD-ROM distribution. By that time, I had already been involved in the hacker culture for fifteen years. My earliest experiences had been with the primitive ARPAnet of the late 1970s; I was even briefly a tourist on the ITS machines. I had already been writing free software and posting it to Usenet before the Free Software Foundation was launched in 1984, and was one of the FSF's first contributors. I had just published the second edition of *The New Hacker's Dictionary*. I thought I understood the hacker culture—and its limitations—pretty well.

Encountering Linux was a shock. Even though I had been active in the hacker culture for many years, I still carried in my head the unexamined assumption that hacker amateurs, gifted though they might be, could not possibly muster the resources or skill necessary to produce a usable multitasking operating system. The HURD developers, after all, had been evidently failing at this for a decade.

But where they had failed, Linus Torvalds and his community had succeeded. And they did not merely fulfill the minimum requirements of stability and functioning Unix interfaces. No. They blew right past that criterion with exuberance and flair, providing hundreds of megabytes of programs, documents, and other resources. Full suites of Internet tools, desktop-publishing software, graphics support, editors, games—you name it.

Seeing this feast of wonderful code spread in front of me as a working system was a much more powerful experience than merely knowing, intellectually, that all the bits were probably out there. It was as though for years I'd been sorting through piles of disconnected car parts—only to be suddenly confronted with those same parts assembled into a gleaming red Ferrari, door open, keys swinging from the lock, and engine gently purring with a promise of power. . . .

The hacker tradition I had been observing for two decades seemed suddenly alive in a vibrant new way. In a sense, I had already been made part of this community, for several of my personal free-software projects had been added to the mix. But I wanted to get in deeper, because every delight I saw also deepened my puzzlement. It was too good!

The lore of software engineering is dominated by Brooks's Law, which predicts that as your N number of programmers rises, work performed scales as N but complexity and vulnerability to bugs rises as N-squared. N-squared is the number of communications paths (and potential code interfaces) between developers' code bases.

Brooks's Law predicts that a project with thousands of contributors ought to be a flaky, unstable mess. Somehow the Linux community had beaten the N-squared effect and produced an OS of astonishingly high quality. I was determined to understand how they did it.

It took me three years of participation and close observation to develop a theory, and another year to test it experimentally. And then I sat down and wrote "The Cathedral and the Bazaar" (CatB)[*] to explain what I had seen.

Memes and Mythmaking

What I saw around me was a community which had evolved the most effective software-development method ever *and didn't know it!* That is, an effective practice had evolved as a set of customs, transmitted by imitation and example, without the theory or language to explain why the practice worked.

---

[*] *http://www.tuxedo.org/~esr/writings/cathedral-bazaar*

In retrospect, lacking that theory and that language hampered us in two ways. First, we couldn't think systematically about how to improve our own methods. Second, we couldn't explain or sell the method to anyone else.

At the time, I was only thinking about the first effect. My only intention in writing the paper was to give the hacker culture an appropriate language to use internally, to explain itself to itself. So I wrote down what I had seen, framed as a narrative and with appropriately vivid metaphors to describe the logic that could be deduced behind the customs.

There was no really fundamental discovery in CatB. I did not invent any of the methods it describes. What is novel in that paper is not the facts but those metaphors and the narrative—a simple, powerful story that encouraged the reader to see the facts in a new way. I was attempting a bit of memetic engineering on the hacker culture's generative myths.

I first gave the full paper at Linux Kongress, in May 1997 in Bavaria. The fact that it was received with rapt attention and thunderous applause by an audience in which there were very few native speakers of English seemed to confirm that I was onto something. But, as it turned out, the sheer chance that I was seated next to Tim O'Reilly at the Thursday night banquet set in motion a more important train of consequences.

As a long-time admirer of O'Reilly's institutional style, I had been looking forward to meeting Tim for some years. We had a wide-ranging conversation (much of it exploring our common interest in classic science fiction) which led to an invitation for me to give CatB at Tim's Perl Conference later in the year.

Once again, the paper was well-received—with cheers and a standing ovation, in fact. I knew from my email that since Bavaria, word about CatB had spread over the Internet like a fire in dry grass. Many in the audience had already read it, and my speech was less a revelation of novelty for them than an opportunity to celebrate the new language and the consciousness that went with it. That standing ovation was not so much for my work as for the hacker culture itself—and rightly so.

Though I didn't know it, my experiment in memetic engineering was about to light a bigger fire. Some of the people for whom my speech was genuinely novel were from Netscape Communications, Inc. And Netscape was in trouble.

Netscape, a pioneering Internet-technology company and Wall Street highflier, had been targeted for destruction by Microsoft. Microsoft rightly feared that the open Web standards embodied by Netscape's browser might lead to an erosion of the Redmond giant's lucrative monopoly on the PC desktop. All the weight of Microsoft's billions, and shady tactics that would later trigger an antitrust lawsuit, were deployed to crush the Netscape browser.

For Netscape, the issue was less browser-related income (never more than a small fraction of their revenues) than maintaining a safe space for their much more valuable server business. If Microsoft's Internet Explorer achieved market dominance, Microsoft would be able to bend the Web's protocols away from open standards and into proprietary channels that only *Microsoft's* servers would be able to service.

Within Netscape there was intense debate about how to counter the threat. One of the options proposed early on was to throw the Netscape browser source open—but it was a hard case to argue without strong reasons to believe that doing so would prevent Internet Explorer dominance.

I didn't know it at the time, but CatB became a major factor in making that case. Through the winter of 1997, as I was working on the material for my next paper, the stage was being set for Netscape to break the rules of the commercial game and offer my tribe an unprecedented opportunity.

The Road to Mountain View

On January 22nd, 1998, Netscape announced that it would release the sources of the Netscape client line to the Internet. Shortly after the news reached me the following day, I learned that CEO Jim Barksdale described my work to national-media reporters as "fundamental inspiration" for the decision.

This was the event that commentators in the computer trade press would later call "the shot heard 'round the world"—and Barksdale had cast me as its Thomas Paine, whether I wanted the role or not. For the first time in the history of the hacker culture, a Fortune 500 darling of Wall Street had bet its future on the belief that *our way was right*. And, more specifically, that *my analysis* of "our way" was right.

This is a pretty sobering kind of shock to deal with. I had not been very surprised when CatB altered the hacker culture's image of itself; that was the result I had been trying for, after all. But I was astonished (to say the least) by the news of its success on the outside. So I did some very hard thinking in the first few hours after word reached me. About the state of Linux and the hacker community. About Netscape. And about whether I, personally, had what it would take to make the next step.

It was not difficult to conclude that helping Netscape's gamble succeed had just become a very high priority for the hacker culture, and thus for me personally. If Netscape's gamble failed, we hackers would probably find all the opprobrium of that failure piled on our heads. We'd be discredited for another decade. And that would be just too much to take.

By this time I had been in the hacker culture, living through its various phases, for twenty years. Twenty years of repeatedly watching brilliant ideas, promising starts, and superior technologies crushed by slick marketing. Twenty years of watching hackers dream and sweat and build, too often only to watch the likes of the bad old IBM or the bad new Microsoft walk away with the real-world prizes. Twenty years of living in a ghetto—a fairly comfortable ghetto full of interesting friends, but still one walled in by a vast and intangible barrier of prejudice inscribed "ONLY FLAKES LIVE HERE."

The Netscape announcement cracked that barrier, if only for a moment; the business world had been jolted out of its complacency about what "hackers" are capable of. But lazy mental habits have huge inertia. If Netscape failed, or perhaps even if they succeeded, the experiment might come to be seen as a unique one-off not worth trying to repeat. And then we'd be back in the same ghetto, walls higher than before.

To prevent that, we needed Netscape to succeed. So I considered what I had learned about bazaar-mode development, and called up Netscape, and offered to help with developing their license and in working out the details of the strategy. In early February I flew to Mountain View at their request for seven hours of meetings with various groups at Netscape HQ, and helped them develop the outline of what would become the Mozilla Public License and the Mozilla organization.

While there, I met with several key people in the Silicon Valley and national Linux community (this part of the history is told in more detail on the Open Source web site's history page*). While helping Netscape was clearly a short-term priority, everybody I spoke with had already understood the need for some longer-term strategy to follow up on the Netscape release. It was time to develop one.

The Origins of "Open Source"

It was easy to see the outlines of the strategy. We needed to take the pragmatic arguments I had pioneered in CatB, develop them further, and push them hard, in public. Because Netscape itself had an interest in convincing investors that its strategy was not crazy, we could count on them to help the promotion. We also recruited Tim O'Reilly (and through him, O'Reilly & Associates) very early on.

The real conceptual breakthrough, though, was admitting to ourselves that what we needed to mount was in effect a *marketing campaign*—and that it would require marketing techniques (spin, image-building, and re-branding) to make it work.

Hence the term "open source," which the first participants in what would later become the Open Source campaign (and, eventually, the Open Source Initiative organization) invented at a meeting held in Mountain View in the offices of VA Research on February 3.

---

* http://www.opensource.org/history.html

It seemed clear to us in retrospect that the term "free software" had done our movement tremendous damage over the years. Part of this stemmed from the well-known "free-speech/free-beer" ambiguity. Most of it came from something worse—the strong association of the term "free software" with hostility to intellectual property rights, communism, and other ideas hardly likely to endear themselves to an MIS manager.

It was, and still is, beside the point to argue that the Free Software Foundation is not hostile to all intellectual property and that its position is not exactly communistic. We knew that. What we realized, under the pressure of the Netscape release, was that FSF's actual position didn't matter. Only the fact that its evangelism had backfired (associating "free software" with these negative stereotypes in the minds of the trade press and the corporate world) actually mattered.

Our success after Netscape would depend on replacing the negative FSF stereotypes with *positive* stereotypes of our own—pragmatic tales, sweet to managers' and investors' ears, of higher reliability and lower cost and better features.

In conventional marketing terms, our job was to re-brand the product, and build its reputation into one the corporate world would hasten to buy.

Linus Torvalds endorsed the idea the day after that first meeting. We began acting on it within a few days after. Bruce Perens had the opensource.org domain registered and the first version of the Open Source web site* up within a week. He also suggested that the Debian Free Software Guidelines become the "Open Source Definition,"† and began the process of registering "Open Source" as a certification mark so that we could legally require people to use "Open Source" for products conforming to the OSD.

Even the particular tactics needed to push the strategy seemed pretty clear to me even at this early stage (and were explicitly discussed at the initial meeting). Key themes:

Forget bottom-up; work on top-down

> One of the things that seemed clearest was that the historical Unix strategy of bottom-up evangelism (relying on engineers to persuade their bosses by rational argument) had been a failure. This was naive and easily trumped by Microsoft. Further, the Netscape breakthrough didn't happen that way. It happened because a strategic decision-maker (Jim Barksdale) got the clue and then imposed that vision on the people below him.

> The conclusion was inescapable. Instead of working bottom-up, we should be evangelizing top-down—making a direct effort to capture the CEO/CTO/CIO types.

---

* *http://www.opensource.edu/*
† *http://www.opensource.org/osd.html*

Linux is our best demonstration case

Promoting Linux must be our main thrust. Yes, there are other things going on in the open-source world, and the campaign will bow respectfully in their direction—but Linux started with the best name recognition, the broadest software base, and the largest developer community. If Linux can't consolidate the breakthrough, nothing else will, pragmatically speaking, have a prayer.

Capture the Fortune 500

There are other market segments that spend more dollars (small-business and home-office being the most obvious examples) but those markets are diffuse and hard to address. The Fortune 500 doesn't merely *have* lots of money, it concentrates lots of money where it's relatively easy to get at. Therefore, the software industry largely does what the Fortune 500 business market tells it to do. And therefore, it is primarily the Fortune 500 we need to convince.

Co-opt the prestige media that serve the Fortune 500

The choice to target the Fortune 500 implies that we need to capture the media that shape the climate of opinion among top-level decision-makers and investors: very specifically, the *New York Times*, the *Wall Street Journal*, the *Economist*, *Forbes*, and *Barron's Magazine*.

On this view, co-opting the technical trade press is necessary but not sufficient; it's important essentially as a pre-condition for storming Wall Street itself through the elite mainstream media.

Educate hackers in guerilla marketing tactics

It was also clear that educating the hacker community itself would be just as important as mainstream outreach. It would be insufficient to have one or a handful of ambassadors speaking effective language if, at the grassroots level, most hackers were making arguments that didn't work.

Use the Open Source certification mark to keep things pure

One of the threats we faced was the possibility that the term "open source" would be "embraced and extended" by Microsoft or other large vendors, corrupting it and losing our message. It is for this reason that Bruce Perens and I decided early on to register the term as a certification mark and tie it to the Open Source Definition (a copy of the Debian Free Software Guidelines). This would allow us to scare off potential abusers with the threat of legal action.

The Accidental Revolutionary

Planning this kind of strategy was relatively easy. The hard part (for me, anyway) was accepting what my own role had to be.

One thing I understood from the beginning is that the press almost completely tunes out abstractions. They won't write about ideas without larger-than-life personalities fronting them. Everything has to be story, drama, conflict, sound bites. Otherwise most reporters will simply go to sleep—and if they don't, their editors will.

Accordingly, I knew somebody with very particular characteristics would be needed to front the community's response to the Netscape opportunity. We needed a fire-brand, a spin doctor, a propagandist, an ambassador, an evangelist—somebody who could dance and sing and shout from the housetops and seduce reporters and hug-germug with CEOs and bang the media machine until its contrary gears ground out the message: *The revolution is here!*

Unlike most hackers, I have the brain chemistry of an extrovert and had already had extensive experience at dealing with the press. Looking around me, I couldn't see anyone better qualified to play evangelist. But I didn't want the job, because I knew it would cost me my life for many months, maybe for years. My privacy would be destroyed. I'd probably end up caricatured as a geek by the mainstream press and (worse) despised as a sell-out or glory-hog by a significant fraction of my own tribe. Worse than all the other bad consequences put together, I probably wouldn't have time to hack any more!

I had to ask myself: are you fed up enough with watching your tribe lose to do *whatever it takes to win*? I decided the answer was yes—and having so decided, threw myself into the dirty but necessary job of becoming a public figure and media personality.

I'd learned some basic media chops while editing *The New Hacker's Dictionary*. This time I took it much more seriously and developed an entire theory of media manipulation which I then proceeded to apply. This is not the place to describe the theory in detail, but it centers around the use of what I call "attractive dissonance" to fan an itchy curiosity about the evangelist, and then exploiting that itch for all it's worth in promoting the ideas.

The combination of the "open source" label and deliberate promotion of myself as an evangelist turned out to have both the good and bad consequences that I expected. The ten months after the Netscape announcement featured a steady exponential increase in media coverage of Linux and the open-source world in general. Throughout this period, approximately a third of these articles quoted me directly; most of the other two-thirds used me as a background source. At the same time, a vociferous minority of hackers declared me an evil egotist. I managed to preserve a sense of humor about both outcomes (though occasionally with some difficulty).

My plan from the beginning was that, eventually, I would hand off the evangelist role to some successor, either an individual or organization. There would come a time when charisma became less effective than broad-based institutional respectability (and, from my own point of view, the sooner the better!). At the time of this writing I am attempting to transfer my personal connections and carefully built-up reputation with the press to the Open Source Initiative, an incorporated nonprofit formed specifically to manage the Open Source trademark. I am currently the president of this organization, but hope and expect not to remain so indefinitely.

Phases of the Campaign

The open-source campaign began with the Mountain View meeting, and rapidly collected an informal network of allies over the Internet (including key people at Netscape and O'Reilly & Associates). Where I write "we" below I'm referring to that network.

From February 3 to around the time of the actual Netscape release on March 31, our primary concern was convincing the hacker community "open source" label and the arguments that went with it represented our best shot at persuading the mainstream. As it turned out, the change was rather easier than we expected. We discovered a lot of pent-up demand for a message less doctrinaire than the Free Software Foundation's.

When the twenty-odd community leaders at the Free Software Summit on March 7 voted to adopt the term "open source," they formally ratified a trend that was already clear at the grass roots among developers. By six weeks after the Mountain View meeting, a healthy majority of the community was speaking our language.

In April after the Summit and the actual Netscape release, our main concern shifted to recruiting as many open-source early adopters as possible. The goal was to make Netscape's move look less singular—and to buy us insurance in case Netscape executed poorly and failed its goals.

This was the most worrying time. On the surface, everything seemed to be coming up roses; Linux was moving technically from strength to strength, the wider open-source phenomenon was enjoying a spectacular explosion in trade press coverage, and we were even beginning to get positive coverage in the mainstream press. Nevertheless, I was uneasily aware that our success was still fragile. After an initial flurry of contributions, community participation in Mozilla was badly slowed down by its requirement of Motif. None of the big independent software vendors had yet committed to Linux ports. Netscape was still looking lonely, and its browser still losing market share to Internet Explorer. Any serious reverse could lead to a nasty backlash in the press and public opinion.

Our first serious post-Netscape breakthrough came on May 7 when Corel Computer announced its Linux-based Netwinder network computer. But that wasn't enough in itself; to sustain the momentum, we needed commitments not from hungry second-stringers but from industry leaders. Thus, it was the mid-July announcements by Oracle and Informix that really closed out this vulnerable phase.

The database outfits joined the Linux party three months earlier than I expected, but none too soon. We had been wondering how long the positive buzz could last without major Independent Software Vendor (ISV) support and feeling increasingly nervous about where we'd actually find that. After Oracle and Informix announced Linux ports other ISVs began announcing Linux support almost as a matter of routine, and even a failure of Mozilla became survivable.

Mid-July through the beginning of November was a consolidation phase. It was during this time that we started to see fairly steady coverage from the elite media I had originally targeted, led off by articles in *The Economist* and a cover story in *Forbes*. Various hardware and software vendors sent out feelers to the open-source community and began to work out strategies for getting an advantage from the new model. And internally, the biggest closed-source vendor of them all was beginning to get seriously worried.

Just *how* worried became apparent when the now-infamous "Halloween Documents"* leaked out of Microsoft.

The Halloween Documents were dynamite. They were a ringing testimonial to the strengths of open-source development from the company with the most to lose from Linux's success. And they confirmed a lot of peoples' darkest suspicions about the tactics Microsoft would consider in order to stop it.

The Halloween Documents attracted massive press coverage in the first few weeks of November. They created a new surge of interest in the open-source phenomenon, serendipitously confirming all the points we had been making for months. And they led directly to a request for me to conference with a select group of Merrill Lynch's major investors on the state of the software industry and the prospects for open source.

Wall Street, finally, came to us.

The Facts on the Ground

While the Open Source campaign's "air war" in the media was going on, key technical and market facts on the ground were also changing. I'll review some of them briefly here because they combine interestingly with the trends in press and public perception.

In the ten months following the Netscape release, Linux rapidly continued to grow more capable. The development of solid SMP support and the effective completion of the 64-bit cleanup laid important groundwork for the future.

---

* *http://www.opensource.org/halloween.html*

The roomful of Linux boxes used to render scenes for *Titanic* threw a healthy scare into builders of expensive graphics engines. Then the Beowulf supercomputer-on-the-cheap project showed that Linux's Chinese-army sociology could be successfully applied even to bleeding-edge scientific computing.

Nothing dramatic happened to vault Linux's open-source competitors into the limelight. And proprietary Unixes continued to lose market share; in fact, by mid-year only NT and Linux were actually gaining market share in the Fortune 500, and by late fall Linux was gaining faster.

Apache continued to increase its lead in the web server market. In November, Netscape's browser reversed its market-share slide and began to make gains against Internet Explorer.

Into the Future

I have rehearsed recent history here only partly to get it into the record. More importantly, it sets a background against which we can understand near-term trends and project some things about the future (I write in mid-December of 1998).

First, safe predictions for the next year:

- The open-source developer population will continue to explode, a growth fueled by ever-cheaper PC hardware and Internet connections.

- Linux will continue to lead the way, the relative size of its developer community overpowering the higher average skill of the open-source BSD people and the tiny HURD crew.

- ISV commitments to support the Linux platform will increase dramatically; the database-vendor commitments were a turning point. Corel's commitment to ship their entire office suite on Linux points the way.

- The Open Source campaign will continue to build on its victories and successfully raise awareness at the CEO/CTO/CIO and investor level. MIS directors will feel increasing pressure to go with open-source products not from below but from *above*.

- Stealth deployments of Samba-over-Linux will replace increasing numbers of NT machines even at shops that have all-Microsoft policies.

- The market share of proprietary Unixes will continue to gradually erode. At least one of the weaker competitors (likely DG-UX or HP-UX) will actually fold. But by the time it happens, analysts will attribute it to Linux's gains rather than Microsoft's.

- Microsoft will not have an enterprise-ready operating system, because Windows 2000 will not ship in a usable form. (At 60 million lines of code and still bloating, its development is out of control.)

Extrapolating these trends certainly suggests some slightly riskier predictions for the medium term (eighteen to thirty-two months out):

- Support operations for commercial customers of open-source operating systems will become big business, both feeding off of and fueling the boom in business use.

- Open-source operating systems (with Linux leading the way) will capture the ISP and business data-center markets. NT will be unable to resist this change effectively; the combination of low cost, open sources, and 24/7 reliability will prove irresistible.

- The proprietary-Unix sector will almost completely collapse. Solaris looks like a safe bet to survive on high-end Sun hardware, but most other players' proprietary will quickly become legacy systems.

- Windows 2000 will be either canceled or dead on arrival. Either way it will turn into a horrendous train wreck, the worst strategic disaster in Microsoft's history. However, this will barely affect their hold on the desktop market within the next two years.

At first glance, these trends look like a recipe for leaving Linux as the last one standing. But life is not that simple (and Microsoft derives such immense amounts of money and market clout from the desktop market that it can't safely be counted out even after the Windows 2000 train wreck).

So at two years out the crystal ball gets a bit cloudy. Which of several futures we get depends on questions like: Will the Department of Justice break up Microsoft? Might BeOS or OS/2 or Mac OS/X or some other niche closed-source OS, or some completely new design, find a way to go open and compete effectively with Linux's 30-year-old base design? Will Y2K-related problems have thrown the world economy into a deep enough depression to throw off everybody's timetables?

These are all fairly imponderable. But there is one such question that is worth pondering: Will the Linux community actually deliver a good end-user–friendly GUI interface for the whole system?

I think the most likely scenario for two years out has Linux in effective control of servers, data centers, ISPs, and the Internet, while Microsoft maintains its grip on the desktop. Where things go from there depend on whether GNOME, KDE, or some other Linux-based GUI (and the applications built or rebuilt to use it) ever get good enough to challenge Microsoft on its home ground.

If this were primarily a technical problem, the outcome would hardly be in doubt. But it isn't; it's a problem in ergonomic design and interface psychology, and hackers have historically been poor at it. That is, while hackers can be very good at designing interfaces for other hackers, they tend to be poor at modeling the thought processes of the other 95% of the population well enough to write interfaces that J. Random End-User and his Aunt Tillie will pay to buy.

Applications were this year's problem; it's now clear we'll swing enough ISVs to get the ones we don't write ourselves. I believe the problem for the next two years is whether we can grow enough to meet (and *exceed!*) the interface-design quality standard set by the Macintosh, combining that with the virtues of the traditional Unix way.

We half-joke about "world domination," but the only way we will get there is by *serving* the world. That means J. Random End-User and his Aunt Tillie; and *that* means learning how to think about what we do in a fundamentally new way, and ruthlessly reducing the user-visible complexity of the default environment to an absolute minimum.

Computers are tools for human beings. Ultimately, therefore, the challenges of designing hardware and software must come back to designing for human beings— *all* human beings.

This path will be long, and it won't be easy. But we owe it to ourselves and each other to do it right. May the Open Source be with you!

Appendix A
The Tanenbaum-Torvalds Debate

What follows in this appendix are what are known in the community as the Tanenbaum/Linus "Linux is obsolete" debates. Andrew Tanenbaum is a well-respected researcher who has made a very good living thinking about operating systems and OS design. In early 1992, noticing the way that the Linux discussion had taken over the discussion in comp.os.minix, he decided it was time to comment on Linux.

Although Andrew Tanenbaum has been derided for his heavy hand and misjudgements of the Linux kernel, such a reaction to Tanenbaum is unfair. When Linus himself heard that we were including this, he wanted to make sure that the world understood that he holds no animus towards Tanenbaum and in fact would not have sanctioned its inclusion if we had not been able to convince him that it would show the way the world was thinking about OS design at the time.

We felt the inclusion of this appendix would give a good perspective on how things were when Linus was under pressure because he abandoned the idea of microkernels in academia. The first third of Linus' essay discusses this further.

Electronic copies of this debate are available on the Web and are easily found through any search service. It's fun to read this and note who joined into the discussion; you see user-hacker Ken Thompson (one of the founders of Unix) and David Miller (who is a major Linux kernel hacker now), as well as many others.

To put this discussion into perspective, when it occurred in 1992, the 386 was the dominating chip and the 486 had not come out on the market. Microsoft was still a small company selling DOS and Word for DOS. Lotus 123 ruled the spreadsheet space and WordPerfect the word processing market. DBASE was the dominant database vendor and many companies that are household names today—Netscape, Yahoo, Excite—simply did not exist.

From: ast@cs.vu.nl (Andy Tanenbaum)
Newsgroups: comp.os.minix
Subject: LINUX is obsolete
Date: 29 Jan 92 12:12:50 GMT

I was in the U.S. for a couple of weeks, so I haven't commented much on
LINUX (not that I would have said much had I been around), but for what
it is worth, I have a couple of comments now.

As most of you know, for me MINIX is a hobby, something that I do in the
evening when I get bored writing books and there are no major wars,
revolutions, or senate hearings being televised live on CNN. My real
job is a professor and researcher in the area of operating systems.

As a result of my occupation, I think I know a bit about where operating
are going in the next decade or so. Two aspects stand out:

1. MICROKERNEL VS MONOLITHIC SYSTEM
   Most older operating systems are monolithic, that is, the whole operating
   system is a single a.out file that runs in 'kernel mode.' This binary
   contains the process management, memory management, file system and the
   rest. Examples of such systems are UNIX, MS-DOS, VMS, MVS, OS/360,
   MULTICS, and many more.

   The alternative is a microkernel-based system, in which most of the OS
   runs as separate processes, mostly outside the kernel. They communicate
   by message passing. The kernel's job is to handle the message passing,
   interrupt handling, low-level process management, and possibly the I/O.
   Examples of this design are the RC4000, Amoeba, Chorus, Mach, and the
   not-yet-released Windows/NT.

   While I could go into a long story here about the relative merits of the
   two designs, suffice it to say that among the people who actually design
   operating systems, the debate is essentially over. Microkernels have won.
   The only real argument for monolithic systems was performance, and there
   is now enough evidence showing that microkernel systems can be just as
   fast as monolithic systems (e.g., Rick Rashid has published papers comparing
   Mach 3.0 to monolithic systems) that it is now all over but the shoutin'.

   MINIX is a microkernel-based system. The file system and memory management
   are separate processes, running outside the kernel. The I/O drivers are
   also separate processes (in the kernel, but only because the brain-dead
   nature of the Intel CPUs makes that difficult to do otherwise). LINUX is
   a monolithic style system. This is a giant step back into the 1970s.
   That is like taking an existing, working C program and rewriting it in
   BASIC. To me, writing a monolithic system in 1991 is a truly poor idea.

2. PORTABILITY
   Once upon a time there was the 4004 CPU. When it grew up it became an
   8008. Then it underwent plastic surgery and became the 8080. It begat
   the 8086, which begat the 8088, which begat the 80286, which begat the
   80386, which begat the 80486, and so on unto the N-th generation. In
   the meantime, RISC chips happened, and some of them are running at over
   100 MIPS. Speeds of 200 MIPS and more are likely in the coming years.
   These things are not going to suddenly vanish. What is going to happen

is that they will gradually take over from the 80x86 line. They will
run old MS-DOS programs by interpreting the 80386 in software. (I even
wrote my own IBM PC simulator in C, which you can get by FTP from
ftp.cs.vu.nl = 192.31.231.42 in dir minix/simulator.) I think it is a
gross error to design an OS for any specific architecture, since that is
not going to be around all that long.

MINIX was designed to be reasonably portable, and has been ported from the
Intel line to the 680x0 (Atari, Amiga, Macintosh), SPARC, and NS32016.
LINUX is tied fairly closely to the 80x86. Not the way to go.

Don't get me wrong, I am not unhappy with LINUX. It will get all the people
who want to turn MINIX in BSD UNIX off my back. But in all honesty, I would
suggest that people who want a **MODERN** "free" OS look around for a
microkernel-based, portable OS, like maybe GNU or something like that.

Andy Tanenbaum (ast@cs.vu.nl)

P.S. Just as a random aside, Amoeba has a UNIX emulator (running in user
space), but it is far from complete. If there are any people who would
like to work on that, please let me know. To run Amoeba you need a few 386s,
one of which needs 16M, and all of which need the WD Ethernet card.

From: torvalds@klaava.Helsinki.FI (Linus Benedict Torvalds)
Subject: Re: LINUX is obsolete
Date: 29 Jan 92 23:14:26 GMT
Organization: University of Helsinki

Well, with a subject like this, I'm afraid I'll have to reply.
Apologies to minix-users who have heard enough about linux anyway. I'd
like to be able to just "ignore the bait", but ... Time for some
serious flamefesting!

In article <12595@star.cs.vu.nl> ast@cs.vu.nl (Andy Tanenbaum) writes:
>
>I was in the U.S. for a couple of weeks, so I haven't commented much on
>LINUX (not that I would have said much had I been around), but for what
>it is worth, I have a couple of comments now.
>
>As most of you know, for me MINIX is a hobby, something that I do in the
>evening when I get bored writing books and there are no major wars,
>revolutions, or senate hearings being televised live on CNN. My real
>job is a professor and researcher in the area of operating systems.

You use this as an excuse for the limitations of minix? Sorry, but you
loose: I've got more excuses than you have, and linux still beats the
pants of minix in almost all areas. Not to mention the fact that most
of the good code for PC minix seems to have been written by Bruce Evans.

Re 1: you doing minix as a hobby - look at who makes money off minix,
and who gives linux out for free. Then talk about hobbies. Make minix
freely available, and one of my biggest gripes with it will disappear.
Linux has very much been a hobby (but a serious one: the best type) for
me: I get no money for it, and it's not even part of any of my studies
in the university. I've done it all on my own time, and on my own
machine.

Re 2: your job is being a professor and researcher: That's one hell of a good excuse for some of the brain-damages of minix. I can only hope (and assume) that Amoeba doesn't suck like minix does.

>1. MICROKERNEL VS MONOLITHIC SYSTEM

True, linux is monolithic, and I agree that microkernels are nicer. With a less argumentative subject, I'd probably have agreed with most of what you said. From a theoretical (and aesthetical) standpoint linux looses. If the GNU kernel had been ready last spring, I'd not have bothered to even start my project: the fact is that it wasn't and still isn't. Linux wins heavily on points of being available now.

>   MINIX is a microkernel-based system. [deleted, but not so that you
> miss the point] LINUX is a monolithic style system.

If this was the only criterion for the "goodness" of a kernel, you'd be right. What you don't mention is that minix doesn't do the micro-kernel thing very well, and has problems with real multitasking (in the kernel). If I had made an OS that had problems with a multithreading filesystem, I wouldn't be so fast to condemn others: in fact, I'd do my damndest to make others forget about the fiasco.

[yes, I know there are multithreading hacks for minix, but they are hacks, and bruce evans tells me there are lots of race conditions]

>2. PORTABILITY

"Portability is for people who cannot write new programs"
            -me, right now (with tongue in cheek)

The fact is that linux is more portable than minix. What? I hear you say. It's true - but not in the sense that ast means: I made linux as conformant to standards as I knew how (without having any POSIX standard in front of me). Porting things to linux is generally /much/ easier than porting them to minix.

I agree that portability is a good thing: but only where it actually has some meaning. There is no idea in trying to make an operating system overly portable: adhering to a portable API is good enough. The very /idea/ of an operating system is to use the hardware features, and hide them behind a layer of high-level calls. That is exactly what linux does: it just uses a bigger subset of the 386 features than other kernels seem to do. Of course this makes the kernel proper unportable, but it also makes for a /much/ simpler design. An acceptable trade-off, and one that made linux possible in the first place.

I also agree that linux takes the non-portability to an extreme: I got my 386 last January, and linux was partly a project to teach me about it. Many things should have been done more portably if it would have been a real project. I'm not making overly many excuses about it though: it was a design decision, and last april when I started the thing, I didn't think anybody would actually want to use it. I'm happy

to report I was wrong, and as my source is freely available, anybody is
free to try to port it, even though it won't be easy.

Linus

PS. I apologise for sometimes sounding too harsh: minix is nice enough
if you have nothing else. Amoeba might be nice if you have 5-10 spare
386's lying around, but I certainly don't. I don't usually get into
flames, but I'm touchy when it comes to linux :)

From: ast@cs.vu.nl (Andy Tanenbaum)
Subject: Re: LINUX is obsolete
Date: 30 Jan 92 13:44:34 GMT

In article <1992Jan29.231426.20469@klaava.Helsinki.FI> torvalds@klaava.Helsinki.
FI (Linus Benedict Torvalds) writes:
>You use this [being a professor] as an excuse for the limitations of minix?
The limitations of MINIX relate at least partly to my being a professor:
An explicit design goal was to make it run on cheap hardware so students
could afford it. In particular, for years it ran on a regular 4.77 MHZ PC
with no hard disk. You could do everything here including modify and recompile
the system. Just for the record, as of about 1 year ago, there were two
versions, one for the PC (360K diskettes) and one for the 286/386 (1.2M).
The PC version was outselling the 286/386 version by 2 to 1. I don't have
figures, but my guess is that the fraction of the 60 million existing PCs that
are 386/486 machines as opposed to 8088/286/680x0 etc is small. Among students
it is even smaller. Making software free, but only for folks with enough money
to buy first class hardware is an interesting concept.
Of course 5 years from now that will be different, but 5 years from now
everyone will be running free GNU on their 200 MIPS, 64M SPARCstation-5.

>Re 2: your job is being a professor and researcher: That's one hell of a
>good excuse for some of the brain-damages of minix. I can only hope (and
>assume) that Amoeba doesn't suck like minix does.
Amoeba was not designed to run on an 8088 with no hard disk.

>If this was the only criterion for the "goodness" of a kernel, you'd be
>right. What you don't mention is that minix doesn't do the micro-kernel
>thing very well, and has problems with real multitasking (in the
>kernel). If I had made an OS that had problems with a multithreading
>filesystem, I wouldn't be so fast to condemn others: in fact, I'd do my
>damndest to make others forget about the fiasco.
A multithreaded file system is only a performance hack. When there is only
one job active, the normal case on a small PC, it buys you nothing and adds
complexity to the code. On machines fast enough to support multiple users,
you probably have enough buffer cache to insure a hit cache hit rate, in
which case multithreading also buys you nothing. It is only a win when there
are multiple processes actually doing real disk I/O. Whether it is worth
making the system more complicated for this case is at least debatable.

I still maintain the point that designing a monolithic kernel in 1991 is
a fundamental error. Be thankful you are not my student. You would not
get a high grade for such a design :-)

>The fact is that linux is more portable than minix. What? I hear you
>say. It's true - but not in the sense that ast means: I made linux as

>conformant to standards as I knew how (without having any POSIX standard
>in front of me). Porting things to linux is generally /much/ easier
>than porting them to minix.
MINIX was designed before POSIX, and is now being (slowly) POSIXized as
everyone who follows this newsgroup knows. Everyone agrees that user-level
standards are a good idea. As an aside, I congratulate you for being able
to write a POSIX-conformant system without having the POSIX standard in front
of you. I find it difficult enough after studying the standard at great length.

My point is that writing a new operating system that is closely tied to any
particular piece of hardware, especially a weird one like the Intel line,
is basically wrong. An OS itself should be easily portable to new hardware
platforms. When OS/360 was written in assembler for the IBM 360
25 years ago, they probably could be excused. When MS-DOS was written
specifically for the 8088 ten years ago, this was less than brilliant, as
IBM and Microsoft now only too painfully realize. Writing a new OS only for the
386 in 1991 gets you your second 'F' for this term. But if you do real well
on the final exam, you can still pass the course.

Prof. Andrew S. Tanenbaum (ast@cs.vu.nl)

From: feustel@netcom.COM (David Feustel)
Subject: Re: LINUX is obsolete
Date: 30 Jan 92 18:57:28 GMT
Organization: DAFCO - An OS/2 Oasis

ast@cs.vu.nl (Andy Tanenbaum) writes:

>I still maintain the point that designing a monolithic kernel in 1991 is
>a fundamental error. Be thankful you are not my student. You would not
>get a high grade for such a design :-)

That's ok. Einstein got lousy grades in math and physics.

From: pete@ohm.york.ac.uk (-Pete French.)
Subject: Re: LINUX is obsolete
Date: 31 Jan 92 09:49:37 GMT
Organization: Electronics Department, University of York, UK

in article <1992Jan30.195850.7023@epas.toronto.edu>, meggin@epas.utoronto.ca
(David Megginson) says:
>
> In article <1992Jan30.185728.26477feustel@netcom.COM> feustel@netcom.COM (David
> Feustel) writes:
>>
>>That's ok. Einstein got lousy grades in math and physics.
>
> And Dan Quayle got low grades in political science. I think that there
> are more Dan Quayles than Einsteins out there... ;-)

What a horrible thought !

But on the points about microkernel v monolithic, isnt this partly an
artifact of the language being used ? MINIX may well be designed as a
microkernel system, but in the end you still end up with a large
monolithic chunk of binary data that gets loaded in as "the OS". Isnt it

written as separate programs simply because C does not support the idea
of multiple processes within a single piece of monolithic code. Is there
any real difference between a microkernel written as several pieces of C
and a monolithic kernel written in something like OCCAM ? I would have
thought that in this case the monolithic design would be a better one
than the micorkernel style since with the advantage of inbuilt
language concurrency the kernel could be made even more modular than the
MINIX one is.

Anyone for MINOX :-)

-bat.

From: kt4@prism.gatech.EDU (Ken Thompson)
Subject: Re: LINUX is obsolete
Date: 3 Feb 92 23:07:54 GMT
Organization: Georgia Institute of Technology

viewpoint may be largely unrelated to its usefulness. Many if not
most of the software we use is probably obsolete according to the
latest design criteria. Most users could probably care less if the
internals of the operating system they use is obsolete. They are
rightly more interested in its performance and capabilities at the
user level.

I would generally agree that microkernels are probably the wave of
the future. However, it is in my opinion easier to implement a
monolithic kernel. It is also easier for it to turn into a mess in
a hurry as it is modified.

                    Regards,
                        Ken

From: kevin@taronga.taronga.com (Kevin Brown)
Subject: Re: LINUX is obsolete
Date: 4 Feb 92 08:08:42 GMT
Organization: University of Houston

In article <47607@hydra.gatech.EDU> kt4@prism.gatech.EDU (Ken Thompson) writes:
>viewpoint may be largely unrelated to its usefulness. Many if not
>most of the software we use is probably obsolete according to the
>latest design criteria. Most users could probably care less if the
>internals of the operating system they use is obsolete. They are
>rightly more interested in its performance and capabilities at the
>user level.
>
>I would generally agree that microkernels are probably the wave of
>the future. However, it is in my opinion easier to implement a
>monolithic kernel. It is also easier for it to turn into a mess in
>a hurry as it is modified.

How difficult is it to structure the source tree of a monolithic kernel
such that most modifications don't have a large negative impact on the
source? What sorts of pitfalls do you run into in this sort of endeavor,
and what suggestions do you have for dealing with them?

I guess what I'm asking is: how difficult is it to organize the source
such that most changes to the kernel remain localized in scope, even
though the kernel itself is monolithic?

I figure you've got years of experience with monolithic kernels :-),
so I'd think you'd have the best shot at answering questions like
these.

Kevin Brown

From: rburns@finess.Corp.Sun.COM (Randy Burns)
Subject: Re: LINUX is obsolete
Date: 30 Jan 92 20:33:07 GMT
Organization: Sun Microsystems, Mt. View, Ca.

In article <12615@star.cs.vu.nl> ast@cs.vu.nl (Andy Tanenbaum) writes:
>In article <1992Jan29.231426.20469@klaava.Helsinki.FI> torvalds@klaava.Helsinki.
>FI (Linus Benedict Torvalds) writes:

>Of course 5 years from now that will be different, but 5 years from now
>everyone will be running free GNU on their 200 MIPS, 64M SPARCstation-5.
Well, I for one would _love_ to see this happen.

>>The fact is that linux is more portable than minix. What? I hear you
>>say. It's true - but not in the sense that ast means: I made linux as
>>conformant to standards as I knew how (without having any POSIX standard
>>in front of me). Porting things to linux is generally /much/ easier
>>than porting them to minix.
....
>My point is that writing a new operating system that is closely tied to any
>particular piece of hardware, especially a weird one like the Intel line,
>is basically wrong.
First off, the parts of Linux tuned most finely to the 80x86 are the Kernel
and the devices. My own sense is that even if Linux is simply a stopgap
measure to let us all run GNU software, it is still worthwhile to have a
a finely tuned kernel for the most numerous architecture presently in
existance.

> An OS itself should be easily portable to new hardware
>platforms.
Well, the only part of Linux that isn't portable is the kernel and drivers.
Compare to the compilers, utilities, windowing system etc. this is really
a small part of the effort. Since Linux has a large degree of call
compatibility with portable OS's I wouldn't complain. I'm personally
very grateful to have an OS that makes it more likely that some of us will
be able to take advantage of the software that has come out of Berkeley,
FSF, CMU etc. It may well be that in 2-3 years when ultra cheap BSD
variants and Hurd proliferate, that Linux will be obsolete. Still, right
now Linux greatly reduces the cost of using tools like gcc, bison, bash
which are useful in the development of such an OS.

From: torvalds@klaava.Helsinki.FI (Linus Benedict Torvalds)
Subject: Re: LINUX is obsolete
Date: 31 Jan 92 10:33:23 GMT
Organization: University of Helsinki

In article <12615@star.cs.vu.nl> ast@cs.vu.nl (Andy Tanenbaum) writes:
>The limitations of MINIX relate at least partly to my being a professor:
>An explicit design goal was to make it run on cheap hardware so students
>could afford it.

All right: a real technical point, and one that made some of my comments
inexcusable. But at the same time you shoot yourself in the foot a bit:
now you admit that some of the errors of minix were that it was too
portable: including machines that weren't really designed to run unix.
That assumption lead to the fact that minix now cannot easily be
extended to have things like paging, even for machines that would
support it. Yes, minix is portable, but you can rewrite that as
"doesn't use any features", and still be right.

>A multithreaded file system is only a performance hack.

Not true. It's a performance hack /on a microkernel/, but it's an
automatic feature when you write a monolithic kernel - one area where
microkernels don't work too well (as I pointed out in my personal mail
to ast). When writing a unix the "obsolete" way, you automatically get
a multithreaded kernel: every process does it's own job, and you don't
have to make ugly things like message queues to make it work
efficiently.

Besides, there are people who would consider "only a performance hack"
vital: unless you have a cray-3, I'd guess everybody gets tired of
waiting on the computer all the time. I know I did with minix (and yes,
I do with linux too, but it's /much/ better).

>I still maintain the point that designing a monolithic kernel in 1991 is
>a fundamental error. Be thankful you are not my student. You would not
>get a high grade for such a design :-)

Well, I probably won't get too good grades even without you: I had an
argument (completely unrelated - not even pertaining to OS's) with the
person here at the university that teaches OS design. I wonder when
I'll learn :)

>My point is that writing a new operating system that is closely tied to any
>particular piece of hardware, especially a weird one like the Intel line,
>is basically wrong.

But /my/ point is that the operating system /isn't/ tied to any
processor line: UNIX runs on most real processors in existence. Yes,
the /implementation/ is hardware-specific, but there's a HUGE
difference. You mention OS/360 and MS-DOG as examples of bad designs
as they were hardware-dependent, and I agree. But there's a big
difference between these and linux: linux API is portable (not due to my
clever design, but due to the fact that I decided to go for a fairly-
well-thought-out and tested OS: unix.)

If you write programs for linux today, you shouldn't have too many
surprises when you just recompile them for Hurd in the 21st century. As
has been noted (not only by me), the linux kernel is a miniscule part of
a complete system: Full sources for linux currently runs to about 200kB
compressed - full sources to a somewhat complete developement system is

at least 10MB compressed (and easily much, much more). And all of that
source is portable, except for this tiny kernel that you can (provably:
I did it) re-write totally from scratch in less than a year without
having /any/ prior knowledge.

In fact the /whole/ linux kernel is much smaller than the 386-dependent
things in mach: i386.tar.Z for the current version of mach is well over
800kB compressed (823391 bytes according to nic.funet.fi). Admittedly,
mach is "somewhat" bigger and has more features, but that should still
tell you something.

      Linus

From: kaufman@eecs.nwu.edu (Michael L. Kaufman)
Subject: Re: LINUX is obsolete
Date: 3 Feb 92 22:27:48 GMT
Organization: EECS Department, Northwestern University

I tried to send these two posts from work, but I think they got eaten. If you
have seen them already, sorry.

Andy Tanenbaum writes an interesting article (also interesting was finding out
that he actually reads this group) but I think he is missing an important
point.

He Wrote:
>As most of you know, for me MINIX is a hobby, ...

Which is also probably true of most, if not all, of the people who are involved
in Linux. We are not developing a system to take over the OS market, we are
just having a good time.

>   What is going to happen
>   is that they will gradually take over from the 80x86 line. They will
>   run old MS-DOS programs by interpreting the 80386 in software.

Well when this happens, if I still want to play with Linux, I can just run it
on my 386 simulator.

>   MINIX was designed to be reasonably portable, and has been ported from the
>   Intel line to the 680x0 (Atari, Amiga, Macintosh), SPARC, and NS32016.
>   LINUX is tied fairly closely to the 80x86. Not the way to go.

That's fine for the people who have those machines, but it wasn't a free
lunch. That portibility was gained at the cost of some performance and some
features on the 386. Before you decide that LINUX is not the way to go, you
should think about what it is going to be used for. I am going to use it for
running memory and computation intensive graphics programs on my 486. For me,
speed and memory were more important then future state-of-the-artness and
portability.

>But in all honesty, I would
>suggest that people who want a **MODERN** "free" OS look around for a
>microkernel-based, portable OS, like maybe GNU or something like that.

I don't know of any free microkernel-based, portable OSes. GNU is still
vaporware, and likely to remain that way for the forseeable future. Do
you actually have one to recomend, or are you just toying with me? ;-)

In article <12615@star.cs.vu.nl> ast@cs.vu.nl (Andy Tanenbaum) writes:
>My point is that writing a new operating system that is closely tied to any
>particular piece of hardware, especially a weird one like the Intel line,
>is basically wrong. An OS itself should be easily portable to new hardware
>platforms.

I think I see where I disagree with you now. You are looking at OS design
as an end in itself. Minix is good because it is portable/Micro-Kernal/etc.
Linux is not good because it is monolithic/tightly tied to Intel/etc. That
is not a strange attitude for someone in the acedemic world, but it is not
something you should expect to be universally shared. Linux is not being written
as a teaching tool, or as an abstract exercise. It is being written to allow
people to run GNU-type software _today_. The fact that it may not be in use
in five years is less important then the fact that today (well, by April
probably) I can run all sorts of software on it that I want to run. You keep
saying that Minix is better, but if it will not run the software that I want
to run, it really isn't that good (for me) at all.

>   When OS/360 was written in assembler for the IBM 360
>25 years ago, they probably could be excused. When MS-DOS was written
>specifically for the 8088 ten years ago, this was less than brilliant, as
>IBM and Microsoft now only too painfully realize.

Same point. MSoft did not come out with Dos to "explore the frontiers of os
research". They did it to make a buck. And considering the fact that MS-DOS
probably still outsells everyone else put together, I don't think that you
say that they have failed _in their goals_. Not that MS-Dos is the best OS
in terms of anything else, only that it has served their needs.

Michael

From: julien@incal.inria.fr (Julien Maisonneuve)
Subject: Re: LINUX is obsolete
Date: 3 Feb 92 17:10:14 GMT

I would like to second Kevin brown in most of his remarks.
I'll add a few user points :
- When ast states that FS multithreading is useless, it reminds me of the many
times I tried to let a job run in the background (like when reading an archive on
a floppy), it is just unusable, the & shell operator could even have been left
out.
- Most interesting utilities are not even compilable under Minix because of the
ATK compiler's incredible limits. Those were hardly understandable on a basic PC,
but become absurd on a 386. Every stupid DOS compiler has a large model (more
expensive, OK). I hate the 13 bit compress !
- The lack of Virtual Memory support prevents people studying this area to
experiment, and prevents users to use large programs. The strange design of the
MM also makes it hard to modify.

The problem is that even doing exploratory work under minix is painful.
If you want to get any work done (or even fun), even DOS is becoming a better
alternative (with things like DJ GPP).
In its basic form, it is really no more than OS course example, a good
toy, but a toy. Obtaining and applying patches is a pain, and precludes further
upgrades.

Too bad when not so much is missing to make it really good.
Thanks for the work andy, but Linux didn't deserve your answer.
For the common people, it does many things better than Minix.

Julien Maisonneuve.

This is not a flame, just my experience.

From: richard@aiai.ed.ac.uk (Richard Tobin)
Subject: Re: LINUX is obsolete
Date: 4 Feb 92 14:46:49 GMT
Reply-To: richard@aiai.UUCP (Richard Tobin)
Organization: AIAI, University of Edinburgh, Scotland

In article <12615@star.cs.vu.nl> ast@cs.vu.nl (Andy Tanenbaum) writes:
>A multithreaded file system is only a performance hack. When there is only
>one job active, the normal case on a small PC, it buys you nothing

I find the single-threaded file system a serious pain when using
Minix. I often want to do something else while reading files from the
(excruciatingly slow) floppy disk. I rather like to play rogue while
waiting for large C or Lisp compilations. I look to look at files in
one editor buffer while compiling in another.

(The problem would be somewhat less if the file system stuck to
serving files and didn't interact with terminal i/o.)

Of course, in basic Minix with no virtual consoles and no chance of
running emacs, this isn't much of a problem. But to most people
that's a failure, not an advantage. It just isn't the case that on
single-user machines there's no use for more than one active process;
the idea only has any plausibility because so many people are used to
poor machines with poor operating systems.

As to portability, Minix only wins because of its limited ambitions.
If you wanted a full-featured Unix with paging, job-control, a window
system and so on, would it be quicker to start from basic Minix and
add the features, or to start from Linux and fix the 386-specific
bits? I don't think it's fair to criticise Linux when its aims are so
different from Minix's. If you want a system for pedagogical use,
Minix is the answer. But if what you want is an environment as much
like (say) a Sun as possible on your home computer, it has some
deficiencies.

-- Richard

From: ast@cs.vu.nl (Andy Tanenbaum)
Subject: Re: LINUX is obsolete
Date: 5 Feb 92 14:48:48 GMT
Organization: Fac. Wiskunde & Informatica, Vrije Universiteit, Amsterdam

In article <6121@skye.ed.ac.uk> richard@aiai.UUCP (Richard Tobin) writes:
>If you wanted a full-featured Unix with paging, job-control, a window
>system and so on, would it be quicker to start from basic Minix and
>add the features, or to start from Linux and fix the 386-specific
>bits?

Another option that seems to be totally forgotten here is buy UNIX or a
clone. If you just want to USE the system, instead of hacking on its
internals, you don't need source code. Coherent is only $99, and there
are various true UNIX systems with more features for more money. For the
true hacker, not having source code is fatal, but for people who just
want a UNIX system, there are many alternatives (albeit not free).

Andy Tanenbaum (ast@cs.vul.nl)

From: ajt@doc.ic.ac.uk (Tony Travis)
Subject: Re: LINUX is obsolete
Date: 6 Feb 92 02:17:13 GMT
Organization: Department of Computing, Imperial College, University of London,
UK.

ast@cs.vu.nl (Andy Tanenbaum) writes:
> Another option that seems to be totally forgotten here is buy UNIX or a
> clone. If you just want to USE the system, instead of hacking on its
> internals, you don't need source code. Coherent is only $99, and there
> are various true UNIX systems with more features for more money. For the
> true hacker, not having source code is fatal, but for people who just
> want a UNIX system, there are many alternatives (albeit not free).

Andy, I have followed the development of Minix since the first messages
were posted to this group and I am now running 1.5.10 with Bruce
Evans's patches for the 386.

I 'just' want a Unix on my PC and I am not interested in hacking on its
internals, but I *do* want the source code!

An important principle underlying the success and popularity of Unix is
the philosophy of building on the work of others.

This philosophy relies upon the availability of the source code in
order that it can be examined, modified and re-used in new software.

Many years ago, I was in the happy position of being an AT&T Seventh
Edition Unix source licencee but, even then, I saw your decision to
make the source of Minix available as liberation from the shackles of
AT&T copyright!!

I think you may sometimes forget that your 'hobby' has had a profound
effect on the availability of 'personal' Unix (ie. affordable Unix) and
that the 8086 PC I ran Minix 1.2 on actually cost me considerably more
than my present 386/SX clone.

Clearly, Minix _cannot_ be all things to all men, but I see the
progress to 386 versions in much the same way that I see 68000 or other
linear address space architectures: it is a good thing for people like
me who use Minix and feel constrained by the segmented architecture of
the PC version for applications.

NOTHING you can say would convince me that I should use Coherent ...

     Tony

From: richard@aiai.ed.ac.uk (Richard Tobin)
Subject: Re: LINUX is obsolete
Date: 7 Feb 92 14:58:22 GMT
Organization: AIAI, University of Edinburgh, Scotland

In article <12696@star.cs.vu.nl> ast@cs.vu.nl (Andy Tanenbaum) writes:
>If you just want to USE the system, instead of hacking on its
>internals, you don't need source code.

Unfortunately hacking on the internals is just what many of us want
the system for... You'll be rid of most of us when BSD-detox or GNU
comes out, which should happen in the next few months (yeah, right).

-- Richard

From: comm121@unixg.ubc.ca (Louie)
Subject: Re: LINUX is obsolete
Date: 30 Jan 92 02:55:22 GMT
Organization: University of British Columbia, Vancouver, B.C., Canada

In <12595@star.cs.vu.nl> ast@cs.vu.nl (Andy Tanenbaum) writes:

>But in all honesty, I would
>suggest that people who want a **MODERN** "free" OS look around for a
>microkernel-based, portable OS, like maybe GNU or something like that.

There are really no other alternatives other than Linux for people like
me who want a "free" OS. Considering that the majority of people who
would use a "free" OS use the 386, portability is really not all that
big of a concern. If I had a Sparc I would use Solaris.

As it stands, I installed Linux with gcc, emacs 18.57, kermit and all of the
GNU utilities without any trouble at all. No need to apply patches. I
just followed the installation instructions. I can't get an OS like
this *anywhere* for the price to do my Computer Science homework. And
it seems like network support and then X-Windows will be ported to Linux
well before Minix. This is something that would be really useful. In my
opinion, portability of standard Unix software is important also.

I know that the design using a monolithic system is not as good as the
microkernel. But for the short term future (And I know I won't/can't
be uprading from my 386), Linux suits me perfectly.

Philip Wu
pwu@unixg.ubc.ca

From: dgraham@bmers30.bnr.ca (Douglas Graham)
Subject: Re: LINUX is obsolete
Date: 1 Feb 92 00:26:30 GMT
Organization: Bell-Northern Research, Ottawa, Canada

In article <12595@star.cs.vu.nl> ast@cs.vu.nl (Andy Tanenbaum) writes:

> While I could go into a long story here about the relative merits of the
> two designs, suffice it to say that among the people who actually design
> operating systems, the debate is essentially over. Microkernels have won.

Can you recommend any (unbiased) literature that points out the strengths
and weaknesses of the two approaches? I'm sure that there is something
to be said for the microkernel approach, but I wonder how closely
Minix resembles the other systems that use it. Sure, Minix uses lots
of tasks and messages, but there must be more to a microkernel architecture
than that. I suspect that the Minix code is not split optimally into tasks.

> The only real argument for monolithic systems was performance, and there
> is now enough evidence showing that microkernel systems can be just as
> fast as monolithic systems (e.g., Rick Rashid has published papers comparing
> Mach 3.0 to monolithic systems) that it is now all over but the shoutin`.

My main complaint with Minix is not it's performance. It is that adding
features is a royal pain -- something that I presume a microkernel
architecure is supposed to alleviate.

> MINIX is a microkernel-based system.

Is there a consensus on this?

> LINUX is
> a monolithic style system. This is a giant step back into the 1970s.
> That is like taking an existing, working C program and rewriting it in
> BASIC. To me, writing a monolithic system in 1991 is a truly poor idea.

This is a fine assertion, but I've yet to see any rationale for it.
Linux is only about 12000 lines of code I think. I don't see how
splitting that into tasks and blasting messages around would improve it.

>Don't get me wrong, I am not unhappy with LINUX. It will get all the people
>who want to turn MINIX in BSD UNIX off my back. But in all honesty, I would
>suggest that people who want a **MODERN** "free" OS look around for a
>microkernel-based, portable OS, like maybe GNU or something like that.

Well, there are no other choices that I'm aware of at the moment. But
when GNU OS comes out, I'll very likely jump ship again. I sense that
you *are* somewhat unhappy about Linux (and that surprises me somewhat).
I would guess that the reason so many people embraced it, is because it
offers more features. Your approach to people requesting features in
Minix, has generally been to tell them that they didn't really want that
feature anyway. I submit that the exodus in the direction of Linux
proves you wrong.

Disclaimer: I had nothing to do with Linux development. I just find
            it an easier system to understand than Minix.
--
Doug Graham   dgraham@bnr.ca   My opinions are my own.

From: hedrick@klinzhai.rutgers.edu (Charles Hedrick)
Subject: Re: LINUX is obsolete
Date: 1 Feb 92 00:27:04 GMT
Organization: Rutgers Univ., New Brunswick, N.J.

The history of software shows that availability wins out over
technical quality every time. That's Linux' major advantage. It's a
small 386-based system that's fairly compatible with generic Unix, and
is freely available. I dropped out of the Minix community a couple of
years ago when it became clear that (1) Minix was not going to take
advantage of anything beyond the 8086 anytime in the near future, and
(2) the licensing -- while amazingly friendly -- still made it hard
for people who were interested in producing a 386 version. Several
people apparently did nice work for the 386. But all they could
distribute were diffs. This made bringing up a 386 system a job that
isn't practical for a new user, and in fact I wasn't sure I wanted to
do it.

I apologize if things have changed in the last couple of years. If
it's now possible to get a 386 version in a form that's ready to run,
the community has developed a way to share Minix source, and bringing
up normal Unix programs has become easier in the interim, then I'm
willing to reconsider Minix. I do like its design.

It's possible that Linux will be overtaken by Gnu or a free BSD.
However, if the Gnu OS follows the example of all other Gnu software,
it will require a system with 128MB of memory and a 1GB disk to use.
There will still be room for a small system. My ideal OS would be 4.4
BSD. But 4.4's release date has a history of extreme slippage. With
most of their staff moving to BSDI, it's hard to believe that this
situation is going to be improved. For my own personal use, the BSDI
system will probably be great. But even their very attractive pricing
is likely to be too much for most of our students, and even though
users can get source from them, the fact that some of it is
proprietary will again mean that you can't just put altered code out
for public FTP. At any rate, Linux exists, and the rest of these
alternatives are vapor.

From: tytso@athena.mit.edu (Theodore Y. Ts'o)
Subject: Re: LINUX is obsolete
Date: 31 Jan 92 21:40:23 GMT
Organization: Massachusetts Institute of Technology
In-Reply-To: ast@cs.vu.nl's message of 29 Jan 92 12: 12:50 GMT

>From: ast@cs.vu.nl (Andy Tanenbaum)

>ftp.cs.vu.nl = 192.31.231.42 in dir minix/simulator.) I think it is a
>gross error to design an OS for any specific architecture, since that is
>not going to be around all that long.

It's not your fault for believing that Linux is tied to the 80386
architecture, since many Linux supporters (including Linus himself) have
made the this statement. However, the amount of 80386-specific code is
probably not much more than what is in a Minix implementation, and there
is certainly a lot less 80386 specific code in Linux than here is
Vax-specific code in BSD 4.3.

Granted, the port to other architectures hasn't been done yet. But if I
were going to bring up a Unix-like system on a new architecture, I'd
probably start with Linux rather than Minix, simply because I want to
have some control over what I can do with the resulting system when I'm
done with it. Yes, I'd have to rewrite large portions of the VM and
device driver layers --- but I'd have to do that with any other OS.
Maybe it would be a little bit harder than it would to port Minix to the
new architecture; but this would probably be only true for the first
architecture that we ported Linux to.

>While I could go into a long story here about the relative merits of the
>two designs, suffice it to say that among the people who actually design
>operating systems, the debate is essentially over. Microkernels have won.
>The only real argument for monolithic systems was performance, and there
>is now enough evidence showing that microkernel systems can be just as
>fast as monolithic systems (e.g., Rick Rashid has published papers comparing
>Mach 3.0 to monolithic systems) that it is now all over but the shoutin'.

This is not necessarily the case; I think you're painting a much more
black and white view of the universe than necessarily exists. I refer
you to such papers as Brent Welsh's (welch@parc.xerox.com) "The
Filsystem Belongs in the Kernel" paper, where in he argues that the
filesystem is a mature enough abstraction that it should live in the
kernel, not outside of it as it would in a strict microkernel design.

There also several people who have been concerned about the speed of
OSF/1 Mach when compared with monolithic systems; in particular, the
nubmer of context switches required to handle network traffic, and
networked filesystems in particular.

I am aware of the benefits of a micro kernel approach. However, the
fact remains that Linux is here, and GNU isn't --- and people have been
working on Hurd for a lot longer than Linus has been working on Linux.
Minix doesn't count because it's not free.   :-)

I suspect that the balance of micro kernels versus monolithic kernels
depend on what you're doing. If you're interested in doing research, it
is obviously much easier to rip out and replace modules in a micro
kernel, and since only researchers write papers about operating systems,
ipso facto micro kernels must be the right approach. However, I do know
a lot of people who are not researchers, but who are rather practical
kernel programmers, who have a lot of concerns over the cost of copying
and the cost of context switches which are incurred in a micro kernel.

By the way, I don't buy your arguments that you don't need a
multi-threaded filesystem on a single user system. Once you bring up a
windowing system, and have a compile going in one window, a news reader
in another window, and UUCP/C News going in the background, you want
good filesystem performance, even on a single-user system. Maybe to a

theorist it's an unnecessary optimization and a (to use your words)
"performance hack", but I'm interested in a Real operating system ---
not a research toy.
=-=
Theodore Ts'o   bloom-beacon!mit-athena!tytso
308 High St., Medford, MA 02155   tytso@athena.mit.edu
    Everybody's playing the game, but nobody's rules are the same!

From: joe@jshark.rn.com
Subject: Re: LINUX is obsolete
Date: 31 Jan 92 13:21:44 GMT
Organization: a blip of entropy

In article <12595@star.cs.vu.nl> ast@cs.vu.nl (Andy Tanenbaum) writes:
>
>   MINIX was designed to be reasonably portable, and has been ported from the
>   Intel line to the 680x0 (Atari, Amiga, Macintosh), SPARC, and NS32016.
>   LINUX is tied fairly closely to the 80x86. Not the way to go.

If you looked at the source instead of believing the author, you'd realise
this is not true!

He's replaced 'fubyte' by a routine which explicitly uses a segment register
- but that could be easily changed. Similarly, apart from a couple of places
which assume the '386 MMU, a couple of macros to hide the exact page sizes
etc would make porting trivial. Using '386 TSS's makes the code simpler,
but the VAX and WE32000 have similar structures.

As he's already admitted, a bit of planning would have the the system
neater, but merely putting '386 assembler around isn't a crime!

And with all due respect:
  - the Book didn't make an issue of portability (apart from a few
    "#ifdef M8088"s)
  - by the time it was released, Minix had come to depend on several
    8086 "features" that caused uproar from the 68000 users.

>Andy Tanenbaum (ast@cs.vu.nl)

joe.

From: entropy@wintermute.WPI.EDU (Lawrence C. Foard)
Subject: Re: LINUX is obsolete
Date: 5 Feb 92 14:56:30 GMT
Organization: Worcester Polytechnic Institute

In article <12595@star.cs.vu.nl> ast@cs.vu.nl (Andy Tanenbaum) writes:
>Don`t get me wrong, I am not unhappy with LINUX. It will get all the people
>who want to turn MINIX in BSD UNIX off my back. But in all honesty, I would
>suggest that people who want a **MODERN** "free" OS look around for a
>microkernel-based, portable OS, like maybe GNU or something like that.

I believe you have some valid points, although I am not sure that a
microkernel is necessarily better. It might make more sense to allow some
combination of the two. As part of the IPC code I'm writting for Linux I am
going to include code that will allow device drivers and file systems to run

as user processes. These will be significantly slower though, and I believe it would be a mistake to move everything outside the kernel (TCP/IP will be internal).

Actually my main problem with OS theorists is that they have never tested there ideas! None of these ideas (with a partial exception for MACH) has ever seen the light of day. 32 bit home computers have been available for almost a decade and Linus was the first person to ever write a working OS for them that can be used without paying AT&T $100,000. A piece of software in hand is worth ten pieces of vaporware, OS theorists are quick to jump all over an OS but they are unwilling to ever provide an alternative.

The general consensus that Micro kernels is the way to go means nothing when a real application has never even run on one.

The release of Linux is allowing me to try some ideas I've been wanting to experment with for years, but I have never had the opportunity to work with source code for a functioning OS.

From: ast@cs.vu.nl (Andy Tanenbaum)
Subject: Re: LINUX is obsolete
Date: 5 Feb 92 23:33:23 GMT
Organization: Fac. Wiskunde & Informatica, Vrije Universiteit, Amsterdam

In article <1992Feb5.145630.759@wpi.WPI.EDU> entropy@wintermute.WPI.EDU (Lawrence C. Foard) writes:
>Actually my main problem with OS theorists is that they have never tested
>there ideas!
I'm mortally insulted. I AM NOT A THEORIST. Ask anybody who was at our department meeting yesterday (in joke).

Actually, these ideas have been very well tested in practice. OSF is betting its whole business on a microkernel (Mach 3.0). USL is betting its business on another one (Chorus). Both of these run lots of software, and both have been extensively compared to monolithic systems. Amoeba has been fully implemented and tested for a number of applications. QNX is a microkernel based system, and someone just told me the installed base is 200,000 systems. Microkernels are not a pipe dream. They represent proven technology.

The Mach guys wrote a paper called "UNIX as an application program." It was by Golub et al., in the Summer 1990 USENIX conference. The Chorus people also have a technical report on microkernel performance, and I coauthored another paper on the subject, which I mentioned yesterday (Dec. 1991 Computing Systems). Check them out.

Andy Tanenbaum (ast@cs.vu.nl)

From: peter@ferranti.com (peter da silva)
Subject: Re: LINUX is obsolete
Organization: Xenix Support, FICC
Date: Thu, 6 Feb 1992 16:02:47 GMT

In article <12747@star.cs.vu.nl> ast@cs.vu.nl (Andy Tanenbaum) writes:
> QNX is a microkernel
> based system, and someone just told me the installed base is 200,000 systems.

Oh yes, while I'm on the subject... there are over 3 million Amigas out there, which means that there are more of them than any UNIX vendor has shipped, and probably more than all UNIX systems combined.

From: peter@ferranti.com (peter da silva)
Subject: Re: LINUX is obsolete
Organization: Xenix Support, FICC
Date: Thu, 6 Feb 1992 16:00:22 GMT

In article <1992Feb5.145630.759@wpi.WPI.EDU> entropy@wintermute.WPI.EDU (Lawrence C. Foard) writes:
> Actually my main problem with OS theorists is that they have never tested
> there ideas!

I beg to differ... there are many microkernel operating systems out there for everything from an 8088 (QNX) up to large research systems.

> None of these ideas (with a partial exception for MACH) has ever
> seen the light of day. 32 bit home computers have been available for almost a
> decade and Linus was the first person to ever write a working OS for them
> that can be used without paying AT&T $100,000.

I must have been imagining AmigaOS, then. I've been using a figment of my imagination for the past 6 years.

AmigaOS is a microkernel message-passing design, with better response time and performance than any other readily available PC operating system: including MINIX, OS/2, Windows, MacOS, Linux, UNIX, and *certainly* MS-DOS.

The microkernel design has proven invaluable. Things like new file systems that are normally available only from the vendor are hobbyist products on the Amiga. Device drivers are simply shared libraries and tasks with specific entry points and message ports. So are file systems, the window system, and so on. It's a WONDERFUL design, and validates everything that people have been saying about microkernels. Yes, it takes more work to get them off the ground than a coroutine based macrokernel like UNIX, but the versatility pays you back many times over.

I really wish Andy would do a new MINIX based on what has been learned since the first release. The factoring of responsibilities in MINIX is fairly poor, but the basic concept is good.

> The general consensus that Micro kernels is the way to go means nothing when
> a real application has never even run on one.

I'm dreaming again. I sure throught Deluxe Paint, Sculpt 3d, Photon Paint, Manx C, Manx SDB, Perfect Sound, Videoscape 3d, and the other programs I bought for my Amiga were "real". I'll have to send the damn things back now, I guess.

The availability of Linux is great. I'm delighted it exists. I'm sure that the macrokernel design is one reason it has been implemented so fast, and this is a valid reason to use macrokernels. BUT... this doesn't mean that microkernels are inherently slow, or simply research toys.

From: dsmythe@netcom.COM (Dave Smythe)

Subject: Re: LINUX is obsolete
Date: 10 Feb 92 07:08:22 GMT
Organization: Netcom - Online Communication Services   (408 241-9760 guest)

In article <1992Feb5.145630.759@wpi.WPI.EDU> entropy@wintermute.WPI.EDU (Lawrence
C. Foard) writes:
>Actually my main problem with OS theorists is that they have never tested
>there ideas! None of these ideas (with a partial exception for MACH) has ever
>seen the light of day.

David Cheriton (Prof. at Stanford, and author of the V system) said something
similar to this in a class in distributed systems. Paraphrased:

  "There are two kinds of researchers: those that have implemented
   something and those that have not. The latter will tell you that
   there are 142 ways of doing things and that there isn't consensus
   on which is best. The former will simply tell you that 141 of
   them don't work."

He really rips on the OSI-philes as well, for a similar reason. The Internet
protocols are adapted only after having been in use for a period of time,
preventing things from getting standardized that will never be implementable
in a reasonable fashion. OSI adherents, on the other hand, seem intent on
standardizing everything possible, including "escapes" from the standard,
before a reasonable reference implementation exists. Consequently, you see
obsolete ideas immortalized, such as sub-byte-level data field packing,
which makes good performance difficult when your computer is drinking from
a 10+ Gbs fire-hose :-).

Just my $.02

D

From: torvalds@klaava.Helsinki.FI (Linus Benedict Torvalds)
Subject: Apologies (was Re: LINUX is obsolete)
Date: 30 Jan 92 15:38:16 GMT
Organization: University of Helsinki

In article <1992Jan29.231426.20469@klaava.Helsinki.FI> I wrote:
>Well, with a subject like this, I'm afraid I'll have to reply.

And reply I did, with complete abandon, and no thought for good taste
and netiquette. Apologies to ast, and thanks to John Nall for a friendy
"that's not how it's done"-letter. I over-reacted, and am now composing
a (much less acerbic) personal letter to ast. Hope nobody was turned
away from linux due to it being (a) possibly obsolete (I still think
that's not the case, although some of the criticisms are valid) and (b)
written by a hothead :-)

        Linus "my first, and hopefully last flamefest" Torvalds

----

From: pmacdona@sanjuan (Peter MacDonald)
Subject: re: Linux is obsolete
Date: 1 Feb 92 02:10:06 GMT
Organization: University of Victoria, Victoria, BC, CANADA

Since I think I posted one of the earliest messages in all this discussion
of Minix vs Linux, I feel compelled to comment on my reasons for
switching from Minix to Linux. In order of importance they are:

1) Linux is free
2) Linux is evolving at a satisfactory clip (because new features
   are accepted into the distribution by Linus).

The first requires some explanation, because if I have already purchased
Minix, what posssible concern could price have for me? Simple.
If the OS is free, many more people will use/support/enhance it.
This is also the same reasoning I used when I bought my 386 instead
of a sparc (which I could have got for just 30% more). Since
PCs are cheap and generally available, more people will buy/use
them and thus good, cheap/free software will be abundant.

The second should be pretty obvious to anyone who has been using Minix
for for any period of time. AST generally does not accept enhancements
to Minix. This is not meant as a challenge, but merely a statement of
fact. AST has good and legitimate reasons for this, and I do not dispute
them. But Minix has some limitations which I just could no longer
live with, and due to this policy, the prospect of seeing them resolved
in reasonable time was unsatisfactory. These limitations include:

    no 386 support
    no virtual consoles
    no soft links
    no select call
    no ptys
    no demand paging/swapping/shared-text/shared-libs... (efficient mm)
    chmem (inflexible mm)
    no X-Windows (advocated for the same reasons as Linux and the 386).
    no TCP/IP
    no GNU/SysV integration (portability)

Some of these could be fixed by patches (and if you have done this
yourself, I don't have to tell you how satisfactory that is), but at
least the last 5 items were/are beyond any reasonable expectation.

Finally, my comment (crack?) about Minix's segmented kernel, or
micro-kernel architecture was more an expression of my frustration/
bewilderment at attempting to use the Minix PTY patches as a guide
of how to do it under Linux. That particular instance was one where
message passing greatly complicated the implementation of a feature.

I do have an opinion about Monlithic vs Message Passing, but won't
express it now, and did not mean to expresss it then. My goals are
totally short term (maximum functionality in the minimum amount of
time/cost/hassle), and so my views on this are irrelevant, and should
not be misconstrued. If you are non-plussed by the lack of the above
features, then you should consider Minix, as long as you don't mind
paying of course :)

From: olaf@oski.toppoint.de (Olaf Schlueter)
Subject: Re: Linux is obsolete
Date: 7 Feb 92 11:41:44 GMT
Organization: Toppoint Mailbox e.V.

Just a few comments to the discussion of Linux vs Minix, which evolved
partly to a discussion of monolithic vs micro-kernel.

I think there will be no aggreement between the two parties advocating
either concept, if they forget, that Linux and Minix have been designed
for different applications. If you want a cheap, powerful and
enhancable Unix system running on a single machine, with the possibility
to adapt standard Unix software without pain, then Linux is for you. If
you are interested in modern operating system concepts, and want to
learn how a microkernel based system works, then Minix is the better
choice.

It is not an argument against microkernel system, that for the time
being monolithic implementations of Unix on PCs have a better
performance. This means only, that Unix is maybe better implemented as
a monolithic OS, at least as long as it runs on a single machine. From
the users point of view, the internal design of the OS doesn't matter at
all. Until it comes to networks. On the monolithic approach, a file
server will become a user process based on some hardware facility like
ethernet. Programs which want to use this facility will have to use
special libraries which offer the calls for communication with this
server. In a microkernel system it is possible to incorporate the
server into the OS without the need for new "system" calls. From the
users point of view this has the advantage, that nothing changes, he
just gets better performance (in terms of more disk space for example).
From the implementors point of view, the microkernel system is faster
adaptable to changes in hardware design.

It has been critized, that AST rejects any improvements to Minix. As he
is interested in the educational value of Minix, I understand his
argument, that he wants to keep the code simple, and don't want to
overload it with features. As an educational tool, Minix is written as
a microkernel system, although it is running on hardware platforms, who
will probably better perform with a monolithic OS. But the area of
network applications is growing and modern OS like Amoeba or Plan 9
cannot be written as monolithic systems. So Minix has been written with
the intention to give students a practical example of a microkernel OS,
to let them play with tasks and messages. It was not the idea to give a
lot of people a cheap, powerful OS for a tenth of the price of SYSV or
BSD implementations.

Resumee: Linux is not better than Minix, or the other way round. They
are different for good reasons.

From: meggin@epas.utoronto.ca (David Megginson)
Subject: Mach/Minix/Linux/Gnu etc.
Date: 1 Feb 92 17:11:03 GMT
Organization: University of Toronto - EPAS

Well, this has been a fun discussion. I am absolutely convinced by
Prof. Tanenbaum that a micro-kernel _is_ the way to go, but the more

I look at the Minix source, the less I believe that it is a micro-kernel. I would probably not bother porting Linux to the M68000, but I want more services than Minix can offer.

What about a micro-kernel which is message/syscall compatible with MACH? It doesn't actually have to do everything that MACH does, like virtual memory paging -- it just has to _look_ like MACH from the outside, to fool programs like the future Gnu Unix-emulator, BSD, etc. This would extend the useful lives of our M68000- or 80286-based machines for a little longer. In the meantime, I will probably stay with Minix for my ST rather than switching back to MiNT -- after all, Minix at least looks like Unix, while MiNT looks like TOS trying to look like Unix (it has to, to be TOS compatible).

David

From: peter@ferranti.com (peter da silva)
Newsgroups: comp.os.minix
Subject: What good does this war do? (Re: LINUX is obsolete)
Date: 3 Feb 92 16:37:24 GMT
Organization: Xenix Support, FICC

Will you quit flaming each other?

I mean, linux is designed to provide a reasonably high performance environment on a hardware platform crippled by years of backwards-compatible kludges. Minix is designed as a teaching tool. Neither is that good at doing the other's job, and why should they? The fact that Minix runs out of steam quickly (and it does) isn't a problem in its chosen mileau. It's sure better than the TOY operating system. The fact that Linux isn't transportable beyond the 386/AT platform isn't a problem when there are millions of them out there (and quite cheap: you can get a 386/SX for well under $1000).

A monolithic kernel is easy enough to build that it's worth doing it if it gets a system out the door early. Think of it as a performance hack for programmer time. The API is portable. You can replace the kernel with a microkernel design (and MINIX isn't the be-all and end-all of microkernel designs either: even for low end PCs... look at AmigaOS) without disturbing the applications. That's the whole point of a portable API in the first place.

Microkernels are definitely a better design for many tasks. I takes more work to make them efficient, so a simpler design that doesn't take advantage of the microkernel in any real way is worth doing for pedagogical reasons. Think of it as a performance hack for student time. The design is still good and when you can get an API to the microkernel interface you can get VERY impressive performance (thousands of context switches per second on an 8 MHz 68000).

From: ast@cs.vu.nl (Andy Tanenbaum)
Subject: Unhappy campers
Date: 3 Feb 92 22:46:40 GMT
Organization: Fac. Wiskunde & Informatica, Vrije Universiteit, Amsterdam

I've been getting a bit of mail lately from unhappy campers. (Actually 10 messages from the 43,000 readers may seem like a lot, but it is not really.)

There seem to be three sticking points:

1. Monolithic kernels are just as good as microkernels
2. Portability isn't so important
3. Software ought to be free

If people want to have a serious discussion of microkernels vs. monolithic kernels, fine. We can do that in comp.os.research. But please don't sound off if you have no idea of what you are talking about. I have helped design and implement 3 operating systems, one monolithic and two micro, and have studied many others in detail. Many of the arguments offered are nonstarters (e.g., microkernels are no good because you can't do paging in user space-- except that Mach DOES do paging in user space).

If you don't know much about microkernels vs. monolithic kernels, there is some useful information in a paper I coauthored with Fred Douglis, Frans Kaashoek and John Ousterhout in the Dec. 1991 issue of COMPUTING SYSTEMS, the USENIX journal). If you don't have that journal, you can FTP the paper from ftp.cs.vu.nl (192.31.231.42) in directory amoeba/papers as comp_sys.tex.Z (compressed TeX source) or comp_sys.ps.Z (compressed PostScript). The paper gives actual performance measurements and supports Rick Rashid's conclusion that microkernel based systems are just as efficient as monolithic kernels.

As to portability, there is hardly any serious discussion possible any more. UNIX has been ported to everything from PCs to Crays. Writing a portable OS is not much harder than a nonportable one, and all systems should be written with portability in mind these days. Surely Linus' OS professor pointed this out. Making OS code portable is not something I invented in 1987.

While most people can talk rationally about kernel design and portability, the issue of free-ness is 100% emotional. You wouldn't believe how much [expletive deleted] I have gotten lately about MINIX not being free. MINIX costs $169, but the license allows making two backup copies, so the effective price can be under $60. Furthermore, professors may make UNLIMITED copies for their students. Coherent is $99. FSF charges >$100 for the tape its "free" software comes on if you don't have Internet access, and I have never heard anyone complain. 4.4 BSD is $800. I don't really believe money is the issue. Besides, probably most of the people reading this group already have it.

A point which I don't think everyone appreciates is that making something available by FTP is not necessarily the way to provide the widest distribution. The Internet is still a highly elite group. Most computer users are NOT on it. It is my understanding from PH that the country where MINIX is most widely used is Germany, not the U.S., mostly because one of the (commercial) German computer magazines has been actively pushing it. MINIX is also widely used in Eastern Europe, Japan, Israel, South America, etc. Most of these people would never have gotten it if there hadn't been a company selling it.

Getting back to what "free" means, what about free source code? Coherent is binary only, but MINIX has source code, just as LINUX does. You can change it any way you want, and post the changes here. People have been doing that for 5 years without problems. I have been giving free updates for years, too.

I think the real issue is something else. I've been repeatedly offered virtual memory, paging, symbolic links, window systems, and all manner of features. I have usually declined because I am still trying to keep the system simple

enough for students to understand. You can put all this stuff in your version,
but I won't put it in mine. I think it is this point which irks the people who
say "MINIX is not free," not the $60.

An interesting question is whether Linus is willing to let LINUX become "free"
of his control. May people modify it (ruin it?) and sell it? Remember the
hundreds of messages with subject "Re: Your software sold for money" when it
was discovered the MINIX Centre in England was selling diskettes with news
postings, more or less at cost?

Suppose Fred van Kempen returns from the dead and wants to take over, creating
Fred's LINUX and Linus' LINUX, both useful but different. Is that ok? The
test comes when a sizable group of people want to evolve LINUX in a way Linus
does not want. Until that actually happens the point is moot, however.

If you like Linus' philosophy rather than mine, by all means, follow him, but
please don't claim that you're doing this because LINUX is "free." Just
say that you want a system with lots of bells and whistles. Fine. Your choice.
I have no argument with that. Just tell the truth.

As an aside, for those folks who don't read news headers, Linus is in Finland
and I am in The Netherlands. Are we reaching a situation where another
critical industry, free software, that had been totally dominated by the U.S.
is being taken over by the foreign competition? Will we soon see
President Bush coming to Europe with Richard Stallman and Rick Rashid
in tow, demanding that Europe import more American free software?

Andy Tanenbaum (ast@cs.vu.nl)

From: ast@cs.vu.nl (Andy Tanenbaum)
Subject: Re: Unhappy campers
Date: 5 Feb 92 23:23:26 GMT
Organization: Fac. Wiskunde & Informatica, Vrije Universiteit, Amsterdam

In article <205@fishpond.uucp> fnf@fishpond.uucp (Fred Fish) writes:
>If PH was not granted a monopoly on distribution, it would have been possible
>for all of the interested minix hackers to organize and set up a group that
>was dedicated to producing enhanced-minix. This aim of this group could have
>been to produce a single, supported version of minix with all of the commonly
>requested enhancements. This would have allowed minix to evolve in much the
>same way that gcc has evolved over the last few years.
This IS possible. If a group of people wants to do this, that is fine.
I think co-ordinating 1000 prima donnas living all over the world will be
as easy as herding cats, but there is no legal problem. When a new release
is ready, just make a diff listing against 1.5 and post it or make it FTPable.
While this will require some work on the part of the users to install it,
it isn't that much work. Besides, I have shell scripts to make the diffs
and install them. This is what Fred van Kempen was doing. What he did wrong
was insist on the right to publish the new version, rather than diffs against
the PH baseline. That cuts PH out of the loop, which, not surprisingly, they
weren't wild about.   If people still want to do this, go ahead.

Of course, I am not necessarily going to put any of these changes in my version,
so there is some work keeping the official and enhanced ones in sync, but I
am willing to co-operate to minimize work. I did this for a long time with
Bruce Evans and Frans Meulenbroeks.

If Linus wants to keep control of the official version, and a group of eager
beavers want to go off in a different direction, the same problem arises.
I don't think the copyright issue is really the problem. The problem is
co-ordinating things. Projects like GNU, MINIX, or LINUX only hold together
if one person is in charge.   During the 1970s, when structured programming
was introduced, Harlan Mills pointed out that the programming team should
be organized like a surgical team--one surgeon and his or her assistants,
not like a hog butchering team--give everybody an axe and let them chop away.

Anyone who says you can have a lot of widely dispersed people hack away on
a complicated piece of code and avoid total anarchy has never managed a
software project.

>Where is the sizeable group of people that want to evolve gcc in a way that
>rms/FSF does not approve of?
A compiler is not something people have much emotional attachment to. If
the language to be compiled is a given (e.g., an ANSI standard), there isn't
much room for people to invent new features. An operating system has unlimited
opportunity for people to implement their own favorite features.

Andy Tanenbaum (ast@cs.vu.nl)

From: torvalds@klaava.Helsinki.FI (Linus Benedict Torvalds)
Subject: Re: Unhappy campers
Date: 6 Feb 92 10:33:31 GMT
Organization: University of Helsinki

In article <12746@star.cs.vu.nl> ast@cs.vu.nl (Andy Tanenbaum) writes:
>
>If Linus wants to keep control of the official version, and a group of eager
>beavers want to go off in a different direction, the same problem arises.

This is the second time I've seen this "accusation" from ast, who feels
pretty good about commenting on a kernel he probably haven't even seen.
Or at least he hasn't asked me, or even read alt.os.linux about this.
Just so that nobody takes his guess for the full thruth, here's my
standing on "keeping control", in 2 words (three?):

I won't.

The only control I've effectively been keeping on linux is that I know
it better than anybody else, and I've made my changes available to
ftp-sites etc. Those have become effectively official releases, and I
don't expect this to change for some time: not because I feel I have
some moral right to it, but because I haven't heard too many complaints,
and it will be a couple of months before I expect to find people who
have the same "feel" for what happens in the kernel. (Well, maybe
people are getting there: tytso certainly made some heavy changes even
to 0.10, and others have hacked it as well)

In fact I have sent out feelers about some "linux-kernel" mailing list
which would make the decisions about releases, as I expect I cannot
fully support all the features that will /have/ to be added: SCSI etc,
that I don't have the hardware for. The response has been non-existant:
people don't seem to be that eager to change yet. (well, one person

felt I should ask around for donations so that I could support it - and
if anybody has interesting hardware lying around, I'd be happy to accept
it :)

The only thing the copyright forbids (and I feel this is eminently
reasonable) is that other people start making money off it, and don't
make source available etc... This may not be a question of logic, but
I'd feel very bad if someone could just sell my work for money, when I
made it available expressly so that people could play around with a
personal project. I think most people see my point.

That aside, if Fred van Kempen wanted to make a super-linux, he's quite
wellcome. He won't be able to make much money on it (distribution fee
only), and I don't think it's that good an idea to split linux up, but I
wouldn't want to stop him even if the copyright let me.

>I don't think the copyright issue is really the problem. The problem is
>co-ordinating things. Projects like GNU, MINIX, or LINUX only hold together
>if one person is in charge.

Yes, coordination is a big problem, and I don't think linux will move
away from me as "head surgeon" for some time, partly because most people
understand about these problems. But copyright /is/ an issue: if people
feel I do a bad job, they can do it themselves. Likewise with gcc. The
minix copyright, however, means that if someone feels he could make a
better minix, he either has to make patches (which aren't that great
whatever you say about them) or start off from scratch (and be attacked
because you have other ideals).

Patches aren't much fun to distribute: I haven't made cdiffs for a
single version of linux yet (I expect this to change: soon the patches
will be so much smaller than the kernel that making both patches and a
complete version available is a good idea - note that I'd still make the
whole version available too). Patches upon patches are simply
impractical, especially for people that may do changes themselves.

>>Where is the sizeable group of people that want to evolve gcc in a way that
>>rms/FSF does not approve of?
>A compiler is not something people have much emotional attachment to. If
>the language to be compiled is a given (e.g., an ANSI standard), there isn't
>much room for people to invent new features. An operating system has unlimited
>opportunity for people to implement their own favorite features.

Well, there's GNU emacs... Don't tell us people haven't got emotional
attachment to editors :)

        Linus

From: dmiller@acg.uucp (David Miller)
Subject: Linux is Obsolete and follow up postings
Date: 3 Feb 92 01:03:46 GMT
Organization: AppliedComputerGroup

As an observer interested in operating system design, I couldn't resist this
thread. Please realize that I am not really experienced with minux
or linux: I have been into unix for many years. First, a few observations:

Minix was written to be an educational tool for ASTs' classes, not a commercial operating system. It was never a design parameter to have it run freely available source code for unix systems. I think it was also a statement of how operating systems should be designed, with a micro kernel and seperate processes covering as much of the required functionality as possible.

Linux was written mostly as a learning exercise on Linus part - how to program the 386 family. Designing the ultimate operating system was not an objective. Providing a usable, free platform that would run all sorts of widely available free software was a consideration, and one that appears to have been well met.

Criticism from anyone that either of these systems isn't what *they* would like it to be is misplaced. After all, anybody that has a computer that will run either system is free to do what Linus and Andrew did: write your own!

I, for one, applaud Linus for his considerable effort in developing Linux and his decision to make it free to everybody. I applaud AST for his effort to make minix affordable - I have real trouble relating to complaints that minix isn't free. If you can afford the time to explore minix, and a basic computer system, $150 is not much more - and you do get a book to go with it.

Next, a few questions for the professor:

Is minix supposed to be a "real operating system" or an educational tool ? As an educational tool it is an excellent work. As a real operating system it presents some terribly rough edges (why no malloc() ?, just for starters) My feeling from reading The Book and listening to postings here is that you wanted a tool to teach your classes, and a lot of others wanted to play with an affordable operating system. These others have been trying to bolt on enough features to make it a "real operating system", with less than outstanding success.

Why split fundemental os functions, such as memory management, into user processes? As all good *nix gurus know, the means to success is to divide and conquer, with the goal being to *simplify* the problem into managable, well defined components. If splitting basic parts of the operating system into user space processes complicates the function by introducing additional mechanisms (message passing, complicated signals), have we met the objective of simplifying the design and implementation?

I agree that *nix has suffered a bad case of feature-itis - especially sysVr4. Perhaps the features that people want for either functionality or compatibility could be offered by run-time loadable modules/libraries that offer these features. The micro-kernel would still be a base-level resource manager that also routes function requests to the appropriate module/library. The modules could be threads or user processes. (I think - os hackers please correct me :-))

Just my $.04 worth - please feel free to post or email responses. I have no formal progressive training in computer science, so I am really asking these questions in ignorance. I suspect a lot of others on the net have similar questions in their own minds, but I've been wrong before.

-- David

From: michael@gandalf.informatik.rwth-aachen.de (Michael Haardt)
Subject: 1.6.17 summary and why I think AST is right.
Date: 6 Feb 92 20:07:25 GMT
Reply-To: u31b3hs@messua.informatik.rwth-aachen.de (Michael Haardt)
Organization: Gandalf - a 386-20 machine

I will first give a summary of what you can expect from MINIX in *near*
future, and then explain why I think AST is right.

Some time ago, I asked for details about the next MINIX release (1.6.17).
I got some response, but only from people running 1.6.16. The following
informations are not official and may be wrong, but they are all I know
at the moment. Correct me if something is wrong:

- The 1.6.17 patches will be relative to 1.5 as shipped by PH.

- The header files are clean.

- The two types of filesystems can be used together.

- The signal handling is rewritten for POSIX. The old bug is removed.

- The ANSI compiler (available from Transmediar, I guess) comes with
  compiler binaries and new libraries.

- There don't seem to be support for the Amoeba network protocol.

- times(2) returns a correct value. termios(2) is implemented, but it's
  more a hack. I don't know if "implemented" means in the kernel, or the
  current emulation.

- There is no documentation about the new filesystem. There is a new fsck
  and a new mkfs, don't know about de.

- With the ANSI compiler, there is better floating point support.

- The scheduler is improved, but not as good as written by Kai-Uwe Bloem.

I asked these things to get facts for the decision if I should upgrade to
MINIX 1.6.17 or to Linux after the examens are over. Well, the decision
is made: I will upgrade to Linux at the end of the month and remove MINIX
from my winchester, when Linux runs all the software I need and which currently
runs under MINIX 1.5 with heavy patches. I guess this may take up to two
months. These are the main reasons for my decision:

- There is no "current" MINIX release, which can be used as basis for
  patches and nobody knows, when 1.6.17 will appear.

- The library contains several bugs and from what I have heard, there is
  no work done at them. There will not be a new compiler, and the 16 bit
  users still have to use buggy ACK.

- 1.6.17 should offer more POSIX, but a complete termios is still missing.

- I doubt that there is still much development for 16 bit users.

I think I will stop maintaining the MINIX software list in a few months.
Anyone out there, who would like to continue it? Until Linux runs
perfect on my machine, each update of Origami will still run on 16-bit
MINIX. I will announce when the last of these versions appears.

In my opinion, AST is right in his decision about MINIX. I read the flame
war and can't resist to say that I like MINIX the way it is, now where
there is Linux. MINIX has some advantages:

- You can start playing with it without a winchester, you can even
  compile programs. I did this a few years ago.

- It is so small, you don't need to know much to get a small system which
  runs ok.

- There is the book. Ok, only for version 1.3, but most of it is still valid.

- MINIX is an example of a non-monolithic kernel. Call it a microkernel
  or a hack to overcome braindamaged hardware: It demonstrates a concept,
  with its pros and cons -- a documented concept.

In my eyes, it is a nice system for first steps in UNIX and systems
programming. I learned most of what I know about UNIX with MINIX, in
all areas, from programming in C under UNIX to system administration
(and security holes:) MINIX grew with me: 1.5.xx upgrades, virtual
consoles, mail & news, text processing, crosscompiling etc. Now it is
too small for me. I don't need a teaching system anymore, I would like
to get a more complicated and featureful UNIX, and there is one: Linux.

Back in the old days, v7 was state of the art. There was MINIX which
offered most of it. In one or two years, POSIX is what you are used to
see. Hopefully, there will be MINIX, offering most of it, with a new
book, for people who want to run a small system to play and experiment with.

Stop flaming, MINIX and Linux are two different systems with different
purposes. One is a teaching tool (and a good one I think), the other is
real UNIX for real hackers.

Michael

From: dingbat@diku.dk (Niels Skov Olsen)
Subject: Re: 1.6.17 summary and why I think AST is right.
Date: 10 Feb 92 17:33:39 GMT
Organization: Department of Computer Science, U of Copenhagen

michael@gandalf.informatik.rwth-aachen.de (Michael Haardt) writes:

>Stop flaming, MINIX and Linux are two different systems with different
>purposes. One is a teaching tool (and a good one I think), the other is
>real UNIX for real hackers.

Hear, hear! And now Linux articles in alt.os.linux (or comp.os.misc
if your site don't receive alt.*) and Minix articles here.

eoff (end of flame fest :-)

Niels

Appendix B
The Open Source Definition, Version 1.0

Open source doesn't just mean access to the source code. The distribution terms of an open-source program must comply with the following criteria:

1. Free Redistribution

   The license may not restrict any party from selling or giving away the software as a component of an aggregate software distribution containing programs from several different sources. The license may not require a royalty or other fee for such sale.

2. Source Code

   The program must include source code, and must allow distribution in source code as well as compiled form. Where some form of a product is not distributed with source code, there must be a well-publicized means of downloading the source code, without charge, via the Internet. The source code must be the preferred form in which a programmer would modify the program. Deliberately obfuscated source code is not allowed. Intermediate forms such as the output of a preprocessor or translator are not allowed.

3. Derived Works

   The license must allow modifications and derived works, and must allow them to be distributed under the same terms as the license of the original software. (rationale)

4. Integrity of the Author's Source Code

   The license may restrict source code from being distributed in modified form only if the license allows the distribution of "patch files" with the source code for the purpose of modifying the program at build time. The license must explicitly permit distribution of software built from modified source code. The license may require derived works to carry a different name or version number from the original software. (rationale)

5. No Discrimination Against Persons or Groups

The license must not discriminate against any person or group of persons. (rationale)

6. No Discrimination Against Fields of Endeavor

The license must not restrict anyone from making use of the program in a specific field of endeavor. For example, it may not restrict the program from being used in a business, or from being used for genetic research. (rationale)

7. Distribution of License

The rights attached to the program must apply to all to whom the program is redistributed without the need for execution of an additional license by those parties. (rationale)

8. License Must Not Be Specific to a Product

The rights attached to the program must not depend on the program's being part of a particular software distribution. If the program is extracted from that distribution and used or distributed within the terms of the program's license, all parties to whom the program is redistributed should have the same rights as those that are granted in conjunction with the original software distribution. (rationale)

9. License Must Not Contaminate Other Software

The license must not place restrictions on other software that is distributed along with the licensed software. For example, the license must not insist that all other programs distributed on the same medium must be open-source software. (rationale)

10. Example Licenses

The GNU GPL, BSD, X Consortium, and Artistic licenses are examples of licenses that we consider conformant to the Open Source Definition. So is the MPL.

Bruce Perens wrote the first draft of this document as "The Debian Free Software Guidelines," and refined it using the comments of the Debian developers in a month-long email conference in June, 1997. He removed the Debian-specific references from the document to create the "Open Source Definition."

GNU General Public License

Table of Contents

* GNU GENERAL PUBLIC LICENSE
+Preamble
+TERMS AND CONDITIONS FOR COPYING, DISTRIBUTION AND MODIFICATION
+ How to Apply These Terms to Your New Programs

GNU GENERAL PUBLIC LICENSE

Version 2, June 1991
Copyright (C) 1989, 1991 Free Software Foundation, Inc. 59 Temple Place—Suite 330, Boston, MA 02111-1307, USA

Everyone is permitted to copy and distribute verbatim copies of this license document, but changing it is not allowed.

Preamble

The licenses for most software are designed to take away your freedom to share and change it. By contrast, the GNU General Public License is intended to guarantee your freedom to share and change free software--to make sure the software is free for all its users. This General Public License applies to most of the Free Software Foundation's software and to any other program whose authors commit to using it. (Some other Free Software Foundation software is covered by the GNU Library General Public License instead.) You can apply it to your programs, too.

When we speak of free software, we are referring to freedom, not price. Our General Public Licenses are designed to make sure that you have the freedom to distribute copies of free software (and charge for this service if you wish), that you receive source code or can get it if you want it, that you can change the software or use pieces of it in new free programs; and that you know you can do these things.

To protect your rights, we need to make restrictions that forbid anyone to deny you these rights or to ask you to surrender the rights. These restrictions translate to certain responsibilities for you if you distribute copies of the software, or if you modify it.

For example, if you distribute copies of such a program, whether gratis or for a fee, you must give the recipients all the rights that you have. You must make sure that they, too, receive or can get the source code. And you must show them these terms so they know their rights.

We protect your rights with two steps: (1) copyright the software, and (2) offer you this license which gives you legal permission to copy, distribute and/or modify the software.

Also, for each author's protection and ours, we want to make certain that everyone understands that there is no warranty for this free software. If the software is modified by someone else and passed on, we want its recipients to know that what they have is not the original, so that any problems introduced by others will not reflect on the original authors' reputations.

Finally, any free program is threatened constantly by software patents. We wish to avoid the danger that redistributors of a free program will individually obtain patent licenses, in effect making the program proprietary. To prevent this, we have made it clear that any patent must be licensed for everyone's free use or not licensed at all.

The precise terms and conditions for copying, distribution and modification follow.

TERMS AND CONDITIONS FOR COPYING, DISTRIBUTION AND MODIFICATION

1. This License applies to any program or other work which contains a notice placed by the copyright holder saying it may be distributed under the terms of this General Public License. The "Program", below, refers to any such program or work, and a "work based on the Program" means either the Program or any derivative work under copyright law: that is to say, a work containing the Program or a portion of it, either verbatim or with modifications and/or translated into another language. (Hereinafter, translation is included without limitation in the term "modification".) Each licensee is addressed as "you".

   Activities other than copying, distribution and modification are not covered by this License; they are outside its scope. The act of running the Program is not restricted, and the output from the Program is covered only if its contents constitute a work based on the Program (independent of having been made by running the Program). Whether that is true depends on what the Program does.

2. You may copy and distribute verbatim copies of the Program's source code as you receive it, in any medium, provided that you conspicuously and appropriately publish on each copy an appropriate copyright notice and disclaimer of warranty; keep intact all the notices that refer to this License and to the absence of any warranty; and give any other recipients of the Program a copy of this License along with the Program.

   You may charge a fee for the physical act of transferring a copy, and you may at your option offer warranty protection in exchange for a fee.

3. You may modify your copy or copies of the Program or any portion of it, thus forming a work based on the Program, and copy and distribute such modifica-

tions or work under the terms of Section 1 above, provided that you also meet all of these conditions:

a. You must cause the modified files to carry prominent notices stating that you changed the files and the date of any change.

b. You must cause any work that you distribute or publish, that in whole or in part contains or is derived from the Program or any part thereof, to be licensed as a whole at no charge to all third parties under the terms of this License.

c. If the modified program normally reads commands interactively when run, you must cause it, when started running for such interactive use in the most ordinary way, to print or display an announcement including an appropriate copyright notice and a notice that there is no warranty (or else, saying that you provide a warranty) and that users may redistribute the program under these conditions, and telling the user how to view a copy of this License. (Exception: if the Program itself is interactive but does not normally print such an announcement, your work based on the Program is not required to print an announcement.) These requirements apply to the modified work as a whole. If identifiable sections of that work are not derived from the Program, and can be reasonably considered independent and separate works in themselves, then this License, and its terms, do not apply to those sections when you distribute them as separate works. But when you distribute the same sections as part of a whole which is a work based on the Program, the distribution of the whole must be on the terms of this License, whose permissions for other licensees extend to the entire whole, and thus to each and every part regardless of who wrote it.

Thus, it is not the intent of this section to claim rights or contest your rights to work written entirely by you; rather, the intent is to exercise the right to control the distribution of derivative or collective works based on the Program.

In addition, mere aggregation of another work not based on the Program with the Program (or with a work based on the Program) on a volume of a storage or distribution medium does not bring the other work under the scope of this License.

4. You may copy and distribute the Program (or a work based on it, under Section 2) in object code or executable form under the terms of Sections 1 and 2 above provided that you also do one of the following:

a. Accompany it with the complete corresponding machine-readable source code, which must be distributed under the terms of Sections 1 and 2 above on a medium customarily used for software interchange; or,

b. Accompany it with a written offer, valid for at least three years, to give any third party, for a charge no more than your cost of physically performing source distribution, a complete machine-readable copy of the corresponding source code, to be distributed under the terms of Sections 1 and 2 above on a medium customarily used for software interchange; or,

c. Accompany it with the information you received as to the offer to distribute corresponding source code. (This alternative is allowed only for noncommercial distribution and only if you received the program in object code or executable form with such an offer, in accord with Subsection b above.) The source code for a work means the preferred form of the work for making modifications to it. For an executable work, complete source code means all the source code for all modules it contains, plus any associated interface definition files, plus the scripts used to control compilation and installation of the executable. However, as a special exception, the source code distributed need not include anything that is normally distributed (in either source or binary form) with the major components (compiler, kernel, and so on) of the operating system on which the executable runs, unless that component itself accompanies the executable.

If distribution of executable or object code is made by offering access to copy from a designated place, then offering equivalent access to copy the source code from the same place counts as distribution of the source code, even though third parties are not compelled to copy the source along with the object code.

5. You may not copy, modify, sublicense, or distribute the Program except as expressly provided under this License. Any attempt otherwise to copy, modify, sublicense or distribute the Program is void, and will automatically terminate your rights under this License. However, parties who have received copies, or rights, from you under this License will not have their licenses terminated so long as such parties remain in full compliance.

6. You are not required to accept this License, since you have not signed it. However, nothing else grants you permission to modify or distribute the Program or its derivative works. These actions are prohibited by law if you do not accept this License. Therefore, by modifying or distributing the Program (or any work based on the Program), you indicate your acceptance of this License to do so, and all its terms and conditions for copying, distributing or modifying the Program or works based on it.

7. Each time you redistribute the Program (or any work based on the Program), the recipient automatically receives a license from the original licensor to copy, distribute or modify the Program subject to these terms and conditions. You may not impose any further restrictions on the recipients' exercise of the rights

granted herein. You are not responsible for enforcing compliance by third parties to this License.

8. If, as a consequence of a court judgment or allegation of patent infringement or for any other reason (not limited to patent issues), conditions are imposed on you (whether by court order, agreement or otherwise) that contradict the conditions of this License, they do not excuse you from the conditions of this License. If you cannot distribute so as to satisfy simultaneously your obligations under this License and any other pertinent obligations, then as a consequence you may not distribute the Program at all. For example, if a patent license would not permit royalty-free redistribution of the Program by all those who receive copies directly or indirectly through you, then the only way you could satisfy both it and this License would be to refrain entirely from distribution of the Program.

   If any portion of this section is held invalid or unenforceable under any particular circumstance, the balance of the section is intended to apply and the section as a whole is intended to apply in other circumstances.

   It is not the purpose of this section to induce you to infringe any patents or other property right claims or to contest validity of any such claims; this section has the sole purpose of protecting the integrity of the free software distribution system, which is implemented by public license practices. Many people have made generous contributions to the wide range of software distributed through that system in reliance on consistent application of that system; it is up to the author/donor to decide if he or she is willing to distribute software through any other system and a licensee cannot impose that choice.

   This section is intended to make thoroughly clear what is believed to be a consequence of the rest of this License.

9. If the distribution and/or use of the Program is restricted in certain countries either by patents or by copyrighted interfaces, the original copyright holder who places the Program under this License may add an explicit geographical distribution limitation excluding those countries, so that distribution is permitted only in or among countries not thus excluded. In such case, this License incorporates the limitation as if written in the body of this License.

10. The Free Software Foundation may publish revised and/or new versions of the General Public License from time to time. Such new versions will be similar in spirit to the present version, but may differ in detail to address new problems or concerns.

    Each version is given a distinguishing version number. If the Program specifies a version number of this License which applies to it and "any later version", you have the option of following the terms and conditions either of that version or of any later version published by the Free Software Foundation. If the Program does not specify a version number of this License, you may choose any version ever published by the Free Software Foundation.

11. If you wish to incorporate parts of the Program into other free programs whose distribution conditions are different, write to the author to ask for permission. For software which is copyrighted by the Free Software Foundation, write to the Free Software Foundation; we sometimes make exceptions for this. Our decision will be guided by the two goals of preserving the free status of all derivatives of our free software and of promoting the sharing and reuse of software generally.

NO WARRANTY

12. BECAUSE THE PROGRAM IS LICENSED FREE OF CHARGE, THERE IS NO WARRANTY FOR THE PROGRAM, TO THE EXTENT PERMITTED BY APPLICABLE LAW. EXCEPT WHEN OTHERWISE STATED IN WRITING THE COPYRIGHT HOLDERS AND/OR OTHER PARTIES PROVIDE THE PROGRAM "AS IS" WITHOUT WARRANTY OF ANY KIND, EITHER EXPRESSED OR IMPLIED, INCLUDING, BUT NOT LIMITED TO, THE IMPLIED WARRANTIES OF MERCHANTABILITY AND FITNESS FOR A PARTICULAR PURPOSE. THE ENTIRE RISK AS TO THE QUALITY AND PERFORMANCE OF THE PROGRAM IS WITH YOU. SHOULD THE PROGRAM PROVE DEFECTIVE, YOU ASSUME THE COST OF ALL NECESSARY SERVICING, REPAIR OR CORRECTION.

13. IN NO EVENT UNLESS REQUIRED BY APPLICABLE LAW OR AGREED TO IN WRITING WILL ANY COPYRIGHT HOLDER, OR ANY OTHER PARTY WHO MAY MODIFY AND/OR REDISTRIBUTE THE PROGRAM AS PERMITTED ABOVE, BE LIABLE TO YOU FOR DAMAGES, INCLUDING ANY GENERAL, SPECIAL, INCIDENTAL OR CONSEQUENTIAL DAMAGES ARISING OUT OF THE USE OR INABILITY TO USE THE PROGRAM (INCLUDING BUT NOT LIMITED TO LOSS OF DATA OR DATA BEING RENDERED INACCURATE OR LOSSES SUSTAINED BY YOU OR THIRD PARTIES OR A FAILURE OF THE PROGRAM TO OPERATE WITH ANY OTHER PROGRAMS), EVEN IF SUCH HOLDER OR OTHER PARTY HAS BEEN ADVISED OF THE POSSIBILITY OF SUCH DAMAGES.

END OF TERMS AND CONDITIONS

How to Apply These Terms to Your New Programs

If you develop a new program, and you want it to be of the greatest possible use to the public, the best way to achieve this is to make it free software which everyone can redistribute and change under these terms.

To do so, attach the following notices to the program. It is safest to attach them to the start of each source file to most effectively convey the exclusion of warranty; and each file should have at least the "copyright" line and a pointer to where the full notice is found.

One line to give the program's name and an idea of what it does. Copyright (C) 19yy name of author

This program is free software; you can redistribute it and/or modify it under the terms of the GNU General Public License as published by the Free Software Foundation; either version 2 of the License, or (at your option) any later version.

This program is distributed in the hope that it will be useful, but WITHOUT ANY WARRANTY; without even the implied warranty of MERCHANTABILITY or FITNESS FOR A PARTICULAR PURPOSE. See the GNU General Public License for more details.

You should have received a copy of the GNU General Public License along with this program; if not, write to the Free Software Foundation, Inc., 59 Temple Place—Suite 330, Boston, MA 02111-1307, USA.

Also add information on how to contact you by electronic and paper mail.

If the program is interactive, make it output a short notice like this when it starts in an interactive mode:

Gnomovision version 69, Copyright (C) 19yy name of author Gnomovision comes with ABSOLUTELY NO WARRANTY; for details type "show w". This is free software, and you are welcome to redistribute it under certain conditions; type "show c" for details.

The hypothetical commands "show w" and "show c" should show the appropriate parts of the General Public License. Of course, the commands you use may be called something other than "show w" and "show c"; they could even be mouse-clicks or menu items—whatever suits your program.

You should also get your employer (if you work as a programmer) or your school, if any, to sign a "copyright disclaimer" for the program, if necessary. Here is a sample; alter the names:

Yoyodyne, Inc., hereby disclaims all copyright interest in the program `Gnomovision' (which makes passes at compilers) written by James Hacker.

Signature of Ty Coon, 1 April 1989 Ty Coon, President of Vice

This General Public License does not permit incorporating your program into proprietary programs. If your program is a subroutine library, you may consider it more useful to permit linking proprietary applications with the library. If this is what you want to do, use the GNU Library General Public License instead of this License.

FSF & GNU inquiries & questions to *gnu@gnu.org*. Other ways to contact the FSF.

Comments on these web pages to *webmasters@www.gnu.org*, send other questions to gnu@gnu.org.

Copyright notice above. Free Software Foundation, Inc., 59 Temple Place—Suite 330, Boston, MA 02111, USA

Updated: 16 Feb 1998 tower

With the Linux kernel, Linus Torvalds includes the following preamble to the GPL:

NOTE! This copyright does *not* cover user programs that use kernel services by normal system calls—this is merely considered normal use of the kernel, and does *not* fall under the heading of "derived work." Also note that the GPL below is copyrighted by the Free Software Foundation, but the instance of code that it refers to (the Linux kernel) is copyrighted by me and others who actually wrote it.

Linus Torvalds

Contributors

BRIAN BEHLENDORF is not the normal person's idea of a hacker. He is a co-founder and a core member of the Apache Group. Apache is the open-source web server that runs a 53% of the web servers on the publicly accessible Internet. This means that this free program enjoys greater market share than offerings from Microsoft, Netscape, and all other vendors combined.

Brian has worked on Apache for four years, helping to guide the growth of the project along with other members of the Apache team. What began as an interesting experiment is now a finely crafted, full-featured web server.

He is not alone in this book in his dedication to music, but he is probably the only one who has organized raves or DJ'd for parties. His web site, *http://hypereal.org*, is a marvelous music, rave, and club resource site. He likes to read, lately reading outside of the computing field and enjoying the Capra's *Tao of Physics* and Chomsky's *Secrets, Lies and Democracy*.

In late 1998, IBM announced support for Apache on its high-end AS/400 line, a true watershed event for the Apache Project. Brian commented on IBM's move by saying he was "Happy that I wasn't the only one who thought there might be a business case for this. Not just fun to work on, but a model for business. People are coming around do see that Open Source is in fact a better way to do things on the computer, that it is healthy and can be profitable."

SCOTT BRADNER has been involved in the design, operation, and use of data networks at Harvard University since the early days of the ARPAnet. He was involved in the design of the Harvard High-Speed Data Network (HSDN), the Longwood Medical Area network (LMAnet), and NEARNET. He was founding chair of the technical committees of LMAnet, NEARNET, and CoREN.

Scott is the codirector of the Transport Area in the IETF, a member of the IESG, and an elected trustee of the Internet Society where he serves as the Vice President for Standards. He was also codirector of the IETF IP next generation effort and is coeditor of *IPng: Internet Protocol Next Generation* from Addison-Wesley.

Scott is a senior technical consultant at the Harvard Office of the Provost, where he provides technical advice and guidance on issues relating to the Harvard data networks and new technologies. He also manages the Harvard Network Device Test Lab, is a frequent speaker at technical conferences, a weekly columnist for *Network World*, an instructor for Interop, and does a bit of independent consulting on the side.

JIM HAMERLY is a Vice President in the Client Products Division of Netscape Communications Corporation. In June of 1997 Netscape acquired DigitalStyle Corporation, where Jim was a co-founder, president, and CEO.

Prior to founding DigitalStyle, he was Vice President, Engineering, of Pages Software, Inc. where he managed the development of Pages, a desktop publishing tool, and WebPages, the first WYSIWYG web authoring tool.

Jim spent 15 years with Xerox in various R&D and product development activities, most recently as Deputy Chief Engineer of XSoft, a software division of Xerox Corporation, where he was responsible for four software product lines.

Jim holds B.S., M.S., and Ph.D. degrees in Electrical Engineering and Computer Science from MIT, UC Berkeley, and Carnegie Mellon University.

KIRK MCKUSICK writes books and articles, consults, and teaches classes on Unix- and BSD-related subjects. While at the University of California at Berkeley, he implemented the 4.2BSD fast file system, and was the Research Computer Scientist at the Berkeley Computer Systems Research Group (CSRG) overseeing the development and release of 4.3BSD and 4.4BSD. His particular areas of interest are the virtual-memory system and the filesystem. One day, he hopes to see them merged seamlessly. He earned his undergraduate degree in Electrical Engineering from Cornell University, and did his graduate work at the University of California at Berkeley, where he received Masters degrees in Computer Science and Business Administration, and a doctoral degree in Computer Science. He is a past president of the Usenix Association, and is a member of ACM and IEEE.

In his spare time, he enjoys swimming, scuba diving, and wine collecting. The wine is stored in a specially constructed wine cellar (accessible from the Web at *http://www.mckusick.com/~mckusick/index.html*) in the basement of the house that he shares with Eric Allman, his domestic partner of 19-and-some-odd years.

TIM O'REILLY is the founder and CEO of O'Reilly & Associates, Inc., the publisher whose books are considered the definitive works on Open Source technologies such as Perl, Linux, Apache, and the Internet infrastructure. Tim convened the first "Open Source Summit" to bring together the leaders of major Open Source communities, and has been active in promoting the Open Source movement through writing, speaking, and conferences. He is also a trustee of the Internet Society.

 TOM PAQUIN first joined IBM Research to work on a project involving parallel processors, but ended up doing a bitmapped graphics accelerator (AMD 29116-based) for the then-new PC. After tinkering on X6 and X9 at MIT and Brown University, he was part of the effort to ship the first-ever commercial X11 with Carnegie Mellon University.

Tom joined Silicon Graphics, Inc. (SGI) in May 1989, where he had the unlucky task of integrating the GL and X. He joined Jim Clark and Marc Andreesson at Netscape in April 1994. He was the very first engineering manager, guiding his team through the 1.0 and 2.0 releases of Mozilla. Now a Netscape fellow, he works on mozilla.org as the manager, problem arbitrator, and mysterious political leader.

 BRUCE PERENS has been a long-time advocate for Linux and open-source software. Until 1997 Bruce headed the Debian Project, an all-volunteer effort to create a distribution of Linux based entirely on open-source software.

While working on the Debian Project, Bruce helped craft the Debian Social Contract, a statement of conditions under which software could be considered sufficiently freely licensed to be included in the Debian distribution. The Debian Social Contract is a direct ancestor of today's Open Source Definition.

After stepping down from the stewardship of Debian, Bruce continued his efforts at Open Source evangelism by creating and leading Software in the Public Interest, and by creating, with Eric Raymond, the Open Source Initiative.

When not actively evangelizing Open Source software, Bruce works at Pixar Animation Studios.

 ERIC STEVEN RAYMOND is a long-time hacker who has been observing and taking part in the Internet and hacker culture with wonder and fascination since the ARPAnet days in the late 1970s. He had lived on three continents and forgotten two languages before he turned fourteen, and he likes to think that this fostered his anthropological way of viewing the world.

He studied mathematics and philosophy before being seduced by computers, and has also enjoyed some success as a musician (playing flute on two albums). Several of his open-source projects are carried by all major Linux distributions. The best known of these is probably fetchmail, but he also contributed extensively to GNU Emacs and ncurses and is currently the termcap maintainer, one of those truly thankless jobs that is important to do well. Eric also holds a black belt in Tae Kwon Do and shoots pistols for relaxation. His favorite gun is the classic 1911-pattern .45 semiautomatic.

Among his writing credits, he has written/compiled *The New Hackers Dictionary* and co-authored the O'Reilly book *Learning GNU Emacs*. In 1997, he posted an essay on the Web titled "The Cathedral and the Bazaar," which is considered a key catalyst in leading Netscape to open the source code up for their browser.

Since then Eric has been deftly surfing the Open Source software wave. Recently, he broke the story on a series of internal Microsoft memos regarding Linux and the threat Microsoft perceives in open-source software. These so-called Halloween Documents (dubbed so because of their date of initial discovery, October 31st) were both a source of humor and the first confirmed reaction that the large software conglomerate has shown to the Open Source phenomenon.

 Every person in this in book one way or another owes a debt to RICHARD STALLMAN (RMS). 15 years ago, he started the GNU project, to protect and foster the development of free software. A stated goal of the project was to develop an entire operating system and complete sets of utilities under a free and open license so that no one would ever have to pay for software again.

In 1991, Stallman received the prestigious Grace Hopper Award from the Association for Computing Machinery for his development of the Emacs editor. In 1990 he was awarded a MacArthur Foundation fellowship. He was awarded an honorary doctorate from the Royal Institute of Technology in Sweden in 1996. In 1998 he shared with Linux Torvalds the Electronic Frontier Foundation's Pioneer award.

He is now more widely known for his evangelism of free software than the code he helped create.

Like anyone utterly devoted to a cause, Stallman has stirred controversy in the community he is a part of. His insistence that the term "Open Source software" is specifically designed to quash the freedom-related aspects of free software is only one of the many stances that he has taken of late that has caused some to label him an extremist. He takes it all in stride, as anyone can testify who as seen him don the garb of his alter ego, Saint GNUtias of the Church of Emacs.

Many have said, "If Richard did not exist, it would have been necessary to invent him." This praise is an honest acknowledgment of the fact that the Open Source movement could not have happened without the Free Software movement that Richard popularizes and evangelizes even today.

In addition to his political stance, Richard is known for a number of software projects. The two most prominent projects are the GNU C compiler (GCC) and the Emacs editor. GCC is by far the most ported, most popular compiler in the world. But far and wide, RMS is known for the Emacs editor. Calling Emacs editor an editor is like calling the Earth a nice hunk of dirt. Emacs is an editor, a web browser, a news reader, a mail reader, a personal information manager, a typesetting program, a programming editor, a hex editor, a word processor, and a number of video games. Many programmers use a kitchen sink as an icon for their copy of Emacs. There are many programmers who enter Emacs and don't leave to do anything else on the computer. Emacs, you'll find, isn't just a program, but a religion, and RMS is its saint.

MICHAEL TIEMANN is a founder of Cygnus Solutions. Michael began making contributions to the software development community through his work on the GNU C compiler (which he ported to the SPARC and several other RISC architectures), the GNU C++ compiler (which he authored), and the GDB debugger (which he enhanced to support the C++ programming language and ported to run on the SPARC). Unable to convince any existing companies to offer commercial support for this new "Open Source" software, he co-founded Cygnus Solutions in 1989. Today, Michael is a frequent speaker and panelist on open-source software and open-source business models, and he continues to look for technical and business solutions that will make the next ten years as exciting and rewarding as the last ten years.

Michael earned a B.S. degree in CSE in 1986 from the Moore School of Engineering, University of Pennsylvania. From 1986 to 1988, he worked at MCC in Austin Texas. In 1988, he entered the Stanford Graduate School (EE) and became a candidate for a Ph.D. in the spring of 1989. Michael withdrew from the Ph.D. program in the fall of 1989 to start Cygnus.

Who is LINUS TORVALDS?

He created Linux, of course. This is like saying "Engelbart invented the mouse." I'm sure the long-term implications of the following email:

```
From: torvalds@klaava.Helsinki.FI (Linus Benedict Torvalds)
Newsgroups: comp.os.minix
    Subject: Gcc-1.40 and a posix-question
Message-ID: <1991Jul3.100050.9886@klaava.Helsinki.FI>
Date: 3 Jul 91 10:00:50 GMT
```

> Hello netlanders,
>   Due to a project I'm working on (in minix), I'm interested in the posix
> standard definition. Could somebody please point me to a (preferably)
> machine-readable format of the latest posix rules? Ftp-sites would be nice.

Never occurred to him.

Linus could not have foreseen that his project would go from being a small hobby to a major OS with from 7 million to 10 million adherents and a major competitor to the enterprise aspirations of the world's largest software company.

Since the mass adoption of Linux and its wildfire growth through the Internet—26% of the Internet's servers run Linux (the closest competitor is Microsoft with 23%)—Linus Torvalds' life has changed. He has moved from his native Finland to Silicon Valley, where he works for Transmeta Corporation. About his work at Transmeta, he will say only that it does not involve Linux, and that it is "very cool."

He has had two children and one patent (Memory Controller for a Microprocessor for Detecting a Failure of Speculation on the Physical Nature of a Component being Addressed), and has been a guest at the most prestigious event in Finland, the President's Independence Day Ball.

His personality won't let him take credit for something as his own when in fact it is not, and Linus is quick to point out that without the help of others, Linux would not be what it is today. Talented programmers like David Miller, Alan Cox, and others have all had instrumental roles in the success of Linux. Without their help and the help of countless others, the Linux OS would not have vaulted to the lofty heights it now occupies.

 PAUL VIXIE is the head of Vixie Enterprises. He is also the President and Founder of the Internet Software Consortium, the home of bind, inn, and the dhcp server. Paul is the head architect of bind, which is the most popular implementation of DNS. Inn is the Internet news server package, and dhcp allows dynamic configuration of networking information.

He is the author of Vixie cron, which is the default cron daemon for Linux, and much of the rest of the world. This means he is probably responsible for the strange noises your computer makes at 1 a.m. every night.

Paul is the author of the book *Sendmail: Theory and Practice*. Paul's company also manages a network for the Commercial Internet Exchange, and leads the fight against spam with MAPS, the Mail Abuse Protection System, which is made up of a real-time blackhole list (where spammers have their email jettisoned into the almighty bit bucket), and a transport security initiative.

LARRY WALL has authored some of the most popular open-source programs available for Unix, including the rn news reader, the ubiquitous patch program, and the Perl programming language. He's also known for metaconfig, a program that writes Configure scripts, and for the warp space-war game, the first version of which was written in BASIC/PLUS at Seattle Pacific University. By training Larry is actually a linguist, having wandered about both U.C. Berkeley and UCLA as a grad student. (Oddly enough, while at Berkeley, he had nothing to do with the Unix development going on there.)

Larry has been a programmer at JPL. He has also spent time at Unisys, playing with everything from discrete event simulators to software development methodologies. It was there, while trying to glue together a bicoastal configuration management system over a 1200-baud encrypted link using a hacked over version of Netnews, that Perl was born.

Presently Larry's services are retained by O'Reilly, where he consults on matters relating to Perl.

BOB YOUNG has always been a something of an enigma and a legend in the Open Source community. He's a businessman, not a hacker, and has long been talked about in Linux circles as the mythical adult who kept those North Carolina kids at Red Hat in line.

Bob spent the first twenty years of his professional life in the computer leasing business, heading up two different firms before getting into the Linux world. He was the original publisher of *Linux Journal* before Phil Hughes and SSC took it over. Bob joined Red Hat with the promise that the then-members, led by Marc Ewing, wouldn't have to worry about managing the money side of the company. He applied the rules of branding more commonly associated with the Gap or Harley-Davidson to the world of free software, which is exactly what was needed for a company that packaged what is essentially a commodity: Open Source software.

Red Hat was originally going to build OEM Linux versions that they would supply to commercial OS companies, rather than directly marketing or retailing its own products. Only after these commercial partners failed to get their products to market on time did Red Hat retail its own distribution, so that the employees of Red Hat (so the story goes) would be assured enough money to eat.

Red Hat recently received funding from the venture capital world, and from Netscape and Intel. There's a nice irony to this confirmation of Red Hat's success, since it was never supposed to have its own retail products.

CHRIS DIBONA has been using Linux since early 1995. He is very active in the Linux community. He volunteers as the Linux International webmaster and is also the Linux International grant development fund coordinator. He is proud to work as the Director of Linux Marketing for VA Research Linux systems (*http://www.varesearch.com*) and is the Vice President of the Silicon Valley Linux Users Group (the world's largest at *http://www.svlug.org*).

In addition to his Linux activities, his writings and book reviews have been featured in *The Vienna Times*, *Linux Journal*, *Tech Week*, *Boot Magazine* (now *Maximum PC*), and a number of online publications. Additionally, he was the editor for two years of the *Terrorist Profile Weekly*, a geopolitcal weekly with a subscriber base numbered at 20,000.

His personal web site can be found at *http://www.dibona.com* and he can be reached via email at *chris@dibona.com*.

SAM OCKMAN is the President of Penguin Computing, a company specializing in custom-built Linux systems. He's the chairman of LINC, the International Linux Conference and Exposition, which has merged with LinuxWorld. Sam is an expert on Linux system installation and configuration, and on Perl, which he has taught at the University of California, Berkeley Extension School. He also coordinates speakers for the Silicon Valley and Bay Area Linux User Groups. Sam has edited books on Unix and Perl, and writes a monthly column on Linux. He graduated from Stanford with degrees in Computer Systems Engineering and Political Science. Sam is very proud that while at Stanford he won the Ram's Head Dorthea Award for Best Actor in a Drama.

MARK STONE has been using Linux as his mainstay operating system since the 1.0.8 version of the kernel. He wrote his first large-scale program in the late 70s: an Algol compiler for the PDP-1170. These day he prefers scripting to compiling; his favorite language is Tcl.

Currently Mark is the Open Source editor for O'Reilly. Prior to joining the world of publishing he was a professor of philosophy, and holds a Ph.D. from the University of Rochester. During his tenure in academia, he studied chaos theory and philosophy of science. So in many ways, his work hasn't changed all that much.

More Titles from O'Reilly

Hand-held Computers

PalmPilot: The Ultimate Guide

By David Pogue
1st Edition June 1998
520 pages, Includes CD-ROM
ISBN 1-56592-420-7

This PalmPilot "bible" covers the
PalmPilot, PalmPilot Professsional,
and the new software and features of
the 1998 PalmPilot model, the Palm
III, as well as OEM models such as
the IBM Workpad. Dense with undocumented information,
it contains hundreds of timesaving tips and surprising tricks
to help both intermediate and advanced users master this
exciting new device. Includes CD-ROM containing 900
PalmPilot programs.

Palm Programming: The Developer's Guide

By Neil Rhodes & Julie McKeeban
1st Edition December 1998
482 pages, Includes CD-ROM
ISBN 1-56592-525-4

Emerging as the bestselling hand-held
computers of all time, PalmPilots
have spawned intense developer
activity and a fanatical following.
Palm Programming, endorsed by
Palm as their official developer's guide, is a tutorial-style
book eagerly awaited by developers and experienced C
programmers. Includes a CD-ROM with source code and
third-party developer tools.

Perl

Learning Perl/Tk

By Nancy Walsh
1st Edition January 1999
376 pages, ISBN 1-56592-314-6

This tutorial for Perl/Tk, the extension
to Perl for creating graphical user
interfaces, shows how to use Perl/Tk
to build graphical, event-driven applications for both Windows and UNIX.
Rife with illustrations, it teaches how
to implement and configure each Perl/Tk graphical element.

Perl

Learning Perl on Win32 Systems

By Randal L. Schwartz, Erik Olson &
Tom Christiansen
1st Edition August 1997
306 pages, ISBN 1-56592-324-3

In this carefully paced course,
leading Perl trainers and a Windows
NT practitioner teach you to program
in the language that promises to
emerge as the scripting language of
choice on NT. Based on the "llama"
book, this book features tips for PC users and new, NT-specific
examples, along with a foreword by Larry Wall, the creator of
Perl, and Dick Hardt, the creator of Perl for Win32.

Mastering Regular Expressions

By Jeffrey E. F. Friedl
1st Edition January 1997
368 pages, ISBN 1-56592-257-3

Regular expressions, a powerful tool
for manipulating text and data, are
found in scripting languages, editors,
programming environments, and
pecialized tools. In this book, author
Jeffrey Friedl leads you through the
steps of crafting a regular expression that gets the job done.
He examines a variety of tools and uses them in an extensive
array of examples, with a major focus on Perl.

Mastering Algorithms with Perl

By Jon Orwant, Jarkko Hietaniemi &
John Macdonald
1st Edition June 1999 (est.)
480 pages, ISBN 1-56592-398-7

There have been dozens of books on
programming algorithms, but never
before has there been one that uses
Perl. Whether you are an amateur
programmer or know a wide range
of algorithms in other languages, this
book will teach you how to carry out traditional programming
tasks in a high-powered, efficient, easy-to-maintain manner with
Perl. Topics range in complexity from sorting and searching to
statistical algorithms, numerical analysis, and encryption.

Perl

Perl in a Nutshell

By Stephen Spainhour, Ellen Siever &
Nathan Patwardban
1st Edition January 1999
674 pages, ISBN 1-56592-286-7

The perfect companion for working
programmers, *Perl in a Nutshell* is a
comprehensive reference guide to the
world of Perl. It contains everything
you need to know for all but the most
obscure Perl questions.This wealth
of information is packed into an efficient, extraordinarily
usable format.

The Perl Cookbook

By Tom Christiansen &
Nathan Torkington
1st Edition August 1998
794 pages, ISBN 1-56592-243-3

This collection of problems, solutions,
and examples for anyone programming
in Perl covers everything from beginner
questions to techniques that even the
most experienced Perl programmers
might learn from. It contains hundreds
of Perl "recipes," including recipes for parsing strings, doing
matrix multiplication, working with arrays and hashes, and
performing complex regular expressions.

Learning Perl, 2nd Edition

By Randal L. Schwartz &
Tom Christiansen
Foreword by Larry Wall
2nd Edition July 1997
302 pages, ISBN 1-56592-284-0

In this update of a bestseller, two
leading Perl trainers teach you to use
the most universal scripting language
in the age of the World Wide Web.
Now current for Perl version 5.004, this hands-on tutorial
includes a lengthy new chapter on CGI programming, while
touching also on the use of library modules, references, and
Perl's object-oriented constructs.

Programming Perl, 2nd Edition

By Larry Wall, Tom Christiansen &
Randal L. Schwartz
2nd Edition September 1996
670 pages, ISBN 1-56592-149-6

Coauthored by Larry Wall, the creator
of Perl, the second edition of this
authoritative guide contains a full
explanation of Perl version 5.003
features. It covers Perl language
and syntax, functions, library
modules, references, and object-oriented features, and
also explores invocation options, debugging, common
mistakes, and much more.

Perl Resource Kit—Win32 Edition

By Dick Hardt, Erik Olson,
David Futato & Brian Jepson
1st Edition August 1998
1,832 pages
Includes 4 books & CD-ROM
ISBN 1-56592-409-6

The *Perl Resource Kit—Win32 Edition* is
an essential tool for Perl programmers
who are expanding their platform
expertise to include Win32 and for Win32 webmasters and
system administrators who have discovered the power and
flexibility of Perl. The Kit contains some of the latest commercial
Win32 Perl software from Dick Hardt's ActiveState company,
along with a collection of hundreds of Perl modules that run
on Win32, and a definitive documentation set from O'Reilly.

Advanced Perl Programming

By Sriram Srinivasan
1st Edition August 1997
434 pages, ISBN 1-56592-220-4

This book covers complex techniques
for managing production-ready Perl
programs and explains methods for
manipulating data and objects that may
have looked like magic before. It gives
you necessary background for dealing
with networks, databases, and GUIs,
and includes a discussion of internals to help you program
more efficiently and embed Perl within C or C within Perl.

Perl

Linux

Perl Resource Kit—UNIX Edition

*By Larry Wall, Nate Patwardhan,
Ellen Siever, David Futato &
Brian Jepson
1st Edition November 1997
1812 pages, ISBN 1-56592-370-7*

The *Perl Resource Kit—UNIX Edition*
gives you the most comprehensive
collection of Perl documentation
and commercially enhanced software
tools available today. Developed in association with Larry
Wall, the creator of Perl, it's the definitive Perl distribution
for webmasters, programmers, and system administrators.

The *Perl Resource Kit* provides:

- Over 1800 pages of tutorial and in-depth reference
  documentation for Perl utilities and extensions, in 4
  volumes.
- A CD-ROM containing the complete Perl distribution,
  plus hundreds of freeware Perl extensions and utilities—
  a complete snapshot of the Comprehensive Perl Archive
  Network (CPAN)—as well as new software written by
  Larry Wall just for the Kit.

Perl Software Tools All on One Convenient CD-ROM
Experienced Perl hackers know when to create their own,
and when they can find what they need on CPAN. Now all the
power of CPAN—and more—is at your fingertips. The *Perl
Resource Kit* includes:

- A complete snapshot of CPAN, with an install program for
  Solaris and Linux that ensures that all necessary modules
  are installed together. Also includes an easy-to-use
  search tool and a web-aware interface that allows you to
  get the latest version of each module.
- A new Java/Perl interface that allows programmers to
  write Java classes with Perl implementations. This new
  tool was written specially for the Kit by Larry Wall.

Experience the power of Perl modules in areas such as CGI,
web spidering, database interfaces, managing mail and
USENET news, user interfaces, security, graphics, math and
statistics, and much more.

Linux in a Nutshell

*By Jessica P. Hekman &
the Staff of O'Reilly & Associates
1st Edition January 1997
438 pages, ISBN 1-56592-167-4*

Linux in a Nutshell covers the core
commands available on common Linux
distributions. This isn't a scaled-down
quick reference of common commands,
but a complete reference containing
all user, programming, administration,
and networking commands. Also documents a wide range
of GNU tools.

Linux Multimedia Guide

*By Jeff Tranter
1st Edition September 1996
386 pages, ISBN 1-56592-219-0*

Linux is increasingly popular among
computer enthusiasts of all types, and
one of the applications where it is
flourishing is multimedia. This book
tells you how to program such popular
devices as sound cards, CD-ROMs, and
joysticks. It also describes the best free software packages that
support manipulation of graphics, audio, and video and offers
guidance on fitting the pieces together.

Running Linux, 2nd Edition

*By Matt Welsh & Lar Kaufman
2nd Edition August 1996
650 pages, ISBN 1-56592-151-8*

Linux is the most exciting development today in the UNIX world—
and some would say in the world
of the PC-compatible. A complete,
UNIX-compatible operating system
developed by volunteers on the
Internet, Linux is distributed freely
in electronic form and for low cost from many vendors.
This second edition of *Running Linux* covers everything you
need to understand, install, and start using your Linux system,
including a comprehensive installation tutorial, complete
information on system maintenance, tools for document
development and programming, and guidelines for network
and web site administration.

Linux

Linux Network Administrator's Guide

By Olaf Kirch
1st Edition January 1995
370 pages, ISBN 1-56592-087-2

One of the most successful
books to come from the Linux
Documentation Project is the *Linux
Network Administrator's Guide*.
It touches on all the essential
networking software included with
Linux, plus some hardware considerations. Topics include
serial connections, UUCP, routing and DNS, mail and News,
SLIP and PPP, NFS, and NIS.

Linux Device Drivers

By Alessandro Rubini
1st Edition February 1998
432 pages, ISBN 1-56592-292-1

This practical guide is for anyone who
wants to support computer peripherals
under the Linux operating system or
who wants to develop new hardware
and run it under Linux. It shows
step-by-step how to write a driver for
character devices, block devices, and
network interfaces, illustrated with examples you can compile
and run. Focuses on portability.

Learning the bash Shell, 2nd Edition

By Cameron Newham &
Bill Rosenblatt
2nd Edition January 1998
336 pages, ISBN 1-56592-347-2

This second edition covers all of
the features of *bash* Version 2.0,
while still applying to *bash* Version
1.x. It includes one-dimensional
arrays, parameter expansion, more
pattern-matching operations, new
commands, security improvements, additions to ReadLine,
improved configuration and installation, and an additional
programming aid, the *bash* shell debugger.

Using Samba

By Peter Kelly, Perry Donham &
David Collier-Brown
1st Edition May 1999 (est.)
300 pages (est.), Includes CD-ROM
ISBN 1-56592-449-5

Samba turns a UNIX or Linux
system into a file and print server
for Microsoft Windows network
clients. This complete guide to
Samba administration covers basic 2.0 configuration, security,
logging, and   troubleshooting. Whether you're playing on
one note or a full three-octave range, this book will help you
maintain an efficient and secure server. Includes a CD-ROM
of sources
and ready-to-install binaries.

Web Server Administration

Building Your Own WebSite™

By Susan B. Peck & Stephen Arrants
1st Edition July 1996
514 pages, Includes CD-ROM,
ISBN 1-56592-232-8

This is a hands-on reference for
Windows® 95 and Windows NT™
users who want to host a site on the
Web or on a corporate intranet. This
step-by-step guide will have you creating
live web pages in minutes. You'll also learn how to connect
your web to information in other Windows applications, such
as word processing documents and databases. The book is
packed with examples and tutorials on every aspect of web
management, and it includes the highly acclaimed WebSite™
1.1 server software on CD-ROM.

Web Server Administration

Stopping SPAM

By Alan Schwartz & Simson Garfinkel
1st Edition October 1998
204 pages, ISBN 1-56592-388-X

This book describes spam—unwanted
email messages and inappropriate
news articles—and explains what you
and your Internet service providers
and administrators can do to prevent
it, trace it, stop it, and even outlaw it.
Contains a wealth of advice, technical tools, and additional
technical and community resources.

Writing Apache Modules with Perl and C

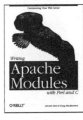

By Lincoln Stein & Doug MacEachern
1st Edition March 1999 (est.)
768 pages (est.), ISBN 1-56592-567-X

This guide to Web programming
teaches you how to extend the
capabilities of the Apache Web server.
It explains the design of Apache,
mod_perl, and the Apache API, then
demonstrates how to use them to
rewrite CGI scripts, filter HTML
documents on the server-side, enhance server log functionality,
convert file formats on the fly, and more.

Web Security & Commerce

By Simson Garfinkel
with Gene Spafford
1st Edition June 1997
506 pages, ISBN 1-56592-269-7

Learn how to minimize the risks
of the Web with this comprehensive
guide. It covers browser vulnerabilities,
privacy concerns, issues with Java,
JavaScript, ActiveX, and plug-ins,
digital certificates, cryptography, web
server security, blocking software, censorship technology, and
relevant civil and criminal issues.

Apache: The Definitive Guide

By Ben Laurie & Peter Laurie
1st Edition March 1997
274 pages, includes CD-ROM
ISBN 1-56592-250-6

Despite all the media attention to
Netscape, Apache is far and away the
most widely used web server platform
in the world. This book, written and
reviewed by key members of the
Apache Group, is the only complete
guide on the market today that describes how to obtain, set
up, and secure the Apache software. Includes CD-ROM with
Apache sources and demo sites discussed in the book.

Web Performance Tuning

By Patrick Killelea
1st Edition October 1998
374 pages, ISBN 1-56592-379-0

Web Performance Tuning hits the
ground running and gives concrete
advice for improving crippled Web
performance right away. For anyone
who has waited too long for a Web
page to display or watched servers
slow to a crawl, this book includes
tips on tuning the server software, operating system, network,
and the Web browser itself.

Building Your Own Web Conferences™

By Susan B. Peck & Beverly Murray Scherf
1st Edition March 1997
270 pages, Includes CD-ROM
ISBN 1-56592-279-4

Building Your Own Web Conferences is
a complete guide for Windows® 95 and
NT™ users on how to set up and manage
dynamic virtual communities that improve
workgroup collaboration and keep visitors coming back to
your site. The second in O'Reilly's "Build Your Own..." series,
this book comes with O'Reilly's state-of-the-art WebBoard™ 2.0
software on CD-ROM.

In a Nutshell Quick References

Perl in a Nutshell

By Stephen Spainhour, Ellen Siever &
Nathan Patwardhan
1st Edition January 1999
674 pages, ISBN 1-56592-286-7

The perfect companion for working programmers, *Perl in a Nutshell* is a comprehensive reference guide to the world of Perl. It contains everything you need to know for all but the most obscure Perl questions. This wealth of information is packed into an efficient, extraordinarily usable format.

SCO UNIX in a Nutshell

By Ellie Cutler &
the staff of O'Reilly & Associates
1st Edition February 1994
590 pages, ISBN 1-56592-037-6

The desktop reference to SCO UNIX and Open Desktop®, this version of *UNIX in a Nutshell* shows you what's under the hood of your SCO system. It isn't a scaled-down quick reference of common commands, but a complete reference containing all user, programming, administration, and networking commands.

Tcl/Tk in a Nutshell

By Paul Raines & Jeff Tranter
1st Edition February 1999 (est.)
480 pages, ISBN 1-56592-433-9

The Tcl language and Tk graphical toolkit are powerful building blocks for applications that feature a variety of commands with a wealth of options in each command. This quick reference briefly describes every command and option in the core Tcl/Tk distribution, as well as the most popular extensions. Keep it on your desk as you write scripts, and you'll be able to quickly find the particular option you need.

UNIX in a Nutshell: System V Edition

By Daniel Gilly &
the staff of O'Reilly & Associates
2nd Edition June 1992
444 pages, ISBN 1-56592-001-5

You may have seen UNIX quick-reference guides, but you've never seen anything like *UNIX in a Nutshell*. Not a scaled-down quick reference of common commands, *UNIX in a Nutshell* is a complete reference containing all commands and options, along with generous descriptions and examples that put the commands in context. For all but the thorniest UNIX problems, this one reference should be all the documentation you need. Covers System V, Releases 3 and 4, and Solaris 2.0.

UML in a Nutshell

By Sinan Si Alhir
1st Edition September 1998
290 pages, ISBN 1-56592-448-7

The Unified Modeling Language (UML), for the first time in the history of systems engineering, gives practitioners a common language. This concise quick reference explains how to use each component of the language, including its extension mechanisms and the Object Constraint Language (OCL). A tutorial with realistic examples brings those new to the UML quickly up to speed.

Year 2000 in a Nutshell

By Norman Shakespeare
1st Edition September 1998
330 pages, ISBN 1-56592-421-5

This reference guide addresses the awareness, the managerial aspect, and the technical issues of the Year 2000 computer dilemma, providing a compact compendium of solutions and reference information useful for addressing the problem.

O'REILLY®

TO ORDER: **800-998-9938** • **order@oreilly.com** • **http://www.oreilly.com/**

OUR PRODUCTS ARE AVAILABLE AT A BOOKSTORE OR SOFTWARE STORE NEAR YOU.

FOR INFORMATION: **800-998-9938** • **707-829-0515** • **info@oreilly.com**

How to stay in touch with O'Reilly

1. Visit Our Award-Winning Site

http://www.oreilly.com/

★ "Top 100 Sites on the Web" —*PC Magazine*
★ "Top 5% Web sites" —*Point Communications*
★ "3-Star site" —*The McKinley Group*

Our web site contains a library of comprehensive product information (including book excerpts and tables of contents), downloadable software, background articles, interviews with technology leaders, links to relevant sites, book cover art, and more. File us in your Bookmarks or Hotlist!

2. Join Our Email Mailing Lists

New Product Releases

To receive automatic email with brief descriptions of all new O'Reilly products as they are released, send email to:
listproc@online.oreilly.com
Put the following information in the first line of your message (*not* in the Subject field):
subscribe oreilly-news

O'Reilly Events

If you'd also like us to send information about trade show events, special promotions, and other O'Reilly events, send email to:
listproc@online.oreilly.com
Put the following information in the first line of your message (*not* in the Subject field):
subscribe oreilly-events

3. Get Examples from Our Books via FTP

There are two ways to access an archive of example files from our books:

Regular FTP

- ftp to:
  ftp.oreilly.com
  (login: anonymous
  password: your email address)
- Point your web browser to:
  ftp://ftp.oreilly.com/

FTPMAIL

- Send an email message to:
  ftpmail@online.oreilly.com
  (Write "help" in the message body)

4. Contact Us via Email

order@oreilly.com
To place a book or software order online. Good for North American and international customers.

subscriptions@oreilly.com
To place an order for any of our newsletters or periodicals.

books@oreilly.com
General questions about any of our books.

software@oreilly.com
For general questions and product information about our software. Check out O'Reilly Software Online at **http://software.oreilly.com/** for software and technical support information. Registered O'Reilly software users send your questions to:
website-support@oreilly.com

cs@oreilly.com
For answers to problems regarding your order or our products.

booktech@oreilly.com
For book content technical questions or corrections.

proposals@oreilly.com
To submit new book or software proposals to our editors and product managers.

international@oreilly.com
For information about our international distributors or translation queries. For a list of our distributors outside of North America check out:
http://www.oreilly.com/www/order/country.html

O'Reilly & Associates, Inc.
101 Morris Street, Sebastopol, CA 95472 USA
TEL   707-829-0515 or 800-998-9938
        (6am to 5pm PST)
FAX   707-829-0104

International Distributors

UK, EUROPE, MIDDLE EAST AND AFRICA (EXCEPT FRANCE, GERMANY, AUSTRIA, SWITZERLAND, LUXEMBOURG, LIECHTENSTEIN, AND EASTERN EUROPE)

INQUIRIES
O'Reilly UK Limited
4 Castle Street
Farnham
Surrey, GU9 7HS
United Kingdom
Telephone: 44-1252-711776
Fax: 44-1252-734211
Email: josette@oreilly.com

ORDERS
Wiley Distribution Services Ltd.
1 Oldlands Way
Bognor Regis
West Sussex PO22 9SA
United Kingdom
Telephone: 44-1243-779777
Fax: 44-1243-820250
Email: cs-books@wiley.co.uk

FRANCE

ORDERS
GEODIF
61, Bd Saint-Germain
75240 Paris Cedex 05, France
Tel: 33-1-44-41-46-16 (French books)
Tel: 33-1-44-41-11-87 (English books)
Fax: 33-1-44-41-11-44
Email: distribution@eyrolles.com

INQUIRIES
Éditions O'Reilly
18 rue Séguier
75006 Paris, France
Tel: 33-1-40-51-52-30
Fax: 33-1-40-51-52-31
Email: france@editions-oreilly.fr

GERMANY, SWITZERLAND, AUSTRIA, EASTERN EUROPE, LUXEMBOURG, AND LIECHTENSTEIN

INQUIRIES & ORDERS
O'Reilly Verlag
Balthasarstr. 81
D-50670 Köln
Germany
Telephone: 49-221-973160-91
Fax: 49-221-973160-8
Email: anfragen@oreilly.de (inquiries)
Email: order@oreilly.de (orders)

CANADA (FRENCH LANGUAGE BOOKS)
Les Éditions Flammarion ltée
375, Avenue Laurier Ouest
Montréal (Québec) H2V 2K3
Tel: 00-1-514-277-8807
Fax: 00-1-514-278-2085
Email: info@flammarion.qc.ca

HONG KONG
City Discount Subscription Service, Ltd.
Unit D, 3rd Floor, Yan's Tower
27 Wong Chuk Hang Road
Aberdeen, Hong Kong
Tel: 852-2580-3539
Fax: 852-2580-6463
Email: citydis@ppn.com.hk

KOREA
Hanbit Media, Inc.
Sonyoung Bldg. 202
Yeksam-dong 736-36
Kangnam-ku
Seoul, Korea
Tel: 822-554-9610
Fax: 822-556-0363
Email: hant93@chollian.dacom.co.kr

PHILIPPINES
Mutual Books, Inc.
429-D Shaw Boulevard
Mandaluyong City, Metro
Manila, Philippines
Tel: 632-725-7538
Fax: 632-721-3056
Email: mbikikog@mnl.sequel.net

TAIWAN
O'Reilly Taiwan
No. 3, Lane 131
Hang-Chow South Road
Section 1, Taipei, Taiwan
Tel: 886-2-23968990
Fax: 886-2-23968916
Email: benh@oreilly.com

CHINA
O'Reilly China
Room 2410
160, FuXingMenNeiDaJie
XiCheng District
Beijing
China PR 100031
Email: frederic@oreilly.com

INDIA
Computer Bookshop (India) Pvt. Ltd.
190 Dr. D.N. Road, Fort
Bombay 400 001 India
Tel: 91-22-207-0989
Fax: 91-22-262-3551
Email: cbsbom@giasbm01.vsnl.net.in

JAPAN
O'Reilly Japan, Inc.
Kiyoshige Building 2F
12-Bancho, Sanei-cho
Shinjuku-ku
Tokyo 160-0008 Japan
Tel: 81-3-3356-5227
Fax: 81-3-3356-5261
Email: japan@oreilly.com

ALL OTHER ASIAN COUNTRIES
O'Reilly & Associates, Inc.
101 Morris Street
Sebastopol, CA 95472 USA
Tel: 707-829-0515
Fax: 707-829-0104
Email: order@oreilly.com

AUSTRALIA
WoodsLane Pty., Ltd.
7/5 Vuko Place
Warriewood NSW 2102
Australia
Tel: 61-2-9970-5111
Fax: 61-2-9970-5002
Email: info@woodslane.com.au

NEW ZEALAND
Woodslane New Zealand, Ltd.
21 Cooks Street (P.O. Box 575)
Waganui, New Zealand
Tel: 64-6-347-6543
Fax: 64-6-345-4840
Email: info@woodslane.com.au

LATIN AMERICA
McGraw-Hill Interamericana
Editores, S.A. de C.V.
Cedro No. 512
Col. Atlampa
06450, Mexico, D.F.
Tel: 52-5-547-6777
Fax: 52-5-547-3336
Email: mcgraw-hill@infosel.net.mx

O'REILLY®

TO ORDER: **800-998-9938** • **order@oreilly.com** • **http://www.oreilly.com/**
OUR PRODUCTS ARE AVAILABLE AT A BOOKSTORE OR SOFTWARE STORE NEAR YOU.
FOR INFORMATION: **800-998-9938** • **707-829-0515** • **info@oreilly.com**

O'REILLY™

O'Reilly & Associates, Inc.
101 Morris Street
Sebastopol, CA 95472-9902
1-800-998-9938

Visit us online at:
http://www.ora.com/
orders@ora.com

O'REILLY WOULD LIKE TO HEAR FROM YOU

Which book did this card come from?

_____

Where did you buy this book?
- ❏ Bookstore
- ❏ Direct from O'Reilly
- ❏ Bundled with hardware/software
- ❏ Computer Store
- ❏ Class/seminar
- ❏ Other _____

What operating system do you use?
- ❏ UNIX
- ❏ Windows NT
- ❏ Other _____
- ❏ Macintosh
- ❏ PC(Windows/DOS)

What is your job description?
- ❏ System Administrator
- ❏ Network Administrator
- ❏ Web Developer
- ❏ Other _____
- ❏ Programmer
- ❏ Educator/Teacher

❏ Please send me O'Reilly's catalog, containing
a complete listing of O'Reilly books and
software.

Name _____ Company/Organization _____

Address _____

City _____ State _____ Zip/Postal Code _____ Country _____

Telephone _____ Internet or other email address (specify network) _____

Nineteenth century wood engraving
of a bear from the O'Reilly &
Associates Nutshell Handbook®
Using & Managing UUCP.

POST CARD

PLACE
STAMP
HERE

NO POSTAGE
NECESSARY IF
MAILED IN THE
UNITED STATES

BUSINESS REPLY MAIL

FIRST CLASS MAIL   PERMIT NO. 80   SEBASTOPOL, CA

Postage will be paid by addressee

O'Reilly & Associates, Inc.
101 Morris Street
Sebastopol, CA 95472-9902